AF540742

METHODS OF TEACHING COMMERCE

By

K. Venkateswarlu

M.A., M.Ed.,
Lecturer
Navya Chaitanya College of Education
Kandukur, Prakasam Distt., A.P

Sk. Johni Basha

B.Com., M.A., M.Ed., M.Phil.
Lecturer
R.V.V.N. College
Dharanikota–Amaravathi
Guntur, Distt, A.P.

General Editor

Dr. Digumarti Bhaskara Rao

M.Sc., M.A., M.A., M.Ed., Ph.D.
Reader
R.V.R. College of Education
Srinivasa Nagar Colony
Guntur–522 006
Andhra Pradesh
India

DISCOVERY PUBLISHING HOUSE
NEW DELHI-110002

Reprinted - 2019

First Published - 2004

ISBN: 978-81-7141-808-4

Methods of Teaching Commerce

Published by:

DISCOVERY PUBLISHING HOUSE PVT. LTD.
4383/4B, Ansari Road, Darya Ganj
New Delhi-110 002 (India)
Phone: +91-11-23279245, 23253475; 43596065
E-mail: discoverybooksindia@gmail.com
discoverypublishinghouse@gmail.com
web: www.discoverypublishinggroup.com

Printed at:
Infinity Imaging Systems
Delhi

Foreword

Teacher education is quantitatively marching ahead towards quality education. The central and state governments through the NCTE and the Directorates of School/Higher Education are rendering their legitimate service in improving the quality of teacher education by formulating and implementing various academic policies and educational programmes. Along with these policies and programmes, the teacher educators and the prospective teachers teaching and studying in teacher education institutions need good curriculum and quality books.

The methods of teaching each subject play a pivotal role in enhancing the efficiency of their practitioners. Identifying the very importance of the methods of teaching and the quality of books, a series of books on the methods of teaching different subjects have been developed by experienced teacher educators for the benefit of teachers in making in teacher education institutions. Thanks to the authors.

Valuable suggestions for the improvement of these books are welcome from fellow teacher educators, prospective teachers and other academicians involved in the arena of teacher education.

The authors and the editor dedicate this series of books on the methodology of teaching to Mr. Tilak Raj Wasan, Proprietor, Discovery Publishing House, New Delhi, for taking up this commendable task of publication to meet the felt needs of teacher education faculty and clientele.

Dr. Digumarti Bhaskara Rao

Research Director in Education

Nagarjuna University

br_digumarti@rediffmail.com

Preface

The movement of modern education in India is almost two century old. It has come of age now. Over the decades, great educationists have contributed towards the development and evolution of education, as a discipline. Thus, education in India has been enriched a lot.

As a result, the Indian education system can be placed at par with any advanced education system in the modern world. In fact, education is a vast sea and Teachers' Training is a stream in it. So, it makes it essential that the responsibilities of the faculty members are focused on the task of providing better training to the future teachers, for their better learning and proper development. And this responsible exercise can only be undertaken, if the trainers are equipped with all the needed skill and knowledge of the subject, they are supposed to teach. Hence, it becomes essential for making adequate provisions, for each course to the teacher-trainees. Methods of Teaching are very important for the successful training of teachers and for their career in future.

In order to provide all related material in one cover, here is this book, on this important subject. Of course there are several books on the subject in the market, but, every book has its own style and way of presentation. Similarly, the present one, too has its own merits and advantages.

During the course of the preparation of this book, the undersigned has done his best for the accomplishment of the job. He would be pleased and feel contented, if this book is acknowledged, as a textbook and a reference tool for the teachers and students, alike.

Author

Contents

1

Introduction

Like the teacher of any other subject a commerce teacher has to perform several roles for the many-sided development of the pupils' personalities. Broadly speaking, he is expected to work for the realization of four objectives namely to enable the child 'to learn' or to gain information and knowledge, 'to be', 'to do' and 'to live' a harmonious life. Some of important roles for the realisation of these objectives are listed below.

Confidant—A teacher is expected to win the confidence of the students so that they express their feelings freely, if need be in private.

Democrat—He is expected to observe democratic values so as to prepare his students for a democratic way of life.

Equaliser—He should treat all students on the basis of equality. He should work for developing an egalitarian outlook in students.

Facilitator of learning—He works for the promotion of significant learning in his students.

Friend and philosopher—He must perform the role of a friend and philosopher to his students.

Group leader—As a leader to the social group in the class, he must develop a suitable climate and cohesion.

Guidance counsellor and helper—He provides an academic career and personal guidance to his students.

Initiator—He is supposed to play the role of an initiator by exploring the new technology to the best advantage of the students and the progress of education. He should play the role of an innovator of educational ideas, practices and systems.

Role model—He is envisaged to behave in a manner whereby traits exemplified by him may be emulated by his students.

Detective—He acts as a detective to find out the shortcomings of the students—committing of offences and law breaking tendencies also.

Judge—He evaluates the academic and other performance of the students in an impartial manner.

Limiter or reducer of anxiety—He can help students control their impulses and reduce anxiety about their conduct and performance in different problematic situations.

Moral educator—His important function is to inculcate attitudes and moral values cherished by society in the students.

Parent surrogate (parent substitute)—He can play the role of ideal parents by treating students with affection and care.

Rationalist—He should set an example of a rationalist by basing his action on reason.

Referee—He is expected to settle disputes among students in an objective manner.

Reformer—His entire work consists of bringing about appropriate changes in his students for their full development.

Resource person—He is expected to serve as a resource person for his students as he possesses knowledge of the subject-matter and skills, better than his pupils.

Secularist—He should play the role of a secularist by having an open mind on the beliefs of students.

Upholder of the norms and values—He must present the norms and values of society in a dignified manner.

Responsibilities of a Teacher

The following are his main functions and responsibilities:

1. Character development.
2. Effective teaching learning.
3. Adjusting individual differences.
4. Class-room management.
5. Evaluation of pupil performance.
6. Curriculum development and implementation.

7. Developing good family and community relationships.
8. Total school effectiveness.
9. Professional growth and ethics.

Character development

For this, the teacher:

1. Creates an atmosphere of purposeful order, enlists pupil's assistance in orderly, friendly, courteous and co-operative interpersonal relation.
2. Develops a respect for the rights, privileges and opinions of others.
3. Creates group situations which will develop desirable leadership and followership qualities in the pupils.
4. Sets a standard of class-room and school environment behaviour which conforms to socially acceptable behaviour.
5. Directs discussion and develops understanding on moral and other ethical issues in order to develop the understanding of the reasons for ethical standard.
6. Encourages each pupil's thinking and action.

Techniques of teaching

(Effective teaching) This includes-

1. Selecting materials, teaching aids and methods which will facilitate the learning process and stimulate the desire for further learning.
2. Meeting the needs, background and capacities of the children being taught.
3. Teaching by use of a suitable variety of lectures, discussions, demonstrations, visual and oral presentations, recitation, directed group effort, experimentation, special projects and field trips.
4. Analysing and evaluating the effectiveness of various teaching techniques in order to improve the learning process.
5. Endeavouring to obtain and maintain pupil interest and attention so that teaching is done in a receptive environment.
6. Endeavouring to assure that material taught is applied in such a manner so as to develop a pattern of understanding for future in other areas.

7. Encouraging and guiding critical thinking by pupils.
8. Developing desirable work and study skills and habits.
9. Enlisting pupil participation in the lesson planning process.
10. Developing broad outlines and objectives to be attained within prescribed limits, for a subject or skill area based upon the needs and interests of a specific group of pupils.
11. Assuring that preparation adequate to assure purposeful and directed teaching precedes all actual class-room teaching.
12. Making suitable lesson plans and other necessary arrangements for substitutes.

Adjusting to individual differences and development levels

This calls for—

1. Drawing upon and applying the basic knowledge of the psychology of the child in order to establish readiness for learning.
2. Making an effort to know as much as possible about the background and out-of-school environment of each child in order to improve the teaching learning process.
3. Developing in each pupil a sense of personal growth and value.
4. Maintaining discipline by being consistently friendly, fair and firm.
5. Handling behaviour problems in a controlled manner.

Techniques of classroom management

This means—

1. Assigning responsibility to pupils for the care and house-keeping of the classroom's physical assets.
2. Developing, preparing or providing material and equipment and displaying it in a manner so as to improve the learning situation.
3. Maintaining the school-room in a healthful and safe condition, assuring proper lighting, ventilation etc.
4. Preparing and maintaining orderly and accurately all required records, such as attendance registers.

Evaluating and reporting of pupil performance

This comprises—

1. Devising and administering appropriate tests to measure the level and quality of pupil learning.

2. Interpreting test results and relating findings to pupil progress or lack of it in order to improve the teaching and learning process.
3. Evaluating pupil performances through reports, recitations, homework and other types of assignment.
4. Reporting pupil achievements and progress to parents by means of conferences and progress reports.
5. Co-operating and enlisting the co-operation of school specialist in the process of pupil evaluation as required.

Curriculum development and implementation

This implies—

1. Participation in grade level or subject matter study of existing curricula and in the development of improved expanded curricula.
2. Determining the object, scope and methods of the grade and subjects to be taught.
3. Devising assignments, when necessary in order to enrich the teaching programme for the pupils.
4. Correlating subject matter with the curriculum of other subjects.

Developing good family and community relations

This envisages—

1. Participating in parent-teacher and similar activities.
2. Participating in community affairs.
3. Making himself available to parents at scheduled times to discuss pupil progress and behaviour.
4. Evincing a sympathetic, helpful and understanding attitude towards parents and their children's schooling problems.
5. Establishing and maintaining a good relationship with parents and reporting of pupil's progress, problems and needs.
6. Assuring through personal behaviour in the community that the school staff-image in the community is favourable.

Total school effectiveness

This consists of—

1. Accepting responsibility for pupil discipline throughout the school and in the interest of the school as a whole.

2. Co-operating with all co-workers and exchanging ideas in order to improve and provide a variety of approach on the teaching situation.
3. Executing all required school regulations and assignments on time.
4. Accepting one's full share of pupil activity participation; such as attending athletic contests etc.
5. Contributing constructively to committees, faculty meetings and other school system groups.
6. Taking positive steps in developing and maintaining faculty and students morale.

Professional growth and ethics

This stipulates—

1. Keeping knowledge upto date.
2. Participating in in-service programmes like seminars and workshops etc.
3. Adhering to professional ethics i.e. not compelling students to take tuition from him and his colleagues, not recommending instructional material to students on some consideration etc.
4. Participating in the activities of professional organisations.

Qualities of a Teacher

These may be categorised as:

I. Scholarship.
II. Professional Training.
III. Personality.
IV. Teaching Skills.
V. Human Relations.

Scholarship

This includes:

1. Acquaintance with problems of present day life.
2. Background of a liberal education.
3. Reader of magazines and newspapers.
4. Reader of books on the subject taught.
5. Sound knowledge of the subject.

Professional training

This incorporates:

(a) Desire for improvement.

(b) Professional attitude.
(c) Reader of professional books.
(d) Reader of educational magazines.
(e) Sound professional training.

Personality

It has three aspects:

A. Physical aspects.
B. Passive virtues.
C. Executive abilities.

Physical aspects

These include:

(i) Personal appearance include dress, carriage, social expression, and personal cleanliness.
(ii) Etiquettee including good manners, observance of social norms, courtesy and refinement.
(iii) Voice, rich and mellow.
(iv) Good language command including pronunciation, enunciation and grammar.
(v) Health.

Passive Virtues

These include:

(i) Enthusiasm.
(ii) Fairness.
(iii) Friendliness.
(iv) Optimism.
(v) Patience.
(vi) Self-control.
(vii) Sincerity.
(viii) Sympathy.
(ix) Tact.
(x) Understanding.

Executive Abilities

These include:

(a) Adaptability.
(b) Directing ability.
(c) Industriousness
(d) Initiative.
(e) Organising ability.
(f) Resourcefulness.

(g) Self-confidence
(h) Self-reliance

Teaching Skills

The Core Training Programme Package (CTPP) of the NCERT (1979) aiming at enabling the teachers to acquire mastery of manipulative skills for making their teaching effective includes the following skills:

1. Skills of class management.
2. Skills of communication (Teacher's Acts).
3. Skills of interaction (Teacher Acts).
4. Skills of the use of Teaching Aids.
5. Skills of Attitude and Behaviour.

Skills of class management

These include as below:

(a) Control and modification of facial expression. The teacher should enter the class as a balanced person. It is necessary to emphasise the need for neatness and simplicity in his dress and appearance. Gaudy dress and shabby appearances have to be avoided. The teacher must maintain his calm and confidence in the face of gesticulation and mimicking of the group.
(b) Greetings and taking up proper position in the class. The teacher is expected to offer the greetings while entering the class and then take the central place facing the class. He is also required to keep moving to the central place when students are offering greetings orally or by standing up in their seats and then face the class and respond to the greetings.
(c) Movements (locomotion in the class-room). Appropriateness of movements lies in providing a balanced supervision to the class and in being available at the right time to the student who needs help.
(d) Use of appropriate gestures in various situations and various stages. Expressions of gestures of approval, appreciation and disapproval also have a great bearing on learning. The tendency of offering undue smile or encouragement or displeasure would form the negative points. Praise like gold and silver owes its utility to scarcity.

Skills of communication (Teacher's Acts)

This comprises five skills, narration, recitation, dramatisation, explanation and demonstration., These skills are teacher-dominated.

Skills of interaction

These include (a) Questions and feedback (b) Discussion and (c) Problem solving.

Skills of the use of teaching aids

This consists of-

(a) Selection of teaching aids as per needs.
(b) Preparation of charts, models, maps and diagrams.
(c) Operation of mechanical aids.
(d) Position in while writing on and explaining from the blackboard.
(e) Writing on the blackboard with reference to size, shape, boldness and colour of letters.
(f) Drawing, sketching, preparing tables and graphs on the blackboard.

Skills of attitude and behaviour

This comprises:

(a) Patient Listening.
(b) Suggesting.
(c) Guiding.
(d) Counselling.

Human Relations

This comprises amicable

1. Relations with students.
2. Relations with colleagues.
3. Relations with parents.
4. Relations with school personnel.
5. Relations with administrators, inspectors, supervisors etc.
6. Relations with the community.
7. Relations with publishers, stationers, sports dealers etc.
8. Relations with professional organisations and workers.

Teacher's Training

Training of a commerce teacher involves the following:

1. University Degree in Commerce.

2. Training course including methodology of teaching Commerce.
3. In-service training through
   (i) Seminars;
   (ii) Symposium;
   (iii) Workshops;
   (iv) Lectures;
   (v) Study of books, newspapers and journals related to commerce and allied subjects;
   (vi) Visits to commercial and industrial establishments;
   (vii) Visits to industrial fairs.

Significance of Each Letter of the Word

C	stands for	Character
O	stands for	Objectivity
M	stands for	Mastery of the subject
M	stands for	Media user
E	stands for	Efficiency
R	stands for	Rational attitude
T	stands for	Tact. Thirst for knowledge. Tolerance. Truth
E	stands for	Enthusiasm. Ethics. Etiquette.
A	stands for	Adaptability. Affection. Alertness
C	stands for	Clarity. Constructiveness. Creativity
H	stands for	Hand work. Honesty. Humility. Human relations Humour.
E	stands for	Emotional Stability. Experimental Attitude.
R	stands for	Resourcefulness.

SYSTEMS APPROACH AND COMMERCE TEACHER

Analysis of the subject-matter,
task or problem

↓

Studying
characteristics of learners

↓

Defining specific communication
problems

↓

Identifying objectives (Stating attainable objectives, terminal objectives, performance criterion)

↓

Exploring available resources (Environmental, human, financial, technological)
Anticipating possible limitations, constraints and alternatives

↓

Specifying methods Method (strategy) and media selection

↓

Constructing prototypes (programme) pre test post test, media production and assembly

↓

Validating programme or prototype
Try out with a representative group

↓

Analysing results

↓

Implementing recycle

QUESTIONS

1. Explain the multifarious roles of the commerce teacher.
2. What specific qualities should a commerce teacher possess to make his work effective?
3. What type of skills are needed in a commerce teacher? Explain.
4. How can a teacher develop his professional competence?
5. Explain the system approach role of the commerce teacher.

2

Scope and Nature

Importance of Education

"There is", as the great philosopher Whitehead (1861-1947) puts it, "only one subject matter of education, and that is life in all its manifestations." Trade, Commerce and industry constitute a vital part of our life's activities. These aspects of our life's experiences are extremely important and if we despise these, all our educational effort will be fruitless toils.

High philosophies apart, the full education for an individual must be both for 'making a living' and for 'making a life'. Thus viewed, the full education of an individual involves both 'vocational education' and 'cultural education'. The individual must be able to earn a living for leading a civilised life. In such a perspective, Commerce or Business Education is to be looked upon as just one phase of education, not inferior or superior to any other phase or branch.

Effects of Information

The explosion of 'information' in science and technology has influenced every area of life, including business and commerce. The increasing complexity of business and commerce organisations in the present day world would make it obligatory for students to be conversant with modern principles and practices of management and accounting. Gone are the days when one could depend on the 'Munims' and their 'Bahi Khatas'. The use of computers and the management techniques of the behavioural sciences have completely revolutionised the running of modern business and commercial enterprises. It therefore, has become very necessary to pay adequate attention to Business and Commerce Education. As observed by the Central Board of Secondary Education, New Delhi (1995), in their scheme of courses in Business Studies: "During the first 10 years of schooling students are not given formal instruction in Commerce and Accountancy subjects. Against this background, it becomes necessary that at this stage, instruction in these two aspects be given in such a manner that students have a good understanding of the principles and practices bearing on business, trade and industry and their relationship to society. They need to be exposed to the realities of the business world as a part of the economic, legal and social environment. This will enable them to understand and appreciate the functions and scope of business activities in the economic set up."

In view of the enlarged functions and scope of commercial activities, the Central Board of Secondary Education has used the terms Business Studies and Accountancy.

That the importance of Commerce Education has gained recognition only in recent years in India is borne out from the fact that the Education Commission 1964-66 which went into all aspects of education and at all stages of education did not include the study of Business and Commerce in the school curriculum. This also accounts for the scanty literature on the education and training of commerce teachers at the school stage.

Socio-economic Factors

Demand for Business Education arose from the private sector of the economy for trained employees. When response from educational institutions did not supply the demand, private enterprise met the challenge by organising profit-making schools, which remained the dominant influence in Business Education for several decades. As the economy expanded; as more opportunities arose for trained business workers; as factories brought more people from farms to the cities, as industrialization spread and increased the demand for clerical and other business workers; and as business began to employ women in their offices, society demanded that this type of education be offered in state or government schools. So Business Education became a part of the Indian system of education. These demands by economy and society formed the socio-economic foundations of Commerce Education.

Significance of Education

A.S. Daughtrey (1974) explains graphically the philosophy and role of Business Education in education.

Role of Business Education in Education

General

Education | Specialised Education

Business Education

Education about Business Basic Business Education		**Education for Business Vocational Business Education**	
Personal Economics	Societal Economics	Occupational Intelligence	Job Training for Business
• Skills, abilities and under-standings to handle personal business and and consumer affairs.	• Understanding the economy of one's own country.	• Good workmen-ship • Job Satisfaction • Occupational selection, efficiency,	• Employable skills and abilities, Stenographic, book-keeping clerical selling, data processing.
	Citizenship res-ponsibilities	adjustment, growth	
• Career education		• Business ethics	• Prevocational Skills

Commercial and Business Education

Different authors, thinkers and writers in different countries have used different terms to convey the same meaning. Sydney Webb (1897) used the expression Commercial Education. The German concept of Business Education is in terms of Applied Economic Education. In Switzerland, the name is Commercial Science. In the U.S.A., the term Business Education is preferable to the term Commercial Education. In the U.K., the term used is Education for Commerce. Prof L.R. Dasgupta (1959) explains the usage in India in these words, "The expression Commercial Education seems to have been identified with education for junior employees in business houses engaged in subordinate occupations, such as clerkships, secretarial (rather ministerial) and book-keeping positions and operation of office appliances." The expression has thus come to mean education for clerical personnel and commercial assistants. The expression "Commerce Education" is often used to indicate college and university grades of Business Education. But then, "Management Education" is being increasingly looked upon as a distinct field in higher Business Education.

The writer prefers to use the word business to cover industry (i.e., production), trade- (i.e., buying and selling) and commerce (i.e., ancillary services like, banking, insurance, warehousing, transport, etc. aiding both industry and trade)... .

We may adopt the expression 'Business Education' as the generic name to cover all types and levels of education for all the business functions or operations, whether in the public or the private sector, except those directly involved in the mechanical extraction or transformation of materials to products and maintenance of machines (i.e., expecting the activities involving technocracy of production and maintenance). The expressions 'Commercial Education', 'Commerce Education' and 'Professional Business Education' may then be used to indicate three levels of 'Business Education' the first to cover the junior level programmes, the second to mean the first degree programmes, and the third to cover all post-graduate and post employment specialist or expert level programmes. The general business knowledge to help the citizens' understanding of the working of economic democracy may be integrated within the general education programmes. Then again, although "Business Education can make some contribution to the training of all workers" such marginal Business Education can better be included within the other specific programmes and need not be covered by the Business Education programmes proper. Lastly, the programmes in Business Education proper at different levels should be such as may serve the needs of both the public and the private sectors of the economy, as also the need of the owner-enterprisers and of the employee-managers. The direction of economic development that the country has adopted seems to suggest that the difference between the two groups or sectors would gradually close up."

Prof. Gupta has made the following groupings at the three levels for determining the dominant role in each curriculum and adoption of appropriate methods of teaching and training.

Commercial Education

(a) Vocationally biased programmes at awareness or acquaintance level.

(b) Specific programmes at skill or specialist level geared to beginning subordinate jobs.

Commerce Education

(a) General Stream. (Pre-professional level through grouped courses)

(b) Functional or Operational Specialisation Stream. (Semi-expert or semi-professional level through grouped courses with elective offerings, and in single-subject courses to aid post-employment betterment of prospects.)

Business Education

(a) Expert level in specific aspects of business operations like, accounting, purchasing, selling, advertising, costing, finance, transport, secretarial work, taxation, business statistics, etc. (Two or three may be elected at a time with some amount of management or say, administrative education on a compulsory basis.)

(b) Advanced General Stream for the teaching professions.

(c) Administrative Specialisation Stream on abroad basis.

No strict adherence to logic is claimed for such classification, but it would be very near the current concepts and usage in India.

The Central Board of Secondary Education has used the terms Business Studies and Accountancy and not Commerce.

Prof Herbert A. Tonne (1955) of the U.S.A. while writing on the purposes of Business Education argues that the term "Business Education" as understood currently is preferable to the term "Commercial Education", as he explains that 'business' is much broader than 'commerce'. The coverage of the expression "Education for Commerce" as delimited by Carr-Saunders Committee (U.K.) is broader than "Commercial Education." Prof. Tonne divides Business Education under the following categories to indicate the specific goals more clearly:

A. General Business Education sub-divided into consumer education and economic education (designated again by some authors as social-business education).

B. Technical Business Education subdivided into occupational intelligence and specific group training.

In 1897, Sydney Webb used the expression Commercial Education to cover "a multitude of things with a vast number of distinct callings from Accountancy and Banking to Typewriting."

Business Education in the Indian context may be described as that broad area of knowledge which deals with the Indian enterprise system which identifies and explains the role of business as an Indian economic institution and which provides content and experiences that prepare the individual for effective participation as a citizen and consumer in the Indian society.

Definitions of Business Education.

Some of the popular definitions of Business Education/Commerce Education are given below.

Freok Hooper and James Graham (1901) defined Commercial Education as "a practical education suited to the needs of present day, and calculated to fit young people intended for business careers for work they will have to perform and to better equip for their work those already in business."

Chessman A. Herrick (1904) defined Commerce Education as, "that form of instruction that both directly and indirectly prepares the businessman for his calling."

Leveret S. Lyon (1922) stated that Commerce Education is "any education which a businessman has and which makes him a better businessman, is for him a business education, no matter whether it was obtained in the walls of a school or not."

Paul S. Lomax (1928) observed that "Commercial Education is fundamentally a programme of economic education that has to do with the requirement, conservation and spending of wealth."

In the words of H.G. Shields (1930), "Real Commerce Education is Economic Education not of academic sort long on theory and short on facts but Economic Education which will give the student a knowledge of basic reality of business life and relationships. The basic science of business is commerce and without a thorough guidance and awareness of economic problems much of the material included in secondary school course is purely additive and essentially superficial. We cannot place technique and socio-business subjects on a dual basic since one is basic and other is supplementary. We cannot accept a two headed definition of the field but must recognise that certain elements must be given most emphasis and these take to be economic factors".

Fredrick G. Nichols (1933) defined Commerce Education in these words," Commerce Education is a type of training which, while playing its part in the achievement of the general aims of education on any given level, has for its primary objective the preparation of people to enter upon a business career or having entered upon such a career, to render more efficient service therein and to advance from their present levels of employment to higher levels."

According to H.E. Tonne (1955), "If education is thought of as the adjustment of the individual to his environment, Business Education must be thought of as the adjustment of the individual to his business environment."

Nanassay and others (1977) define Business Education as, "Ordinarily when speaking of programmes in colleges or schools of business in universities or divisions of business in liberal arts colleges, the general term Business Administration will be used. We will reserve the term Business Education for these business programmes and courses taught ordinarily at the secondary level and "Business Teacher Education" will be used to describe professional preparation."

The Dictionary

In the Policies Commission on Business and Economic Education Statement (1977) it is noted," Business Education represents a broad and diverse discipline that is included in all types of educational delivery systems – elementary and secondary schools, one and two year schools and colleges, and five-year colleges and universities. Business Education can begin at any level; it can be interpreted for varying periods of time, and it can be continued throughout life span of an individual. Business Education includes education for office occupations, distribution and marketing occupations, business teaching, business administration, and economic undertakings".

Business and Economic Policies

International Dictionary of Education (1978) edited by G. Terry Page and J.B. Thomas uses Business Education "as Commercial Studies or Business studies, Studies of Commercial and Management subjects. The term can sometimes be misleading because it tends to be used for a wide range of levels from office skills for school leavers to postgraduate or graduate studies in the more sophisticated management and business subjects and techniques.... Commercial subjects (or education) 1. Such school subjects as typing, shorthand, book keeping and elementary accounting 2. In tertiary education, a wider range of subjects, in the economics and business studies fields."

Calhour (1980) tends to look more at educational content than at educational level and he defines Business Education as, "Business Education is interpreted in many ways. To some, it pertains only to those occupations that are carried out in the office by office workers. Others interpret its scope to include not only the jobs performed by office workers but also the functions by management and/or advancement in occupations related to the office. In addition, business education provides the student with the understanding and knowledge needed for handling personal affairs and using the service of the business world."

According to *A Dictionary of Education* edited by P.J. Hills (1982), the term Business Studies "covers a wide range of activities in education and training. It usually means all those activities that educate and train people at all levels who work in organisations that deal in the purchase and sales of goods and services."

Mohd. Sharif Khan (1982) defines Commerce Education as "that phase of the economic system which is devoted to the management and distribution of the products of industry and the professions.; as such it is the essential integrating element in the whole economic structure."

Hopkins, C. and Lambrecht (1988) note the confusion in the use of the term Business Education and observe, "In spite of a long history in the public and private education sector, many people, including school leaders, other vocational educators and the public understand neither the overriding goals nor the fundamental content of business education. This is not surprising since there is neither consensus nor complete understanding among business educators on these topics."

Definitions and Concepts

The analysis made by Prof Dasgupta in 1959 holds good even today to a considerable extent. Defining business of economic organisation, "chiefly for gratifying human wants," some writers have identified the term "Business Education" with all Vocational Education. But such an approach seems to be too broad for evolving programmes in Business Education, although it is admitted that "Business Education can make some contribution to the training of all workers." The coverage of Vocational Education is broader, and Business Education can be only one branch of Vocational Education if the term vocation is understood in a broad sense.

Some writers again have asserted that "real Business Education is Economic Education-Economic Education not of academic sort, long on theory and short on facts-but Economics Education which will give the students a knowledge of basic realities of business life and relationships". Such identification of Business Education with education in applied Economic or Social Science is found in many countries at the university level. The German concept of "Enterprise economics" is based on such idea. But then, different branches of knowledge like law, cost accountancy, etc., are brought within the domain. In Britain, the majority of the Carr-Saunders Committee recommended the Applied Economics and Social Science approach in this branch of education at university level. In Switzerland the name is 'Commercial Science', presumably to widen the coverage on the argument of scientific study.

Business Education in U.S.A.

In the U.S.A., Business Education at university level is being identified with "Management Education" or "Business administration", and Business Education, at less than the college level is being intended to be covered by "Vocational Business Education" and similar other terms. The Harvard programmes are claimed to mark a break away from the applied economics approach in higher business education. Another British writer on the objectives of Commerce Education states that "the whole programme of commercial teaching then aims at the provision of training for the whole of the commercial and administrative aspects of industry, and not only for the narrower aspects of buying selling, banking transporting, warehousing, and recording." (Mr. A.B. Lowndes)

Nature

Commerce Education is not inferior education. The Scottish Education Department in its booklet on the commercial subjects in secondary schools, stresses that "the function of Commercial Education is not merely to satisfy the vocational need of the pupils but also to foster an understanding of the economy of the community in which they will be called to play a part. In commerce no less than in industry, it is of primary importance that prospective entrants should have a sound general education." Mr. Graham Savage of the London County Council in his pamphlet on "Commercial Studies in Secondary Schools" explains that "the essential function of a secondary school commercial course should be to give the pupils a knowledge of the background of commerce and of the way it affects the life of the community; the pupil's interest in commerce cannot, therefore, be confined to subjects which are specially commercial, but will influence their approach to other subjects." The commercial curriculum in secondary education in Switzerland and Not-way, are also found to include sufficient number of the so-called general subjects.

In this integration approach to the liberal and vocational education, we have the support of many modern thinkers on education. Prof. Whitehead observes in his book The Alms of Education and other Essays (p. 74) that "the antithesis between the technical and liberal education is fallacious. There can be no adequate technical education which is not liberal, and no liberal education which is not technical; that is, no education which does not impart both technique and intellectual vision. In simple language, education should turn the people to something he knows well and can do well. This intimate union of practice and theory aids both. The intellect does not work best in vacuum." The Mudaliar Commission (1952-53) also rightly stressed another aspect of the issue, namely, "that the intellectual and cultural development of different individuals take place best through a variety of media, that the book or the study of traditional academic subjects is not the only door to the education of the personality and that, in the case of many-perhaps the majority-of the children, practical work intelligently organised can unlock their latent energies much more successfully than the traditional subjects which address themselves only to the mind, or worse still, the memory". The Commissioners for Secondary Education in Britain observed as far back as 1895 that "all education is development and discipline of faculty by the communication of knowledge and whether the faculty may be eye or hand or the reason and imagination and whether the knowledge be so communicated as evoke and exercise a disciplined faculty, the process is rightly termed education."

It may be remembered that Commerce is both an academic discipline and a vocational subject.

Commerce area is both a knowledge subject and a skill subject. The objectives of the study of commerce are both preparatory to further studies in colleges or high education and terminal to enter into the careers of middle level lines of employment.

Subject Matter

The Special Committee on Education for Commerce in Britain (1949) delimited the coverage of Commerce Education thus: "Education for Commerce must therefore embrace educational facilities for those preparing for or engaged in business occupations of every kind, professional or otherwise, from office routine such as typewriting and shorthand to the positions of great responsibility... . It is in the sense that we understand the breadth of our enquiry; it includes education for wholesale and retail trade, for import and export trade, for transport and shipping, for general commerce, for profession so-called, for higher functions of management and administration, and for the move modest 'hand-maidens' of commerce, shorthand and typewriting."

In the U.S.A., where the expression Business Education is in vogue, it is not meant to cover technical or technological education for industry. In both the countries U.K. and U.S.A. as also elsewhere, industrial organisation and management, industrial economics etc. are now considered as business or commercial subjects.

Scope

Scope of Commerce Education has changed radically during the past six decades. In this context it would be of interest to note what Abbot-Wood Report (1937) said about Commerce Education.

"This branch (Education for Commerce) of vocational education differs so greatly from education for industry, that it demands separate consideration. It must be so framed as to meet the needs of both the two main groups into which we have divided workers in commercial occupations, that is, (a) of the group of which the members have the responsibility for transacting business on an important scale or for performing the professional functions of banking, accountance and the like, and (b) of the very large group engaged in recording the transactions of the member of the first group".

Scope of Commerce Education at College Level

According to the University Education Commission 1948-49, Professional Business Education should include mathematics, statistics; theory of organisation; business structure; finance, including manangement and budgeting of assets and of expenses; philosophy, history and theory of law; and organisation of work, including economy, process analysis and procedures, standardisation of skills, cost analysis, and the like. The structure of distribution should also be studied. In industrial cases this training can be slanted towards factory practice, office management institutional management, agriculture, or marketing, according to the student's chief interest. While industrial relations should be included in every business course it is so important as to constitute a profession of itself.

Tonne, Popham and Freeman (1965) illustrate the scope of Commerce Education as under:

COMMERCE EDUCATION

General commerce	Education	Job Training for Education	
Basic Commerce education for all	Pre-Vocational commerce education for those planning to enter commerce	Occupational intelligence	Specific skills training

Scope of Commerce at the Senior Secondary Stage

The Central Board of Secondary Education, Delhi (1996) has outlined the following subject matter in Business Studies and Accountancy, the terms used by it in lieu of Commerce.

Business Studies

1. Economic Activities and Business
2. Nature and Purpose of Business
3. Structure of Business
4. Service Sector and Business
5. Forms of Business Enterprise
6. Corporate Organisation
7. Formation of a Company
8. Sources of Business Finance
9. Stock Exchange
10. Internal Trade
11. External Trade
12. (a) Functional Management
    (b) Factory or Organisation
    (c) Office or Administration

Accountancy

1. Accounting-Meaning, Objectives and Basic Accounting Terms
2. Theory Base of Accounting
3. Origin and Recording of Functions
4. Trial Balance and Errors
5. Financial Statements—Trading Account Profit.
6. Loss Account and Business sheet
7. Computer Awareness
8. Depreciation, Reserves and Provision
9. Bills of Exchange
10. Accounts of Non-profit Organisations
11. Accounts from Incomplete Records

Commerce Education as an academic discipline and a vocational discipline includes the following subjects at the senior secondary stage:

1. Business Studies
2. Book Keeping and Accountancy
3. Applied Economics
4. Advertising and Publicity, etc.
5. Commercial English
6. Commercial Law
7. Commercial Mathematics
8. Office, Clerical and Secretarial Practice

9. Salesmanship
10. Shorthand
11. Typewriting

Relationship between Commerce and Education

Commerce and Economics are closely related to each other. Economics provides the base of Commerce as a subject of study. The development of commerce is linked with the economic development of the society. Likewise the development of Commerce as a discipline is looked with the development of Economics as a discipline. Sometimes commerce is regarded as a practical application of economic principles.

Arthur Malthy in Economics and Commerce explains the relationship of Economics and Commerce in these words, "Economics is fundamentally concerned with the problem's arising from the production of goods and services and the demand for them. Commerce, on the other hand, is essentially involved with their distribution and the various processes and services which make distribution fully efficient. But while the economist may study the reasons by which one method of distribution can he more advantageous than another, the allied activities of commercial enterprise deal with the way in which distribution is actually achieved. The commerce student examines what is done in retailing, transport in its forms, advertising and so forth rather than what 'might' or 'should be done of economic gain is to be maximised. The student of Commerce is more concerned with the 'how' than 'why' of economic activity."

Study of Commerce is based on production and exchange which are important economic factors.

The development of special agencies like insurance, banking, agency system, ware housing goes to indicate the close relationship of commerce to economic factors. The fact is that the economic basis of Commerce remains unquestioned.

Business Administration

Commerce education is not mere business administration as commerce involves enterprise and risk taking.

The administration of modern business is now concerned with the analysis of problems, the making of decisions, the formulation of policies and the management of daily operation. It draws upon all departments of knowledge, sponsors research on a prodigious scale, and makes use of staff experts in a variety of fields, and is itself an intellectual activity that now calls for talents of the highest order.

Business education should be so organised as to prepare youth for the management of economic institutions whether those institutions be business firms, labour unions, government economic agencies or other types of operating organisations.

As in engineering the technician deals chiefly with empirical skills, while the professional works not only with skills but natural laws, organised knowledge, and the application of general principles; so in business there is a difference between commerce courses and the profession of business.

For a businessman, as for an engineer, the first requirement is that he shall be an educated man and citizen, so that in his business he can act with informed, social minded statesmanship, and not simply as a business technician.

QUESTIONS

1. Explain the importance and meaning of Commerce Education.
2. State the Significance and nature of Commerce Education.
3. Elucidate the meaning of Commerce Education. What should be its scope at different stages of education?
4. Explain the relationship between Commerce Education and Economics.
5. State various definitions of Commerce Education and give your arguments in favour of definition of your choice.
6. "Commerce Education is not merely vocational education". Explain and state its nature and scope.

3

Basic Issues

Co-curricular activities are also very helpful in the study of commerce. Commerce teachers should try to achieve a balanced development of different tasks and abilities of the students by involving them according to their interest in the variety of activities. Students may be taken to different banks, insurance companies and other commercial and industrial establishments. Various office appliances and accounting machines used in an establishments have valuable educative values.

Education is not merely concerned with a mastery of the 3 R's. It is concerned with integrated development of the personality of an individual; his physical, cultural, aesthetic, social, mental and emotional aspects. The Secondary Education Commission observed, "We would like the school to see if it can provide a richly varied pattern of activities to cater to the development of children's entire personality."

'Learning by Doing', 'Learning by Living', 'Learning without Tears', are the main characteristics of the modern concept of education.

Education accordingly is seen in terms of 7 R's i.e, Reading, Writing, Arithmetic, Rights, Responsibilities, Recreation, and Relationship.

The remarks of the Secondary Education Commission in respect of the cocurricular activities are worth noting: "The school is not merely a place of formal learning whose main concern is to communicate a certain prescribed quantum of knowledge but rather as a living and organic community which is primarily interested in training its pupils, in what we have called the 'gracious art of living'. Knowledge and learning are undoubtedly of value but they must be acquired as a by-product of activity because it is only then that they can become a vital part of the student's mind and personality and influence his behaviour. But the, 'Art of living' is much more comprehensive concept than the acquisition of knowledge, however intelligently planned. It includes training in the habit and graces of social life and the capacity for cooperative group work. It calls for patience, good temper, sincerity, fellow-feeling and discipline. These objective can only be cultivated in the context of the social life and the many cocurricular activities must find a recognised place in any school.

Important co-curricular activities related to commerce teaching are as under:

1. Commerce Club
2. Commerce magazine or School Magazine with a section on Commerce
3. Market Studies and Surveys Field Trips.
4. Debates, Discussions and Symposiums etc.
5. Running of School Bank Running of School Cooperative Store.
6. Educational visits to place of Commercial Importance.
7. Essay Competitions.
9. Book Reading Contests.
10. Undertaking Projects.

Students' Club

Commerce clubs may be formed for undertaking several types of co-curricular activities relating to commerce work. They may organise debates and discussions on current topics in Commerce. Essay competitions on various topics may be conducted. Speakers from outsides may be invited. Wall magazine may be published. In fact scope of work is quite vast.

Following are the chief values of a well-organised club:

a. It provides opportunities to the students for enriching their experiences.
b. It supplements the curricular work.
c. It provides opportunities for the development of pupil abilities.
d. Club is very helpful in making the constructive use of leisure time.

e. Club may help in the exploration of occupational interest of the students.
f. Club provides opportunities for the practice of group planning and decision.

Teacher-in-Charge

He must possess the following qualities.

(i) He should enlist the co-operation of the students.
(ii) He must be able to offer constructive suggestions for activities of the club.
(iii) He must be able to guide without dictation.
(iv) He must have the ability to plan systematically.
(v) He must be willing to give time and thought in making the work of the club a success.
(vi) He must be democratic in spirit.
(vii) He must possess a sense of humour.
(viii) He must have the necessary talent and skill so that pupils look upon as a model.
(ix) He should help the clubs and societies to make a wise choice of office bearers indicating what qualities are necessary in an office bearer but should do nothing to force his choice in favour of any individual student.
(x) He should make as careful a preparation for participation in co-curricular activities as he does for his teaching work.

Magazine by the Students

Values. A school magazine is the embodiment of the corporate life of an institution and affords suitable opportunities to the students for giving expression to their thoughts and ambitions. It develops their power of expression and trains them in the art of writing. It develops a literary taste through writing short stories, essays, etc.

In the words of Jacobson, "The school magazine offers great opportunities for those who participate in it. It is not uncommon to find that pupils and their parents consider the editorship of the school paper the most valuable experience which has come to a pupil, particularly when directed by a wise sponsor who makes it a very purposive educative experience. All pupils who serve on the magazine secure some experience in creative writing. Usually the form of their writing improves because a powerful incentive for correct form exists when the material is to be printed or memeographed for public examination."

It serves as a link between the school and the parents as it reaches them through the students.

A foundation for interstate and international understanding can be laid by exchanging magazines with schools in other states and countries.

Class-room work is supplemented to some extent through it. The students learn to write their thoughts in an effective, clear and concise manner. Study habits are developed as the students consult some books or journals to write for their school magazine and make the best use of their leisure time.

It helps in giving publicity to the school.

Spears and Lawshe list the following functions of the school paper as an aid to the school:

1. To educate the community as to the work of the school.
2. To publish school news.
3. To create and express school opinion.
4. To capitalise the achievements of the school.
5. To act as a means of unifying the school.
6. To express the idealism and reflect the spirit of school.
7. To encourage and stimulate worthwhile activities.
8. To aid in developing right standards of conduct.
9. To promote understanding of other schools.
10. To provide an outlet for student suggestions for the betterment of the school.
11. To develop better inter-school relationships.
12. To increase school spirit.
13. To promote co-operation between parents and school.

Essentials for its Success. Contribution from the students should be corrected before their publication. The school magazine should include a variety of articles. Student editors should be carefully appointed. Prizes for the best contributions may be given to the students to give them an incentive to write. The teachers should not make the school magazine as their organ.

The teacher incharge of the magazine should be well-versed with the current events.

In schools where the number of students is small and the financial position does not permit the publication of a fulfledged magazine, it will be advantageous to take resort to wall magazine.

Blackboard or wall-magazine greatly helps in the preparation of printed magazine. News on boards may be written every day in the morning. Daily news should be illustrated with the help of a map. Important places where important events take place should be shown on the map. Other boards dealing with facts and figure regarding our natural resources, development projects, inspiring thoughts from religion, history or ethics may be prepared weekly or fortnightly as the case may be. The students should be made responsible for preparing these boards.

Community Field Trips, Educational Tours, Market Studies and Surveys

These are practical activities that greatly help in enriching instruction by introducting practical aspects of the subject as application of classroom theory. Field trips to business establishments and industries in the community provide first hand information to the students. They permit students to analyse problems through their own efforts. They supplement class work. They acquaint the pupils with the environment. They develop qualities of citizenships.

It may be remembered that careful planning on the part of the teacher is very essential to make the optimum use of out-of-class activities. Following points deserve careful attention in this regard.

1. The teacher should brief students before hand so that they become aware of the salient features which are of special importance and the aspects to which special attention should be given.
2. Some idea of the organisation of the place or establishment to be visited, the various departments to be visited, the various departments it consists of and the types of jobs in each department should be given to the student.
3. In addition to briefing the students, it is also necessary to brief the managers or heads of the establishments to be visited. They should be well informed with the purpose of the visit and the kinds of information which they are expected to provide to the students during the visit.
4. During the visit the student's attention should be drawn to the kind of work performed, the hierarchy of the

organisation, the machines and tools used by different workers, the working conditions etc.

5. If a talk by a representative of the organisation is to be arranged during the trip, students should be prepared in advance to ask him questions on various aspects of the organisation.
6. Students should be asked to observe work carefully.
7. After the visit, the teacher should have a follow-up discussion with the students.
8. A guide sheet for the students should be prepared and given to them. Check lists inventories and questionnaires should be prepared thoughtfully while planning market surveys and field trips.
9. Students should be advised to maintain proper decorum during field trips.

W.M. Gregory evaluates school trips and excursions in these words: "Education has been too far removed from the basic experiences of modern life. Many schools are quite deficient in opportunities for some perception exploration and raw experiences. They need fewer words and more activities with things, situations, conditions and relations. For useful learning, pupils require experiences with the raw materials of life. A garden, a shop, a live animal collection, a trip to a farm, a mill, a store, a park, a museum all must have a place in the modern school."

Significance of Commerce-room

A modern teacher of commerce has come a long way from those old days when 'chalk' and 'talk' were the only aids of teaching. Modern technology has placed different types of instructional aids at his disposal. Apart from text books, there are different types of reference books, pamphlets, magazines, maps, charts, projects, etc. which must be used to make the teaching-learning process effective.

A Commerce room or what a few subject specialists -would like to term as Commerce laboratory, fully equipped with modern aids, will provide a pleasant social and cooperative environment where the teachers and the learners feel homely. It is a must for every school. Class-room furnishings and their arrangements have direct bearing upon the quality of results obtained. Satisfactory outcomes can be expected from any class-room situation only when adequate facilities are provided. It should be furnished to provide a suitable environment for acquiring and practising skill needed in commerce.

It has been recognised that like sciences, social studies also require a specially equipped room or laboratory. This alone can facilitate the use of modern methods and techniques like Play-way Method, Problem Method, Project Method and the Socialized Recitation Method, etc. Special setting and equipment are needed for utilising these methods.

A commerce laboratory should serve the purpose of a classroom, a library, workshop, an amateur theatre, a students' club, a stock room, all combined into one. It may grow steadily and constantly as regards equipment. It should become the exciting 'hub' of activity for the students and teacher of commerce. It should be so planned and arranged that it provides an inviting and stimulating environment. It should be a place of 'doing' rather than of 'talking'. Commerce library is the treasure vault of the store house of ideas. In fact, it is flowing stream of living thought. It provides suitable opportunities to the student to use facts in a creative and productive way to arrive at their own independent conclusions and enable them to grow in enriched knowledge, abilities, skills and interests.

Following are some of the considerations which necessitate the provision of a special room or laboratory for commerce.

1. Providing 'home of their own' to teachers teaching commerce for developing enthusiasm for the subject and faith in themselves and the students.
2. Creating and maintaining an effective teaching- learning environment.
3. Providing a quick and ready functional environment by making available work room for the students.
4. Introduction variety in teaching methods and facilitating the use of teaching aids readily and conveniently.
5. Saving energy and time in carrying round equipment like charts, maps, models, pictures and project work etc.

Essential Equipment of the Commerce Room: The room should be well equipped so that functional environment is created and the teacher and the students are motivated to work. It should have the following equipment.

1. Audio-visual material which includes epidiascope, filmstrip, magic lantern, projector, tape-recorder etc.
2. Bulletin Boards.
3. Charts and Graphs.
4. Flags.
5. Maps and Atlases.
6. Models.
7. Graphs.
8. Reference books.
9. Textbooks
10. Periodicals and magazines dealing with current events.

A school having Vocational courses based on Commerce may have the following three rooms:

1. One room to be used as a general classroom for teaching Commerce.
2. One room for teaching shorthand and typewriting, transcription and business machines.
3. One room for business machines—calculating machines, tape-recording machine, duplicating machine, record player, etc.

Library in the Department

If resources of an institution permit, there should be a separate Commerce Department Library. A Commerce Library is not only a source of learning and inspiration for students but it also serves the various—needs of the teachers, especially of keeping themselves abreast of the latest developments in the subject. Commerce library can be housed in the Commerce room and can be put under the charge of a commerce teacher.

Commerce library should contain the following material:-

1. Visual aids needed in the teaching of Commerce-charts diagrams, tables, video-cassettes etc.
2. Prescribed and recommended textbooks.
3. Books on the teaching of Commerce.
4. Journals and magazines on Commerce and related disciplines.
5. Reference books.
6. Government notifications regarding trade and commerce.

7. Career literature pertaining to the subject.
8. Course prescribed by the Examination Board.

Resources of the Community

Importance. A community provides 'concrete', 'seeable', and 'tangible' resources which are extrernal-v 'dynamic', 'interesting', and 'meaningful' for the teaching and learning of Commerce. It is not enough for a child to have 'knowledge' about the factories, farms, council sessions, museums and commercial enterprises etc. He must have the acquaintance with all these. A community is a child's laboratory for having first hand learning about the ways of living. The Community with its rich and varied resources can enrich and supplement learning. A well planned programme can bring the school and the community quite close to each other. A school cannot remain an 'ivory tower'.

Important Resources. Ordinarily we include only those community resources which are within the "walking distance'. Following are the important community resources:

1. *Places of civic interest.* These include the village panchayat, State legislature etc.
2. *Place of cultural interest.* These include art theatres, clubs, emporium galleries, Kala Kendras, museums, radio stations, T.V. Centres, Zoos etc.
3. *Places of commercial and economic interest.* These include agricultural farms, banks, commercial centres, factories, telephone exchanges etc.
4. *Places of geographical interest.* These comprise dams, hills, lakes, rivers, river valley projects, springs, tea gardens, water falls etc.
5. *Places of historical interest.* These include caves, churches excavations, forts, gurdwaras, inscriptions, mosques, pillars and temples etc.
6. *Places of scientific interest.* These consist of broadcasting stations, engineering institutes, thermal and hydro-power generating stations, television centres etc.
7. *Government buildings.* These include fire stations, law courts, military installations, police stations, public libraries etc.
8. *Forms of social control.* These comprise attitudes, beliefs, customs, ceremonies, rituals, traditions etc.

Utilising Methods

These are basically two ways:

I. Taking the school to the community.
II. Bringing the community to the school.

I. Taking the school to the community. This includes:

1. Field trips to places of civic, cultural, geographical, social and scientific places. These trips are very helpful in integrating classroom instruction, stimulating imagination and providing learning by sensory perceptions, seeing life vividly, learning in the art of living with others and expanding emotional and intellectual horizons.
2. Community service which includes cleanliness of community, attending on the sick, social service in fairs, planting of trees, digging of manure pits, making of drains etc. All these activities help in developing a sense of dignity of labour, fellow-feeling etc.
3. Social survey clubs. Social survey clubs should be organised in schools which could undertake to investigate some of the pressing needs and problems of the surrounding areas, e.g., the condition of roads, the percentage of literacy, the drainage of the village, street or town etc.

The study of the community will help the child:

(a) to develop new interests in occupations;
(b) to develop a more sympathetic attitude towards other people;
(c) to develop a desire to take more active part in community affairs;
(d) to have a recognition of certain forces that shape personal, economic and social living;
(e) to have a greater sensitivity to the need for accepting social responsibility;
(f) to have a more intelligent concern for democratic institutions, their functions and contributions.

The study of the community will help the teacher:

(i) to correlate his teaching with the life of the community;
(ii) to utilise a rich source of instructional aids and material;
(iii) to fit the curriculum to the personal and social needs of pupils;

(iv) to develop better public relations;
(v) to co-operate with all other agencies engaged in school and community improvement.

Community to the School

Following are the important means of bringing the community to the school:

1. Utilising experiences of the experts in the community by arranging talks on vocations.
2. Organising exhibition.
3. Inviting parents to career conferences.
4. Forming parent-teacher associations.
5. Making school a centre of community service.

Use of Computer

Like books, films, blackboards, and laboratory equipments and maps, computer-also can serve the teacher to communicate to the student. But it is a very sophisticated monster aid and requires careful preparation for use and higher prerequisite for understanding. Apart from this the computer does some of the teachers' work.

Computer-assisted instruction has two major levels of impact on the teacher. First, the teachers' ability to work in an efficient way in increased, because the strenuous works of correcting work books, comparing exercise, maps etc., can be given to the computer. Second, the computer makes the teacher to be more critical and active, because the work is synthesised and regulated by the computer.

Computer is very helpful in preparing balance sheets and maintenance of several types of account books needed in commerce.

To the student it gives immense opportunities for learning more and to rationalise thinking. The learning will become sharp and not speculative. The serious student involved with facts, ideas and logics, will find fast sequences in learning. The most important factor is that the computer is a 'flexible' teacher not like 'rigid' human teacher. With a level of flexibility, the computer will give alternatives to the learner so that depending upon learning capacity and imaginative power, different options are available to the students.

Aims and Objectives

The basic objective of CML is to relieve the teacher from tedious time-consuming tasks so that he can more profitably utilise his time and energy for instructional work. Here the teacher, the students and the computer work in close coordination, each doing the tasks most suitable to him/it. The teacher prepares course materials, teaches and helps the students in their learning. The student learns through course materials selected to suit his/her individual needs and the computer processes information quickly and accurately and maintains records. A general model of computer managed learning showing the roles of the student, the computer and the teacher is shown in the figure.

Present Situation

Importance of Current Affairs. There is a general consensus among the educators that teaching of current affairs must form an integral part of commerce curriculum as current events increase the power of discrimination, comprehension, critical and constructive analysis—qualities needed for enlightened citizenship. Current affairs generally fall within the commerce field. In fact, current 'affairs respresent 'an extension' and 'exemplification' of the major topics in the curriculum of Commerce. Teaching of Commerce is likely to remain lifeless and meaningless without the study of current affairs.

Defining current affairs. R.S. Kimbal states, "It is a field, which is concerned with all these happenings, both domestic and international, social, political or economic, a knowledge, an understanding of which is necessary as a basis for citizenship of loyalty and service."

Current events are a living history and are part of the learning activities of 'social living' for the child. Only a well informed and well intentioned people can have a government which looks after the economic, social and individual welfare of the people who make it.

Main Objectives

1. Expanding popular information.
2. Helping pupils to identify important problems and issues to see how these affect their lives and to sense what they can do about them.

3. Helping pupils recognise democratic values in reacting to problems and issues.
4. Encouraging pupils to develop habits of continued reading, listening, enquiring and observing ways of keeping well informed about current affairs.
5. Helping pupils acquire proficiency in locating, organising and evaluating information on important issues and in evaluating and analysing the judgement of others on these issues.
6. Helping pupils acquire the greatest possible proficiency in the skills needed for obtaining and using economic and social information.
7. Helping pupils develop facility in the discussion of issues; orally and in writing.
8. Helping pupils to see the importance of revising judgement in the light of new evidence.
9. Affording pupils a variety of opportunities for action to implement conclusions reached on important issues.
10. Promoting the ability of the pupils to distinguish between more important and less important news items.
11. Promoting the ability of the pupils to take a position on controversial issues.
12. Developing the ability of the pupils to foretell the likely consequences in terms of present developments.
13. Helping the pupils -relate school learning to life outside the school.
14. Promoting the critical appraisal of information obtained from the newspapers, magazines, radio, television etc.
15. Promoting discrimination in the choice of authors and sources of information.
16. Promoting understanding and tolerance.
17. Promoting the ideals and values of national oneness and unity.
18. Promoting the cause of international understanding and world peace.

Scope of Current Affairs. Current Afflairs in commerce include ideas, changes, movements and trends in parties and politics, election results, change in governments and government policies, defence, international relations and foreign policies etc. Reforms – Cultural, economic, educational and social etc., amendments in the constitution etc., all constitute current affairs in one or the other form in commerce.

Current affairs may be included in the following manner in school curriculum:

1. Teaching current affairs in addition to commerce.
2. Utilising current affairs for supplementing the teaching of Commerce.
3. Utilising current affairs as a basis for Commerce unit.

Nature of Current Affairs. There are broadly speaking four methods to use current affairs in commerce.

1. ***Current affairs as a subject.*** This implies including current affairs as a separate discipline of school curriculum. This approach is not very, conducive as it will unnecessarily entail the study of additional subject and the student will treat it as an examination subject.
2. ***Current affairs as a resource.*** This view considers current affairs a reservoir of illustrations which may be utilised to clarify the events, movements and topics described in the textbooks. Here, it is not obligatory on the part of the teacher to devote definite time from his daily schedule to the study of current affairs. He may do so occasionally.
3. ***Current affairs as a method.*** According to this view, current affairs should be used as a method or as a means or approach or procedure of simplifying difficult portions of the textbook and linking the present with the past.
4. ***Current affairs as a means of motivation.*** Children by nature are interested in what is happening now. They are interested in new inventions, new discoveries, elections, electricity projects etc. These topics can serve as motivation as this is the natural procedure of going from known to unknown,, concrete to abstract, definite to indefinite and from immediate to distant.

Selection of Current Events

1. Continuity of the process of any cultural, economic, political and social event.
2. Consequence of the effects or result of a particular news or report in the press.

3. Nationally regarding the countries, groups and persons influencing events.
4. Recency of discoveries and inventions etc., groups and persons influencing events.
5. Reliability of sources, distinction between rumour and truth, fact and fiction.
6. Scope regarding the impact of an event-local, national or international.
7. Suitability regarding the age, ability, aptitude and interest of the students.
8. Utility of events for students.

Related Current Affairs

1. Bulls and Bears in Stock Exchange.
2. Role of Multinational Companies (MNCs) in the Economy.
3. Role of Exim Bank in Foreign Trade.
4. Role of Indigenous Bankers in Rural India.
5. Role of Public Sector Enterprises in Indian Economy.
6. Bank Rates.
7. Tram System in a Metropolitan city.

Current Events Taught

1. Chart Making.
2. Debates on Broadcasting and T.V. Programmes.
3. Discussions.
4. Dramatising New Events.
5. Drawing Cartoons to illustrate events.
6. Map Drawing.
7. Youth Parliament.
8. Morning Assembly Talks.
9. News Bulletin Board and pinning clippings on it, pinning strips of yarn from each clipping to the place on the map where the event occurred etc.
10. Preparation of Note-books and Files.
11. Quiz Competitions.
12. Round Table Discussion.
13. Talks of Experts.
14. Visits to banks, transport offices etc.
15. Wall of World-depiction of current events on the walls of the Commerce room through various types of visual material.

Teacher's Role

The role of Commerce teacher is that of a guide and a leader. For playing this role he must be wide awake, an active, enlightened and well informed person. He must listen to news broadcasts and telecast, read current events, attend lectures and discussions, study and analyse reports and editorials, participate in school and community relations and see good newsreels and documentaries. R.S. Kimball has observed, "Current affairs can be taught successfully when a teacher is sufficiently interested himself. The varying degrees of success, however, seem to indicate that the ability of the teacher, rather than the quality of the medium or the method is the determining factor. Almost any device can be used effectively. The teacher's own interest his own enthusiasm, his own understanding of what should be accomplished, are the matters which determine the failure or success of current events teaching. The best available media fail in their purpose when used by a class guided by a teacher unskilled in methods of current events instruction.

Controversial Issues

Teachers are under close scrutiny of the public as they form the core of democratic action. It is widely believed that the standard of behaviour set by them in and out of the school stands examination and can be worthy of emulation by the impressionable youngsters who make up their student body. The teachers of commerce should have opinions but opinions derived in an objective manner from a weighing of evidence. The Commerce teacher is expected to discuss issues that are considered controversial. Most of the current issues are controversial since they demand choice. If there is no ground for choice and, therefore, no problem of controversial treatment. The Commerce teacher must be very careful to pursue his investigations with objectivity. The Commerce teacher must operate within the limits set by his profession and the pursuit of truth. He should not air his views without any proportion.

Academic freedom implies that the Commerce teachers should be willing to exercise, good judgment, hold objectivity in high esteem and encourage reflective thought in themselves.

The teachers of commerce must also bear in mind that just as they are involved in academic freedom; students too equally and more importantly hope to learn to evaluate facts and human relationship for which they must have academic freedom to learn. Freedom of enquiry must be followed by free and objective instruction.

Academic Liberty

Academic freedom does not imply the right of indoctrination. James High of the University of California has explained this as "An opinion, derived by any means, if made the sole content of teaching and set up as the 'right' answer, constitutes indoctrination and cannot be countenanced under the guise of academic freedom." Schools are for the purpose of broadening the horizons of the students. Means employed must be objective and honest differences of opinion accepted. It is the duty of the school system to encourage reflected thought. Continued interest in the preservation of academic freedom throughout all ranks of society must stem originally from the schools. Reflection is the only unique and original tool man has. Reflected thought concentrated on the records of the human past results in wisdom of the exercise of human choice in the future. After reflecting, man does not always make the best choices, but without it any good choice would be totally accidental. Critical, constructive and tolerant attitude is a great part of adequate citizenship and all efforts have to be made in teaching of commerce to realize this objective. A Commerce teacher has to perform this task very intelligently and skilfully.

One school of thought tends to hold the view that school is a temple of learning and its devotees i.e., children should be kept away from controversial issues. They point out that the conflicts of the real world must not enter into the portals of this temple and conflicting issues must not find their way in it. If they enter, they are likely to vitiate the classroorn environment.

Rechard E. Servey points out that basically teaching acts comprise the following:

(1) Clarifying with the children the issue that lies at the heart of their concern.

(2) Guiding them in identifying the different choices possible for deciding the issues.

(3) Encouraging them to explore the facts and ideas which support the issues.

(4) Guiding them in an analysis of the facts and ideas to determine bases for opinions.

(5) Guiding them towards suspended judgement.

The Commerce teacher should encourage the students to make their own choice, but to think more about it and to be on the alert for more pertinent information. The teacher should feel free to express his own favoured choice for action and to substantiate it but should point out that he too is limited in what he can do about making the final decision. He can somewhat assuage fears by suggesting that the other choices for action have strengths to be considered. In no case, a teacher should make provocated statements or make derogatory remarks directly or indirectly.

The history of Bookkeeping, the only and the earliest from of Commerce Education is very old. It has been found that systematic records of business transactions were maintained in early times by Babylonians, Egyptians, Greeks, Indians and Romans.

The year 1494 is considered to be a landmark in the history of book-keeping in the world as Fra Luca Pacioli, called the father of book-keeping published his classical book on bookkeeping, known as *Everything about Arithmetic, Geometry and Proportion*. This book contained principles of book-keeping. Fra Luca Pauoli was an Italian and therefore double Entry Bookkeeping is called the Italian Method.

During the Middle Ages, tradesmen taught book-keeping to their children in the form of apprenticeship. Later on private teachers began to teach book-keeping. In India, Hindustani Bahi-Khata was taught by 'munims' through apprenticeship. In due course, reputed 'munims' started some Bahi Khata Schools.

In India, the formal teaching of bookkeeping was started in 1886 in the first commercial school established in Madras by the Trustees of Pachyappa Charities. The Madras Government instituted examinations in Bookkeeping and Accountancy at the same time.

In 1895, the Government of India made provisions for the teaching of Bookkeeping in the school of Commerce at Calcutta.

In 1903, the Presidency College, Calcutta started Book-keeping classes.

In the first decade of the 20th century, teaching of Book-keeping and Accountancy was started in several commercial institutes.

In 1913, the Sydenham college of Commerce and Economics, Bombay was founded with provision also made for teaching Bookkeeping and Accountancy.

The Indian Institute of Bankers, established in 1926 had Bookkeeping and Accountancy as one of the subjects.

In 1928, the Hartog Committee recommended diversified courses at the secondary stage and included Bookkeeping and Accountancy as a subject in the curriculum.

In 1935, the Central Advisory Board of Education recommended the inclusion of Book-keeping and Accountancy at the secondary level.

In 1936, a Committee on Vocational Education recommended that teaching of Bookkeeping should be included along with other vocational subjects.

In 1939, was started the Registered Accountants Examination.

The Sargent Committee, (1943-44) appointed by the Government of India, recommended the establishment of academic high schools and technical high schools. The teaching of Bookkeeping found a place in both types of schools.

In 1944, the Institute of Costs and Works Accountants of India was started.

In 1945, the Delhi Polytechnic introduced Commerce Education which included Bookkeeping and Accountancy.

In 1949, the Registered Accountants' Examination was changed into Chartered Accountants' Examination and the Institute of Chartered Accountants was established in New Delhi, through an Act of Parliament.

On the recommendations of the Secondary Education Commission 1952-53, the teaching of Bookkeeping and Accountancy got a prominent place when Commerce was included as one of the streams at the secondary level. The Commercial Stream included the following subjects.

(i) Commercial Practice
(ii) Book Keeping
(iii) Commercial Geography or Elements of Economics and Civics
(iv) Shorthand and Typewriting.

In 1957, the Central Advisory Board of Education (C.A.B.E.) recommended that the Teachers' Training Colleges should provide for teaching of Bookkeeping and Accountancy.

In 1961, the C.A.B.E. recommended for the setting up of four Regional Training Colleges for preparing teachers of practical subjects.

In 1961 also, the V.K.R.V. Rao Committee recommended that Commerce should be taught from class eleven rather than nine and it should consist of elements of Bookkeeping and Commercial Geography.

The teaching of Commerce was introduced in the Regional Colleges of Education in 1964.

The Education Commission 1964-66 which made recommendations at almost all levels and areas of education including curriculum at the secondary and higher secondary stages did not include Commerce (including Bookkeeping and Accountancy) as a subject at the school stage.

According to the Fifth All India Educational Survey (1989), 5585 higher secondary schools offered Commerce courses, 10,608 Science and 13245 Arts courses as on 30th September 1986. Break-up of the commerce course into Bookkeeping and Accountancy etc. is not available.

The Central Board of Secondary Education includes courses of Business Studies and Accountancy in classes XI and XII. Incidentally it does not mention the term 'commerce'.

The present position of teaching of Commerce appears to be quite sound. Besides schools, it is taught at the degree and post-graduate levels. Several professional examinations are conducted by State level and All India level bodies.

As for teaching of Commerce in Training Colleges is concerned, it is available in about a dozen colleges only.

Development of Business Education

Daughtrey, A.S. (1974) has very rightly 'observed, "if a single greatest influence on the early development of Business Education had to be named, it would undoubtedly be the private school."

A business college was first established in Philadelphia in 1834. Haynes and Jackson (1935) report three periods in the development of private business schools in the U.S.A.

1. Experimental-when the first schools were being organised and developed (1834-50)
2. Monopolistic-when the private business school dominated the field of business education (1850-90)
3. Modern-when Business Education took its place in many types of schools and the private business school had to compete for its place in the educational scheme. (1890-to date)

The first public high school of commerce in U.S.A. according to S.J. Wanous, was opened in 1890 in Washington D.C.

QUESTIONS

1. Explain the role of any two co-curricular activities in the teaching of Commerce.
2. What is the scope of out-door activities in the teaching of Commerce? Give examples.
3. Write notes on:
   (i) Commerce Room; (ii) Community resources and their use in Commerce teaching.
4. What is the role of the computer in Commerce? Explain the concept of CAI.
5. Elucidate the role of the Commerce teacher in current affairs and controversial topics in Commerce. Give four examples of such topics.
6. Describe briefly the history of Commerce Education.
7. Write a short note on the available current facilities for Commerce Education in India.

4

Objectives and Aims

The Determination

Objectives are the 'crux' and 'key' of the entire process of teaching and learning and therefore, objectives of teaching and learning will be in consonance with the philosophy of education which in itself reflects the philosophy of a nation.

The work on determining the objectives may follow the pattern indicated below:

Overall objectives of a Nation
(as reflected in its Constitution)
↓
Overall objectives of Education
(Primary, Secondary and University etc.)
↓
Subjectwise Objectives
(Objectives of teaching Commerce, Social Studies etc.)
↓
Classwise Objectives in General
↓
Instructional Objectives
(Classwise and Subject-wise)

Objective Functions

Instructional objectives in Commerce

1. provide the desired 'directions' of instructional activities involvedin the teaching-learning of commerce.
2. determine the nature of instructional activities.
3. provide a basis for systematising or planning an instructional programme.
4. decide on points of emphasis in an instructional activity.
5. give unity and coherence to an instructional programme.
6. provide the basis for the measurement growth and thus guard valid evaluation.
7. help distinguish between various aspects of learning.
8. help focus attention on proper attributes of teaching and learning.
9. help grade learning experiences.
10. help maintain a balance between different aspects of an instructional programme.
11. help fix priorities in an instructional programme.
12. guide instructional decision in curricular and co-curricular areas.
13. guide in the selection of relevant content.
14. give meaning to and clarify the structure and content of.
15. help make learning functional.
16. help articulate learning at various levels.
17. help discover and evolve properly learning situations.
18. help define instructional process.
19. help make the intangibles in instruction tangible.
20. help identify weaknesses and strengths of pupils in learning.
21. facilitate communication among instructional workers.
22. guide improvements in instruction.

Objectives of Teaching at the Senior Secondary Stage

The Central Board of Secondary Education (CBSE) has listed the following objectives of teaching commerce (Business Studies and Accountancy) at the Senior Secondary Stage:

1. to develop in the students an interest in the theory and practice in business, trade and industry.
2. To acquaint students with the theoretical foundations and practices of organising, managing and handling routine operations of a business firm.

3. To inculcate attitudes and values leading to the integration of business with the social system with a positive approach.
4. To enable students to apply the principles and functions of management to specific aspects of business.
5. To equip the students with essential fundamental knowledge for setting up, organising and handling routine operations of a small scale factory.
6. To equip the students with basic information on modern methods of office operations for effectively carrying out paper work in a business office.
7. To impart knowledge of methods considered useful in maintaining records of proprietory and partnership firm companies and nontrading organisations.
8. To generate and promote awareness of students in modern techniques of maintaining accounting records with the help of computers.
9. To enable the students to analyse financial statements and interpret the results for decision making.
10. To acquaint the students with practice and procedure of determination of cost from the point of its elements.
11. To create an awareness of the necessity of auditing the datection/rectification of errors/frauds in the process of accounting.

[Note. It may be noted that the Central Board of Secondary Education has used the term 'Business Studies' and not 'Commerce' although it implies the same meaning.]

Objectives of Teaching at the College Stage

The Curriculum Development Centre in Commerce of the University Grants Commission in 1989 made these observations regarding the nature of Commerce as a discipline, "Commerce as a discipline is not properly understood by administrators, common men and even by educationists. This is being equated with one subject like Physics or Chemistry or Maths or History etc. In the university system, by and large, there is only one Department of Commerce while under Science discipline that are Departments of Physics, Chemistry, Botany, Biology and so on. There is an urgent need to treat Commerce Discipline at par with Science for its proper development and growth."

The UGC Curriculum Development Centre in Commerce has divided the Commerce Discipline into three major areas: Accounting, Business Studies and Business Economics.

The Centre has suggested the objectives of teaching Commerce at various stages as under.

B. Com. (Hons) I Year

1. To acquaint students with the fundamentals of business organisation and management as a body of knowledge.
2. To impart to the students basic knowledge of important laws applicable to business, trade and industry.
3. To acquaint the students with principles of Business Economics.
4. To provide the students a general understanding of the various aspects of business environment of the country.
5. To provide knowledge to the students of accounting principles and their application in different situations.
6. To develop in the students basic mathematical skills and provide an awareness of computer applications.
7. To develop the ability of the students to communicate clearly and correctly in English and also in the regional languages on matters relevant to day-to-day business operations with emphasis on quality of presentation.

B. Com.(Hons) II Year

1. To provide knowledge and develop skills in the construction of accounts of companies and specialised business entities.
2. To make the students familiar with the basic production process and make them understand the dimensions of production function.
3. To familiarise the students with the finance function and acquaint them with working knowledge of various techniques of financial decision making.
4. To impart knowledge of the application of money in the modern context and monetary theories systems and policies including national income.
5. To acquaint students with the techniques of statistical measures and analysis.

B. Com. (Hons) III Year

1. To provide an understanding of the main provisions of Income Tax Act, 1961 and their application.
2. To impart knowledge of the principles, methods and techniques of auditing and their application.
3. To impart knowledge and understanding of various aspects of personal policies, problems and management.
4. To impart knowledge of various aspects of marketing and acquaint the students with the applied problems of marketing, with special reference to India.
5. To provide an insight into the concepts, theories, agreements and regulatory framework relating to international trade, and to expose the students to the contemporary problems in the area.
6. To impart knowledge of the concept and theories of public finance and their application in India.

B. Com. (Professional) I Year

1. To acquaint the students with the fundamentals of business organisation and management as a body of knowledge.
2. To impart to the students basic knowledge of important laws applicable to business, trade and industry.
3. To acquaint the students with principles of business economics.
4. To provide a general understanding of the various aspects of business environment of the country.
5. To provide knowledge of accounting principles and their application in different business situations.
6. To develop basic mathematical skills and provide an awareness of computer applications.
7. To develop ability to communicate clearly and correctly in English and also in the regional languages, on matters relevant to day-to-day business operations with emphasis on quality of presentation.

B. Com. (Professional) II Year

1. To acquaint the students with the basic concepts and tools used in cost accounting management control.
2. To make students conversant with the local environment in which the small business units and other professions

operate and to familiarise them with their special accounting requirements.

3. To familiarise the students with the finance function and acquaint them with working knowledge of various techniques of financial decision making.
4. To acquaint the students with practical and operational problems relating to factory organisation and operational management.
5. To acquaint students with the techniques of statistical measures and analysis.
6. To familiarise students with the organisation and functioning of various bank and non-bank institutions in the money and capital market of India.

B. Com. (Professional) III Year (Accounting)

1. To provide students with the knowledge of some higher aspects and problems of company accounts.
2. To create among students an awareness of the potentialities of electronic data processing in various stages of cost recording, ascertainment, and improvement. They are to use computer as a working tool for preparing budgets and other accounts through cobol programming.
3. To impart knowledge of the principles, methods and techniques of auditing and their application.
4. To make students conversant with the taxation system and to provide detailed knowledge of customs and central excise duties in India.
5. To provide an understanding of the main provisions of Income Tax Act 1961 and their applications.
6. To prepare students for practising in the Wealth Tax, Gift Tax and Sales Tax.

B. Com. (Professional) III Year (Business Studies)

1. To provide students understanding of the problems, techniques and administration of personal management and human resource development.
2. To provide knowledge of various labour laws which are applicable to business units.
3. To impart knowledge about the handling of industrial disputes and maintaining industrial relations.

4. To familiarise the students with the basic concepts and practices of marketing.
5. To impart knowledge of the concepts, techniques and management of advertising.
6. To impart knowledge of policies procedures and techniques of sales management.

B. Com. (Professional) III Year (Business Economics)

1. To impart to the students knowledge of the important aspects of foreign trade and its financing.
2. To acquaint the students with the main aspects of import policy and procedures as prevalent in India.
3. To prepare students for the professional career in the management of export procedures and policy.
4. To impart knowledge to the students with the basic concepts and principles of commercial banks and their operations.
5. To provide knowledge to students of the main provisions of various banking laws and their application.
6. To impart knowledge to the students of the organisation, management and functioning of cooperative banking institutions.

M.Com. (Accounting)

1. To develop the understanding and skills to prepare accounts of corporate sector and also to impart knowledge in current issues in the area of accounting.
2. To acquaint the students with a coherent set of logical principles and a general frame of reference for the evaluation and development of sound accounting practices.
3. To develop understanding of accounting tools and information and their use in managerial decision making.
4. To develop an understanding of the analytical tools necessary for developing a basic framework for designing and operating a management control system.
5. To give an exposure to various accounting issues in international business operations and corporate reporting.
6. To acquaint the participants with some major operations, research techniques as also the application of computer in business systems.

7. To develop an understanding of the finance function and relevant techniques of financial administration.
8. To acquaint students with the application of statistical tools in the area of business decision-making.
9. To provide understanding of direct tax laws including the rules, notifications and case law pertaining thereto and their application to different like business situations.
10. To give an integrated view of tax laws and finance to assess and apply direct tax measures in managerial decisions.
11. To develop a conceptual framework for the study of security analysis and portfolio management.

M.Com. (Business Studies)

1. To provide understanding of the general theory of management.
2. To provide knowledge of organisation behaviour, group dynamics and various important aspects related to industrial psychology.
3. To develop an understanding of the finance function and relevant techniques of financial administration.
4. To develop understanding of the marketing functions and strategies.
5. To provide an understanding of the problems and techniques employed in the field of personnel management.
6. To impart knowledge about production techniques, process and operations management tools.
7. To provide an insight into process of decision-making, policy formulation and strategic management.
8. To provide knowledge and develop skills in the use of tools and techniques of accounting.
9. To give an understanding of concepts, design and practice of management information system.
10. To provide understanding of the rationale, growth problems and policies of public enterprises, with special reference to India.

11. To provide an understanding of the methods of security analysis and various theories and problems related to portfolio management.
12. To acquaint students with the application of statistical tools in the area of business decision making.

M.Com. (Business Economics)

1. To provide knowledge of production function, theory of firm, factor pricing and economic problems at unit level.
2. To provide understanding of economic principles and issues at macro-level and to develop ability to analyse and apply them to current economic issues.
3. To provide understanding of the economic factors governing the operation of industry.
4. To acquaint students with the application of statistical tools in the area of business decision making.
5. To provide understanding of growth models planning process and its methodology.
6. To provide understanding of the functioning of financial markets and institutions and their role in Indian economy.
7. To provide understanding of international economic environment, international monetary mechanism and institutions.
8. To develop an understanding of the current industrial relations situation and the role of personnel management.
9. To provide an understanding to the students of the rationale, growth, problems and policies of public enterprises, with special reference to India.
10. To provide understanding of the public finance and budgetory practices in India.
11. To provide understanding of monetary theory, policies and practices and also problems of international money.

Post-Graduate Diploma in Insurance

1. To acquaint students with the basic principles of life insurance protection, its need and operation.
2. To acquaint students with details of operational aspects of fire and marine insurance business.

3. To acquaint students with operation of different types of insurance protection available to individuals and organisations.
4. To acquaint students with insurance finance, growth of insurance legislation in India and present administrative structure of insurance business in India.

Post-Graduate Diploma in Accountancy and Internal Audit

1. To acquaint the students with accounting tools and techniques for decision making.
2. To acquaint the students with the tools and techniques of financial management of business enterprises.
3. To provide basic knowledge of accounting and auditing principles.
4. To provide understanding of tools and techniques of conducting internal audit of manufacturing and non-manufacturing organisations, including government departments.

Post-Graduate Diploma in Cost Accounting

1. To provide an insight into the factory management, engineering economics and production planning.
2. To make the students aware of the format and procedures and develop skills in accounting of major elements of cost.
3. To provide a working knowledge of the various methods and techniques of costing as employed in present day business enterprises for cost entertainment and cost control.
4. To provide students an insight into the dimension of the cost and management audit.

Post-Graduate Diploma in Personnel Management

1. To provide knowledge of various aspects of personnel policies, management and problems.
2. To provide knowledge of industrial relations and its impact on national economy.
3. To acquaint the students with the legal framework governing Indian labour.
4. To provide knowledge of how to develop human resources in a modern organisation so as to enhance their contribution to organisation.

Post-Graduate Diploma in Portfolio Management

1. To acquaint the students with the theory and practice of portfolio management.
2. To familiarise the students with the functioning and development of the Indian capital market.
3. To acquaint the students with the techniques of preparing, analysing and interpreting the annual accounts.
4. To make the students conversant with the principal provisions of various enactments as they affect the investment and portfolio decisions of the investors.

Post-Graduate Diploma in Entrepreneurship and Small Scale Unit Management

1. To give exposure to the students to entrepreneurship culture and industrial growth and with a view to enabling them to set up and manage small units.
2. To provide knowledge of techniques of formulation and appraisal of viable units.
3. To acquaint the students with functional areas of management as applied to small ventures.
4. To acquaint the students with the concept and tools of accounting and finance and the relevant provision of taxation.

Post-Graduate Diploma in Public Enterprise

1. To acquaint the students with various aspects of growth of public enterprises in India and problems of their management.
2. To provide knowledge about the various issues related to the human resource management in public enterprises, with special reference to India.
3. To impart knowledge about the role and source of financing public enterprises and problems and policies related to investment, budgeting and pricising.
4. To acquaint the students with the nature, problems and modes of control over public enterprises in India.

Post-Graduate Diploma in Foreign Trade

1. To acquaint the students with planning, techniques and organisation of international marketing and appraise them with managerial problems in this regard.

2. To impart knowledge about import and export procedures and make the students familiar with related documents.
3. To impart knowledge about international economic systems and cooperation and various aspects of foreign trade in India.
4. To acquaint the students with various legal provisions affecting foreign trade and also to impart knowledge of overseas marketing research.

QUESTIONS

1. What is the significance of objectives? How are they determined? State the objectives of teaching Commerce at the senior secondary level?
2. What are the functions of instructional objectives?
3. State the objectives of teaching Commerce at the college stage.

5

Objectives of Instructions

Definition. An instructional objective may be defined as desirable change in behaviour through instruction (teaching). The change may be in the following domains:

(i) Cognitive domain
(ii) Affective domain
(iii) Psycho-motor domain

Comparison of Educational and Instructional Objectives

Educational objectives	*Instructional Objectives*
1. Educational objectives are very broad.	1. Instructional objectives are very specific.
2. Educational objectives are determined by philosophy and sociology.	2. Psychology is the main basis of instructional objectives.
3. All school subjects may have common educational objectives.	3. Each school subject has specific instructional objectives.
4. Educational objectives include instructional objectives.	4. Instructional objectives form a part educational objectives.
5. Examples of educational objectives are : development of character, emotional and national integration, democratic values and ideals of secularism, etc.	5. Examples of instructional objectives are : development of knowledge, understanding skills etc. related to a subject.

Taxonomy

Prof B.S. Bloom of the University of Chicago (USA) is considered to be a pioneer in the taxonomy of objectives. Taxonomy implies a classification of an idea or an object. Taxonomy of instructional objectives means an analysis of instructional objectives in terms of the precise teaching outcome and specific or learning appropriate to classroom action. The hierarchy of taxonomy can be depicted in the following manner:

Knowledge (K) Comprehension (C) Application (A) Analysis (AN)

Synthesis (S) Evaluation (E)

Objective and mental process or ability in Bloom's taxonomy may be represented as under:

Objective	*Mental Process or Ability*
1. Knowledge	1. Recall 2. Recognise
2. Comprehension	1. See relationship 2. Cite example 3. Discriminate 4. Classify 5. Interest 6. Verify 7. Generalisation
3. Application	1. Reason 2. Formulate 3. Establish 4. Infer 5. Predict
4. Analysis	Analyse
5. Synthesis	Synthesise
6. Evaluation	Evaluate

According to taxonomy of objectives, objectives may be classified into the following categories:-

1. Congnitive domain objectives. These include knowledge, understanding, application, analysis, synthesis and evaluation.
2. Affective domain objectives. These include the appreciation, values, attitudes, interests and feelings.
3. Psychomotor domain objectives: Those include skills.

In the light of knowledge domain objectives, objectives of teaching Commerce are given below.

Classifications

1. *Knowledge objective:* To acquire the knowledge (information) of facts, terms, concepts, conventions, trends, principles, generalisations, assumptions, hypotheses process, etc. in Commerce.
2. *Understanding Objective:* To develop an understanding of facts, terms, concepts, conventions, trends, principles, generalisations, assumptions, hypotheses, processes, etc. in Commerce.
3. *Application objective:* To apply the acquired knowledge of Commerce and its understanding to unfamiliar situations.
4. *Skill objective:* To acquire practical skills essential for the study of Commerce.
5. *Interest objective:* To develop interest in the subject and problems related to commerce and commercial life of the people of one's country and of those of the world.
6. *Application objective:* To develop desirable positive attitudes necessary for developing a broader outlook as a commerce entrepreneur and, as a citizen.

1.0 Objective: To acquire the knowledge (information) of facts, terms, concepts, conventions, trends, principles, generalisations, assumptions, hypothesis, process, etc. in commerce.

Specification of the Objective: To demonstrate the achievement of the above objective, the pupil:

1.1 recalls facts, terms, concepts, principles, trends, etc. in commerce.

1.2 recognises facts, terms concepts, principles, trends, etc. in commerce.

1.3 reads information from various forms of representation of data i.e. maps, charts, diagrams, graphs etc. in commerce.

2.0 Objective: To develop an understanding of facts, terms, concepts, conventions, trends, principles, generalizations, assumptions, hypotheses, process, etc. in commerce.

Specification of the Objective: To demonstrate the achievement of the above objective, the pupil:

2.1 discriminates.
2.2 classifies.
2.3 compares and contrasts.
2.4 identifies relationships.
2.5 detects the points of emphasis and the trends of arguments.
2.6 cites illustrations.
2.7 detects errors and fallacies and corrects them.
2.8 explains (analyses or gives meaning or clarifies or elucidates).
2.9 gives reasons or advances arguments.
2.10 interprets data presented in different forms.

3.0 Objective: To apply the acquired knowledge and its understanding to unfamiliar situations.

Specification of the Objective: To demonstrate the achievement of the above objective, the pupil:

3.1 analyses the unfamiliar situations or problems and:
(a) finds out what is given and what is required.
(b) recalls knowledge relevant to the situation.
(c) judges the sufficiency or insufficiency, adequacy or inadequacy of data or any other evidence for solving the problem.
3.2 establishes relationships
3.3 suggests alternative methods for solving a particular problem.
3.4 selects the most appropriate method of attack.
3.5 draws inferences and makes generalizations.
3.6 makes predictions regarding the probable outcome of a given situation.

4.0 Objective: To acquire practical skills essential for the study of Commerce.

Specification of the Objective: To demonstrate the achievement of the above objective, the pupil:

4.1 draws maps, charts, tables, diagrams, graphs etc. from the given data.
4.2 translates data from one form of presentation to another.
4.3 prepares models.

5.0 Objective: To develop interest in the subject and problem related to commerce and commercial life of the people of one's country and those of the world.

Specification of the Objective: To demonstrate the achievement of the above objective, the pupil:

5.1 voluntarily studies literature related to commerce and tries to know about the inherent issues and problems.

5.2 spends leisure in trying to know about commercial problems and issues and exerts in finding solutions to them.

5.3 closely observes commercial processes and changes at local, national and international levels.

5.4 discusses and is able to communicate various aspects to every day civic problem and their implications.

5.5 enthusiastically participates in excursions, visits and field-trips to places of commercial activities (e.g. Chambers of Commerce etc.)

5.6 enjoys attending and participating in debates, symposium, discussions on commercial problems.

5.7 enjoys writing articles and preparing pamphlets, brochures, etc. on topics related to commerce.

5.8 enjoys preparing display-materials related to commercial life and events.

5.9 enjoys collecting information about other commercial system and facts about other locations, regions and countries.

6.0 Objective: To develop desirable positive attitudes necessary for developing a broader outlook.

Specification of the Objective: To demonstrate the achievement of the above objective, the pupil:

6.1 respects the views, opinions and problems of others and displays sympathy and fellow feeling towards them:

a) shows tolerance.

b) controls emotions and displays restraint.

c) develops social awareness.

6.2 is able to examine the present situations in the light of a historical perspective.

6.3 develops a sense of law-abidingness.

6.4 assumes responsibility in cooperative and civic activities.

6.5 judges issues objectively and on their merits.

6.6 displays abhorrence towards commercial malpractices like hoarding, profiteering, black marketing, smuggling, bribery for obtaining favours.

6.7 shows sympathetic understanding of the problems of people belonging to different social, religious, linguistic and cultural groups.

6.8 realises the importance of the contributions made by the leaders of the nation in different spheres.

6.9 develops a sense of respect for the National Flag, the National Anthem, the National Emblem and the Constitution of one's country and those of other countries of the world.

6.10 develops faith in democratic and secular values.

QUESTIONS

1. What is an instructional objective? Explain the difference between an educational objective and instructional objective.
2. Write a note on the taxonomy of instructional objectives.
3. State the meaning of the instructional objective. What is the significance of objectives in Commerce.
4. What are the objectives of teaching Commerce at the senior secondary stage? How are these objectives different from specific objectives of teaching Commerce?
5. State the specific objectives of teaching Commerce.

6

Dynamic Method

The Secondary Education Commission 1952-53 has emphasised the need for using right methods of teaching in these words, "Every teacher and educationist of experience knows that even the best curriculum and the most perfect syllabus remain dead unless quickened into life by the right methods of teaching and the right kind of teachers. Sometimes even an unsatisfactory and unimaginative syllabus can be made interesting and significant by the gifted teacher who does not focus his mind on the subject-matter to be taught or the information to be imparted but on his students-their interests and aptitudes, their reactions and response. He judges the success of his lesson not by the amount of matter covered but by the understanding, the appreciation and the efficiency achieved by the students." The Commission has further observed, "Any method, good or bad links up the teacher and his pupils into an organic relationship with constant mutual interaction, it reacts not only on the mind of the students but on their entire personality; their standards of work and judgement, their intellectual and emotional equipment, their attitudes and values. Good methods which are psychologically and socially sound may raise the whole quality of their life; bad method debase it. So, in the choice and assessment of Methods, teachers must always take into consideration their end products, namely, the attitudes and values inculcated in them consciously or unconsciously."

The Importance

James Welton has stressed the significance of good methods of teaching, "The teacher is like a guide and the pupil like a traveller in an unknown country. The traveller knows where he wanted to go, but knows neither the way nor the exact character of the place he wishes to go.... But unless the traveller that is that pupil takes the journey himself, nothing is accomplished. Many a lesson is too much like a guide describing the journey to the would-be traveller who sits and listens but does not leave his chair to undertake it. In other lessons, the guide himself laboriously takes the journeys again and again, but the traveller that should be, remains inert. In short, no matter how admirably a lesson is planned, there is no really methodical teaching unless the pupils by their own efforts pass along the road tacit for them. True teaching is nothing but arousing and directing activity."

In the words of Herbard Ward and Frank Rosceor, "While it is true that good method is not merely a collection of artifices or mechanical devices and that every teacher must devise his own method, it is important to remember that good methods can result only from the constant observation of certain broad principles. These include orderly procedure in teaching, an arrangement of the subject matter which will avoid waste of time and of energy and a distribution of emphasis which will secure the greatest cooperation froth the pupils and maintain their active interest."

The effect of recent developments in educational philosophy and educational psychology upon the methods of teaching has been revolutionary. The central place in the school, in theory at least, has been given to the student. Any process that is not based upon the 'student-activity' is not in accord with recent educational theories. The present century has been termed as 'The Century of the Child'. Rousseau considers that 'child' is a 'hero' in 'the drama of education' and as such he must play the dominant role.

The Origin

The origin of modern methodology may be traced to 'Great Diadic' of Johann Amos Comenius who lived in the seventeenth century. Comenius believed that all instruction should be carefully graded and arranged in a natural order. He advocated that the teacher, in his methods, should appeal through sense perception to the understanding of the child. He set forth his principles in his 'Great

Didactic'. The world of Comenius, however, like that of other educators of his time was buried beneath the sea of religious, controversy and bigotry of his age.

'Emile' of Rousseau in the second half of the eighteenth century laid the foundations of the methodology and became the inspiration of forward looking and progressive educators. Comenius provided some ideas, Rousseau improved and enlarged and others worked them and put them into practice. In his chief educational work 'Emile', Rousseau begins with his principle "Everything is good as it comes from the hands of the Author of Nature; but everything degenerates in the hands of man." He points out that there are three great teachers, "nature, man and things."

Johann Heinrick Pestalozzi attempted to "psychologise instruction". He declared that the basis of all education was a drawing out process and not a pouring in process and that the basis of all education lay in the nature of the child and that methods of instruction must be sought and constructed to that end.

Wilhelm August Froebel and Johann Friedrich Herbart, disciples and followers of Pestalozzi developed elaborate systems of education. The work of Froebel dealt largely with the Kindergarten stage. Herbart gave his famous 'Herbartian Steps' which cast a flood of light on existing methods. Herbartian steps became the stimulators of various other movements in the field of education. Herbart condemned the rote method and stressed comprehension and association. The concept that the outcome of education was not the strengthening of the mental faculties but rather the building up of an "apperceptive mass" of ideas was very revolutionary. Herbartian theory and practice became popular in Germany between 1865 and 1885. Teachers and students from many lands studied at Jena, a centre of Herbartian teaching. By 1890, these ideas were brought to America where they received an almost universal acceptance.

The period of Herbartian influence, on the whole, was a transitional one. It prepared the way for newer and better concepts of education. By 1910, Herbartian as a system of education was quite generally criticised. Herbartianism stressed the teacher and the formal procedure of teachings; the new theories of educational philosophy emphasised the pupils. Emphasis during recent years has been on individual instruction in the classroom but the socialisation of the individual is not to be neglected. Almost all modern methods and procedures can be used to promote both.

Dewey endeavoured to substitute bookish learning by experience. He strongly recommended investigation and experimentation. According to him the school is a 'special environment' where a certain quality of life and certain types of activities and occupations are provided with the object of securing children's development along desirable lines. "The teacher", according to him, "is a guide and director, he steers the boat but the energy that propels it must come from those who are learning."

Nature's Commodity

Children have been endowed by nature with tremendous vitality. They have within themselves the springs of youth, joy and vigour. They possess curiousity and wish to know things for themselves. In the words of T.S. Avinashilingam, "The Great Ganga of life flows majestically on. But if anyone tries to retain and dam it, the dam will break unless attempts are simultaneously made to divert it into other channels. These waters can only be diverted, but cannot be dammed indefinitely. If anyone tried to do the impossible, it would be at his peril, for the dam will break, sooner or later. So is the nature of children. The great vitality of our children cannot be permanently restrained without providing a positive purpose. In ordinary bookish classroom education, the teacher teaches, students are but passive listeners. Their energy has not to be restrained by fear, inducement or punishment. This is against their nature and that is why we see much outbursts of so-called indiscipline. But, on the other hand, if we provide such activities in which the children themselves can take part we will find that discipline becomes natural. Thus, providing for various types of activities which will interest the children and give them opportunities for observation and the use of their hands is to offer them the fulfilment and satisfaction, which nothing else confers."

The principle of 'Learning by Doing' has been accepted by all the progressive educators and in all the progressive countries. All educationists recognise that activity is an important instrument of education.

Main Characteristics

These may be listed as under:

1. They should aim at inculcating 'love of work'.
2. They should aim at developing the desire to do work with the highest measure of efficiency of which one is capable. The motto of every school and his pupils should be 'Everything that is worth doing at all is worth doing well'. Whether it be making a speech, writing a composition, drawing a map, cleaning the class-room, making a book, rack of forming a queue.
3. They should provide numerous opportunities of participation in freely accepted projects and activities in which discipline and cooperation are constantly in demand.
4. They should aim at developing the capacity for 'clear thinking' which distinguishes every truly educated person, "whether a student is asked to make a speech in a debating society or to write an essay or to answer a question in Commerce, History, Geography, or Science or an experiment,' the accent should always be on clear thinking and on lucid expression which is a mirror of clear thought."
5. The methods of teaching should expand the range of students' interest. "We should urge all schools to provide in the time-table, at least one free period every day in which students may pursue their favourite hobbies and creative activities individually or in groups, preferably under the guidance of some interested teacher", recommended the Secondary Education Commission.
6. They should aim at providing opportunities to pupils to apply practically the knowledge that has been acquired by them. They should aim at transforming present bookish schools into "work schools" or "activity schools."
7. They should aim at the quickening of interest and training in efficient techniques of learning and study.
8. They should train the students in the art of study. They should train the students in the use of reference material such as the list of contents and index in books, the dictionary, the atlas, and reference books like the encyclopaedia.

9. They should be adapted to suit different levels of intelligence.
10. They should be such as they balance the claim of individual work with co-operative or group effort. The training of emotions, attitudes and social capacities take place best in the context of projects and units of work undertaken co-operatively. The Secondary Education Commission has recommended that the teachers should be so trained that they are able to visualise and organise at least a part of the curriculum in the form of projects and activity-Units which groups of students may take up and carry to completion.

Telling Methods. Classification on the basis of technique. These include lecture method, debates and discussions, panel discussion, oral quiz, story telling etc.

Showing Methods. These comprise using demonstration, charts, diagrams, observation of on-site operations etc.

Doing Methods. These consist of assignments, committee work, guided experiences, projects work, written tests etc.

Exercise of Classification

Large Group Instruction. This includes descriptive method, lecture method, telelecture etc.

Medium Group Instruction. This denotes informal lecturing such as discussions in medium groups, dialogue, buzz groups, brain storming, role playing, demonstration, field trips etc.

Small Group Instruction. Seminars and discussions in small groups are the important methods covered in this category.

Independent Study. Under this mention may be made of the assignments, use of Dalton Plan, programmed learning, computerised instruction, committee work, work experiences etc.

Classification of Methods

Methods of teaching Commerce may be classified as under.

Discovery Methods. These methods are high on all the three dimensions: learner activity, experience and experimentation by the learner, and cognitive understanding. Simulations primarily come under this category. The main emphasis of methods in this category is on problem-solving and providing necessary framework to the learner, so that while solving the problem the learner is also able to learn the rationale and logic of what he has done.

Encounter Methods. Carl Rogers popularised the term 'encounter' Since the emphasis is on providing experience through confrontation or through encounter, and not through cognitive understanding, these methods are affective for change in basic behavioural patterns and developing new ways of looking at things. Role play also involves some amount of encounter.

Expository Methods. In these methods cognitive emphasis is very high, while emphasis on experience is low. One good example of expository method is the lecture method in which the main emphasis is on imparting cognitive information to the learners.

Individualized Methods. These methods are quite well known mainly through the popularity of programmed instruction. The main characteristic of these methods is the guided search encouraged by the instructor or the teacher. In addition to programmed instruction, self-study, computer-oriented instruction, case method, and prescribed experiements in science are other examples of individualized learning in which the main emphasis is for each learner to learn at his own pace.

Inspirational Methods. These methods are primarily based on high activity on the part of the instructor or the teacher. Giving a sermon to the students or to any group of learners is a good example of this methodology.

Natural Learning Methods. The main rationale of these methods is that learning takes place in a natural way and planning for learning is not necessary. Learners are left on their own, with free and unplanned activity. Thus, the emphasis on learning activity is high, whereas it is low on planned experience and on cognitive inputs.

Project Method. This is discussed in detail separately.

Whether the method is activity-centred, life-centred, pupil-centred, teacher-centred or even subject-centred, there must be the abiding enthusiasm and interest of the teacher which would make teaching learning efficient, enjoyable and pleasant.

7

Project Method

The project method is the outcome of the pragmatic educational philosophy of Dewey, the well-known American philosopher-cum-educationist. It was developed and perfected by Dr. William Head Kilpatric of the Universily of Columbia. It is a revolt against the traditional environment of the school which is usually marked by listlessness and passivity and which lacks keenness and real life. Much of the subject-matter taught and many habits formed in school do not conform to desirable social life in the outside world. The project method is the expression of the widespread dissatisfaction against the bookish, encyclopaedic passive method, whereby children as obedient masses are carefully drilled and spoon-fed with fact and information. The modern educators speak in no uncertain terms about disconnected facts, disconnected subjects, water-tight compartments and pigeonhole time tables "Ignore these" they say, "Give the class a real life project to bite at and watch the result."

The Definition. Project Method has been defined by various educationists as:

1. **Ballard.** A project is a bit of real life that has been imported into the school.
2. **Burton.** The problem is a project which results in doing. The motor element is not what makes the activity a project, but the problem-solving of a practical nature accompanying the activity.
3. **J.A. Stevenson.** A project is a problematic act carried to completion in its natural setting.

4. **Snedden.** Project is a unit of educative work in which the most prominent feature is some form of positive and concrete achievements.
5. **W.W. Charters.** In the topical organisation principles are learned first while in the projects the problems are proposed which demand in the solution the development of principles by the learner as needed.

The following points have been stressed in the above-mentioned definitions of the project:

1. A Project is a Problematic Act.
2. A Project is a Purposeful Activity.
3. A Project is a Whole-hearted Activity.
4. A Project is an Activity in a Natural Setting.
5. A Project is an Activity in a Social Setting.
6. A Project is a Bit of Real Life introduced in School.
7. A Project is a Problem-solving of a Practical Nature.
8. A Project is a Positive and Concrete Achievement.
9. A Project is an Activity through which Solution of various problems are found out.

Basic Principles

The principle of purpose. Knowledge of purpose is a great stimulus which motivates the child to realize his goal. The child must have an ideal. "Why is he doing certain things" ? Purpose motivates learning. Interest cannot be aroused by aimless and meaningless activities.

The principle of activity. Children are active by nature. They love activity. The instincts of curiosity, construction, pugnacity and herd make them active by nature. Therefore, such opportunities should be provided to them that make them active and learn things by doing. Physical as well as mental activities are to be provided to them. They are to be allowed to 'do' and to 'live through doing'.

The principle of experience. Experience is the best teacher. What is real must be experienced. The children learn new facts and information through experience.

The principle of social experience. The child is a social being and we have to prepare him for social life. Training for a corporate life must be given to him in his childhood. In the project method, the child works in groups.

The principle of reality. Life is real and education to be meaningful must be real. The child who is to live in a life of reality must be trained as such through his education. The project method is a method of educating the child and, therefore, it must also be real. Real life situations should be presented in the life of the school.

The principle of freedom. The desire for an activity must be spontaneous and not forced by the teacher. The child should be free from imposition, restrictions or obstructions so that he may express himself fully and freely. He must be given the freedom to choose an activity, to do an activity according to his interests, needs and capacities.

The principle of utility. Knowledge will be worthwhile only when it is useful and practical. The traditional system of instruction simply stressed formal and vital information for its own sake and was of little utility. The project method develops various attitudes and values which are of great significance from the practical point of view.

Different Types. W. H. Kilpatrick mentions four types of projects:

1. 'The Producer Type', in which -the emphasis is directed towards actual construction of a material object or article.
2. 'The Consumer Type'. Where the objective is to obtain either direct or vicarious experience, such as reading and learning from stories, listening to a musical delectation etc.
3. 'The Problem Type', in which the chief purpose is to solve a problem involving the intellectual processes, such as determining the density of a certain liquid.
4. 'The Drill Type', where the objective is to attain a certain degree of skill in a reaction-as learning a vocabulary.

Various Steps

These are given below:

Providing a situation. It is not right to force a project on the unwilling students. The students themselves should define, state and choose their problems. Of course, the teacher's function would be to provide real and worthwhile situations. He would discover the tastes, temperaments and need of the students and provide situations wherein the students feel a spontaneous urge to carry out projects according to their felt needs. Stevenson taught the uses of the electric bell to his high school students by the Project Method. The necessity of completely overhauling the bell system in the school building arose and this occasion was utilised in providing a situation.

Choosing and purposing. Purposing is very important. It is the centre around which a project moves. The project selected must be such as to satisfy a definite need or purpose. This purpose, as far as possible, must be acceptable to all the students of class. Dr. Kilpatrick remarks, "The part of the pupil and the part of the teacher in most of the school work depend largely on who does the purposing. It is practically the whole thing." The students themselves should choose the project. The teacher should not be in a hurry to choose the project. Better results and better satisfaction can be had only through self-choice. Many situations should be provided to children. These situations should be discussed and the teacher should give useful suggestions. Decision should always be democratic. The teacher should merely guide and not thrust his opinion. The children must feel that the project is of their own choice.

Planning. When the decision of a project has been arrived at, the next problem is of planning. The teacher should draw the attention of the students to the need of planning before undertaking any activity. The task of planning is quite difficult. Good Planning leads to better results. Each child should be encouraged to give his suggestions. The teacher should point out to the students to take into consideration their resources. Different proposals should be discussed and alternatives considered. The best plan is agreed upon after a good deal of discussion, suggestions and counter suggestions, rejections, and then students should be asked to write down the plan in their project book.

It must be stressed that the teacher must be ready with some proposals regarding the plan beforehand so that it may be possible for him to help the students in the best possible manner.

Executing the plan. This step is the longest of all and requires a lot of work. The whole project is to be executed through the cooperative efforts of all students. The various activities of the project should be divided according to the individual interests and abilities of the different children in the class.

The teacher should give sufficient guidance to the students. He should not dictate them.

This is the state at which the students perform many activities and learn various useful experiences. The children keep themselves busy in collecting information, reading and writing in various languages, keeping accounts, calculating prices, looking up maps, collecting specimens of different things, measuring length and area, visiting markets, museums and zoos, visiting fields and crops, seeking help from others and the like.

Judging. The work is to be reviewed when it is completed. Lessons must be learnt from the mistakes that have been made in the various steps of a project. The students must learn to criticise constructively their own work. Self-criticism is a valuable form of training. The students should find out what things they have learnt from the project.

Recording. A complete record of all activities connected with the project must be maintained. The project book should be well maintained. All the details in the various steps should be noted down. The project book should give a comprehensive picture of the project as a whole. It should give the procedure of providing a situation and of choosing the project, duties assigned, difficulties felt and experience gained etc.

A Good Project

These factors are given below:

Timely. A project should be related directly to the lesson and vocational interest. Projects should suit the particular mental and chronological ages of the students.

Environmental and seasonal factors should also be taken into consideration. It is a well-known fact that there are definite relationships between the seasons of the year and current community interests and those of pupils. Projects should be timely.

Usefulness. Practical aim of the project should not be lost sight of. It must fulfil a long-standing need. The learning experiences in a project must be capable of being applied in life.

Interesting. Project should be interesting to students. They must make an appeal to the emotional hungers or drives of the students.

Challenging. Projects should neither be too simple and easy nor too long and difficult. They should be challenging. It is an admitted fact that the youth wants to do tasks which are challenging in nature.

Economical. The projects should be economical. They should not unnecessarily tax the energy and pocket of the students. There should be no wastage of time also.

Rich in experiences. Many experiences of the sociable nature should be provided in a project. The project selected should be capable of correlating different subjects and practical activities of life.

Co-operativeness. The students should be allowed to think and plan independently as well as co-operatively. The projects should be executed in such a way as the students are kept active both physically as well as mentally.

Merit

These merits are given below:

Based on the laws of learning. It is in accordance with the psychological laws of learning. It is based upon:

(a) *The law of readiness.* According to this law, we learn most when our minds are ready to receive. The project method prepares the mind of the students by providing them with suitable situations.

(b) *The law of exercise.* Learning to be effective must be practised. The project method affords many opportunities to the students to learn by doing.

(c) *The law of effect.* This laws states that if learning is to be effective and fruitful, it must be accompanied by satisfaction and happiness. The students derive immense pleasure when they manipulate their own activities.

Related with life. Learning becomes practical and intimately related with life when meaningful and purposeful activities are provided to the students. The children get opportunities to acquaint themselves with the real problems of life. The students learn the practical usefulness of different subjects of the curriculum.

Correlation with all the subjects. The project method gives unity to the curriculum. The water-tight treatment of the various subjects which is commonly found in our schools gives way to an integrated programme. Subjects do not remain isolated. Learning comes as a bye-product of purposeful activity.

Training for a democratic way of life. The method provides sufficient opportunities to the students to work co-operatively for a common purpose. Decisions are arrived at democratically. The students have a say in the activities they choose, plan and execute.

Training in citizenship. This method imparts training to the students to inculcate in them primary virtues like tolerance, independence, open-mindedness, resourcefulness, etc.

Upholding dignity of labour. Dignity of labour is engendered through the project method. The students have to perform their activities with their own hands and thus they develop a taste for all kinds of work. They learn that there is nobleness in working and doing things with their own hands.

Stressing problem-solving. It discourages cramming and memory work. It stresses problem-solving. It develops the thinking and reasoning powers of the students.

A source of happiness for the backward. The project method provides a great relief to the backward children by providing them opportunities of participation in practical situation. Such children as are incapable of thinking abstract things keep themselves busy in concrete and practical situations.

Providing freedom. The students work with great enthusiasm for the completion of their self-chosen project. They do not feel tired as there is a good deal of variety in their work and atomosphere is full of freedom.

Solving the problem of indiscipline. As the children remain busy with their self-chosen work they do not get opportunities to think of anti-social ways.

Demerits

These are given below:

Neglecting intellectual work. There is a widespread belief that the project method glorifies hand work at the cost of intellectual work. The critics argue that the children are kept busy in model making and the like.

Haphazard and unconnected teaching. Projects many a time do not keep the examination and curriculum in view.

It is not possible to deal with all the subjects in a single project. There are many topics which cannot be taught through this method.

This difficulty can be met with by setting aside some periods in which the gaps may be covered up.

Upsetting of the time-table. In a project method it is not possible to follow a rigid time-table. It upsets the routine work of the school.

Neglect of drill work. This method neglects practice and the development of skills in various subjects.

Difficulty in getting suitable text-books. Preparation of books suitable for the project method is by no means as easy task. Moreover, material required for the implementation of a project is very costly. The method is not suitable for ordinary schools.

Artificial correlation. Sometimes teachers show over enthusiasm in stretching the projects upon which the class is working beyond its natural limits and try to connect those topics which have remote connections with the project in hand.

Unsuitable for the shirkers and shy. Some students who are not inclined to take responsibility may remain in the background and do very little work.

Too much reliance on young children. It is not wise to depend too much on the choice of the children.

Lack of competent teachers. For the successful working of this method, very learned, efficient and resourceful teachers are needed. The method imposes heavy burden and responsibility upon the teachers.

Unsuitable for transfers. A child reading in an ordinary school finds it very difficult to adapt himself to a school that follows project method and vice versa.

Concluding observations. A review of the above brings us to the conclusion that most of the limitations are unreal and without much significance. Whenever a new method is suggested, criticisms are unnecessarily levelled.

Traditional methods have been tried and found unsuitable to the changing needs of the time. New methods must be tried and if found suitable should be accepted even if they are a bit expensive.

Classroom Teaching

The project to be successful must be based on a definite procedure. The first and the main responsibility of the teacher is to provide those situations to the students wherein they should feel a spontaneous urge to solve some of their practical problems. The teacher must be on the lookout of discovering their interests, tastes, aptitudes and needs. There are different methods of providing situations. As far as possible, problems or situations which are provided to the students should be social ones. These provide better social training and give more satisfaction.

The teacher may converse with the class on different topics of interest to them. Pictures of different scenes may be shown to them. Surveys of the local conditions may be undertaken. The projects for study and work may arise out of the festivals like Diwali or Dussehra. The teacher is to tap all resources to provide worthwhile situations.

Most of the educators are of the view that the projects should be selected by the students themselves. They think that this will stimulate pupil purposing and that they will be more interested in their work if they have a share in determining what they are to make.

Others who think that teachers should select the projects argue that this method will ensure that the students undertake only those projects which are within their reach. Students are immature and they require adequate guidance to select their projects.

Relation with Problem Method

The focus of both the methods is on student involvement in the lesson. Activity on the part of the student is the key-note of these methods. However in the problem method, intellectual activity is more predominant whereas in the project method practical work predominates. Problem method involves lively intellectual discussion and project method involves lot of outside class activities.

Project No 1: Functioning of a Rural Bank

Objectives

1. To enable the students know about the long-term, medium term and short term needs of the rural people for finance.
2. To enable the students know about the various agencies which provide finance in the rural areas and their merits and demerits.
3. To enable the students know about the various banking operations.

Hints.

1. A visit to a local bank.
2. Listing of the operations in the bank.
3. Short description of each operation.
4. Listing of the facilities available in the bank.
5. Teacher to explain the distinction in different types of cheques. Students to fill up specimen of cheques.
6. A short session of question-answer with the manager or some other functionary of the bank.

Project No 2: A Visit to Local Transport Depot

Objectives

1. To enable the students know the different modes of transport.
2. To enable the students know about private and public transport.
3. To enable the students understand why different modes of transports are used for different purposes.
4. To enable the students understand how transport aids commerce.
5. To enable the students to study the freight/fare structure and comparative study of freight/structure/fare of different transport modes.

Hints

1. Individual or group project.
2. Noting down the freight charges.
3. Noting down the fare/freight charges.
4. Destination of passengers or goods.
5. Total amount of goods handled.
6. Finding out relative charges of different modes of transport.

QUESTIONS

1. What is a project method? How would you make use of it in Commerce teaching?
2. Select any project and prepare a lesson plan accordingly.
3. State the role of the teacher in the project method.
4. Define a project. What are the limitations of a project method in the teaching of Commerce? How can it be used effectively in our schools?
5. Explain the various steps that you would follow in using the project method.

8

Problem Method

Problem solving may be defined as a planned attack upon a difficulty or perplexity for the purpose of finding a solution. It is a method in which a person uses his ability to solve problems which confront him. It enables a person to exercise control over his activities and environment. It is an instructional device whereby the teacher and the pupils attempt in a conscious, planned, purposeful effort to arrive at explanation or solution to some educationally significant difficulty. Yoakam and Simpson define it as "a problem occurs in a situation in which a felt difficulty that is clearly present and recognised by the thinker. It may be a purely mental difficulty or it may be physical and may involve the manipulation of data. The distinguishing thing about a problem, however, is that an individual who meets it as needing a solution. He recognises it as a challenge." It is a method in which some difficulty to act in an educational setting is felt and an attempt is made in a conscious, planned and purposeful way to find its solution.

Dewey observes, "Whenever-no-matter how slight and common place in character-perplexes and challenges the mind so that it makes belief at all uncertain there is a genuine problem." He further explains problem solving in these words, "The problem fixes the end of thought and the end controls the process of thinking."

Gates has, defined the problem thus," A problem exists for an individual when he has a definite goal he cannot reach by the behaviour pattern which he already has available."

Problem solving is not merely a method of teaching. It is, in fact a method of organisation of subject matter. It is an approach to deal with subject matter.

Problem Solving

Life is full of problems and the successful man in life is he, who is fully equipped with adequate knowledge and reasoning power to tackle these problems successfully. There are problems and puzzling situations which are a normal feature of a child's everyday life. These problems grow in complexity as he grows older and older. The solution of these problems enables him to have a mastery of the environment. Therefore, if the function of education is to enable the child to prepare him for life, problem solving must be encouraged in school life.

Curious by Nature

They want to find out answers of many questions which sometimes are puzzling even to the adults; nevertheless they must be helped to satisfy their curiosity, whenever possible, by solving various problems. We must teach the pupils, how to think so that they are able to transfer these techniques to a vast number of varied problem situations.

Various Steps

The steps of problem solving are given below.

Formation and appreciation of the problem. The nature of the problem should be made very clearly to the students. They must also feel the necessity of finding out a solution for the problem.

Collection of relevant data and information. The students should be stimulated to collect data in a systematic manner. Full cooperation of the students should be secured. They may be invited to make suggestions as to how they could collect the relevant data. The teacher may suggest many points to them. He may ask them to read extra books. He may also ask them, to organise a few educational trips to gather the relevant information.

Organisation of data. The students should be asked to sift the relevant material from the superficial one and put it in a scientific way.

Drawing of conclusions. Discussions should be arranged collectively and individually with each pupil. Panton suggests that the teacher's aim should be to secure that, as far as possible, the essential thinking is done by the pupils-themselves and that their educative process produces the particular solution where formulation of generalizations is at stake. "Care should be taken that judgement is made only when sufficient data is collected."

Testing conclusions. No conclusion should be accepted without being properly verified. The correctness of the conclusion must be proved. The students must be taught to be critical, to examine the "truths"' which they "discover" to see "whether they fit all the known data." We should have our minds free from every bias in the process of problem-solving.

Teacher's Role

Valentine Davis quotes Prof. Pasher who suggests the following points in problem-solving:

1. Get them (the students) to define the problem clearly.
2. Aid them to keep the problem in mind.
3. Get them to make many suggestions by encouraging them: (a) to analyse the situation in parts, (b) to recall previously known similar cases and general rules that apply, (c) to guess courageously and formulate guesses clearly.
4. Get them time to evaluate each suggestion carefully by encouraging them : (a) to maintain a state of doubt or suspended conclusion, (h) to criticise the suggestion by appeal to know facts, minister experiments, and scientific treatises.
5. Get them to organise the material by proceeding: (a) to build an outline on the board, (b) to use diagrams and

graphs, (c) to formulate concise statement of the net outcome of the discussion.

It has been stated that for the success of the problem-solving teachning technique we need "a teacher who has the ability to see problem clearly, the power to analyse with a keen discernment and the faculty to synthesize and draw conclusions with an uncanny accuracy."

Procedures in Problem-Solving. There are two procedures in problem-solving and they are the Inductive, and (H) the Deductive.

Essential features of a problem. Following are the essential features of a problem:

1. The problem should be meaningful, interesting and worthwhile for children.
2. It should have some correlation with life.
3. It should have some correlation with other subjects.
4. It should arise out of the real needs of the students.
5. The children must possess some background of the problem which they are going to discuss.
6. The problem should be clearly defined.
7. The solution of the problem should be found out by the students themselves working under the guidance and supervision of the teacher.
8. The problem must have some educational value.

Merits

Following are the merits of problem solving.

1. It helps in stimulating thinking.
2. It develops reasoning power.
3. It helps to improve knowledge.
4. It helps in developing good study habits.
5. It affords opportunities for participation in social activities. Problems are solved with the joint efforts of many students. The students learn to appreciate the different points of view and thus become tolerant.
6. The students learn to be self-dependent.
7. Discussions help to develop the power of expression of the students.
8. The method provides opportunities to the teachers to know in detail their pupils. They learn which students

are shy in nature and which are very active and accordingly they assist the students.

9. Students learn facts which are meaningful and which have been discovered by their own efforts.
10. It helps in the maintenance of discipline. The students remain busy in finding out the answers to their own problem.
11. Knowledge is easily assimilated as it is the result of a purposeful activity.
12. Learning becomes more interesting in place of a dread.
13. It develops the power of critical judgement.
14. It helps to verify an opinion.
15. It satisfies curiosity.
16. It helps to learn how to act in a new situation.

Demerits

The demerits are given below:

1. Generally speaking problem-solving involves mental activity only. There is less of bodily activity.
2. A large number of children do not possess sufficient background information and therefore they do not take interest in discussions.
3. There is a lack of suitable reference and source books for children.
4. It involves a lot of time and the teachers find it difficult to cover the prescribed syllabus.

Deductive and Inductive Approaches

Broadly speaking, there are two general approaches or procedures in problem-solving-the Inductive and the Deductive. The whole method of teaching and learning is based on induction and deduction.

Inductive Method

The inductive methods is a method of development. In the inductive method, the child is led to discover truth for himself. The various processes in the inductive method are: (i) observation of the given material: (ii) Discrimination and analysis noting differences and similarities, (iii) Classification, (iv) Abstraction and generalization, and (v) Application or verification.

In the inductive method, the pupils are led from particular instances to general conclusion. Concrete examples are given and with their help students are helped to arrive at certain conclusions or principles.

Merits

Following are the merits of the Inductive Method:

1. Knowledge is self-acquired and is soon transformed into wisdom. 'General truths in order to be learned must be earned' is a famous saying and the inductive method is true to it.
2. It promotes mental activity on the part of the pupils and makes them active participants in the learning teaching process.
3. It makes the lesson interesting by providing challenging situations to the students.
4. The method affords opportunities to the students to be self-dependent and develops self-confidence.
5. The student's curiosity is well-kept up till the end when generalisations are arrived at.
6. This method is very natural because the knowledge in possession of man has been acquired in this way from the practical side of experience.
7. The child learns how to tackle problems. He not only acquires more facts but also learns the process of acquiring facts which proves him useful for practical life.
8. The method is based on sound psychological principles. Learning by doing is the basis of this method.

Demerits

Following are the demerits of Inductive Method:

1. There is every possibility that the students may draw conclusions very hastily and these may be based on insufficient data and, therefore, may be wrong.
2. The method is very slow and lengthy.
3. It is not very helpful in the case of small children.
4. It is not suitable in the teaching of subjects in which there is more stress on the teaching of facts. It is not possible for us to experience facts in history and in so many other subjects.

5. The inductive method is not a complete method in itself. It has been said, "Induction does not prove but only provides the material to prove, it only discovers." When we have discovered a principle, we have to apply it again on some concrete instances for its verification. Therefore, we need deductive method to ensure the value of inductive process.

Deductive Method

This method is the other way round. In the deductive method rules, generalisation and principles are provided to the students and then they are asked to verify them with the help of particular examples.

Merits

The merits of the Deductive Method are as below:

1. The teacher's work is simplified. He gives general principles and the students verify them.
2. This method is very economical. It saves time and energy both of the students and the teachers. Many principles for the discovery of which mankind has taken a lot of pains can be told to the students easily.
3. It is very suitable for small children who cannot discover truths for themselves. They get ready-made material.

Demerits

These are as follows:

1. Knowledge is not self-acquired and, therefore, not assimilated properly.
2. The child is deprived of the pleasure of self-activity and self-effort as ready-made formulae, principles and rules are given to him.
3. It encourages memorisation of facts which are soon forgotten and, therefore, knowledge is rendered useless.
4. This method is unnatural and unpsychological for the students who do not possess ability to appreciate abstract ideas in the absence of concrete examples.
5. It fails to develop motivation and interest in learning.
6. It fails to develop self-confidence and initiative in the students.

Combination of Deductive and Inductive Method. According to I.E. Miller, induction is the making of the tools of thought and deduction is the using of tools. Both supplement each other and are not opposite things. Both are wanted for the discovery of truth as both legs are wanted for walking.

The only method for the teacher is the method by which mind adds to its knowledge.

Induction should be followed by deduction and deduction by induction. Our approach should be inductive-cum-deductive.

Comparison of Deductive and Inductive Method

Deductive	*Inductive*
1. General laws are first stated and particular cases are taken as examples to prove them from them.	1. First particular cases are dealt with and then laws are derived.
2. It does not lead to new knowledge.	2. It leads to new knowledge.
3. It is a method of verification and explanation and, therefore, it is a method of instruction.	3. It is a method of discovery and, therefore, it is a method of education.
4. This method is very quick. The child gets ready-made knowledge and he makes use of knowledge acquired by others.	4. This method is very slow. The child acquires first-hand information by actual observation.
5. This method encourages dependence upon others as it is based on borrowing from others.	5. This method gives training to the child to depend upon himself and to develop self-confidence and initiative.
6. It is downward movement of thought and leads to a more perfect comprehension of the principle or generalisation.	6. It is an upward movement of thought and leads to rules, definitions or principles.

Fundamental Problems

1. Public sector enterprises are required in India.
2. Banks provide you with a large number of services.
3. Foreign trade is an integral part of an economy.
4. Co-ordination is the essence of management.
5. Finance is the lifeblood of a business.
6. Delegation of authority is required for the efficient working of an organisation.

7. "No risk, no gains." Discuss from the 'point of view of a business.
8. 'Planning and controlling go together". Discuss.
9. Ware-housing helps in price stabilisation.
10. 'Management is the life spark' of an organisation.
11. What are the careers open for commerce students? What qualifications are required for each?

QUESTIONS

1. What is a problem method? How would you make use of it in the teaching of Commerce?
2. State any problem in Commerce and prepare a lesson plan on it.
3. Explain the merits and demerits of deductive and inductive approach in the teaching of Commerce.
4. Elucidate the role of the commerce teacher in problem solving method. Is it possible to use it in the teaching of every topic in Commerce? Explain.

9

Socialised Method

Group dynamics is a method which aims at the socialisation of the pupils by developing in them the traits of initiative and responsibility within a group membership and in harmony with group interests. 'Cooperative' enterprise is the 'key-note' of this method. In this method, children are discussing, questioning, reporting, planning and wing in natural ways. The teacher plays the role of an adviser, counsellor and guide in the best sense of the word, trying to get children discover things for themselves rather than to have them merely listening. Group dynamics method develops techniques useful in group work to stimulate creative expression, to develop desirable social attitudes by providing practice in a large variety of socialised stimulus and above all, practice in the techniques of cooperative thinking. It develops social consciousness among the students.

Group dynamics method has the following forms:

1. Group Discussion
2. Panel Discussion
3. Seminar Technique
4. Symposium
5. Workshop

Group Discussion

Meaning and Significance of Discussion Method. This method has been used in the teaching-learning process from time immemorial. It was widely used at the famous Nalanda University. The Greek scholars in their used to discuss various problems and issues with their disciples. Discussion has been described as a thoughtful consideration of the relationships involved in a topic or problem under study. It is concerned with the analysis, comparison, evaluation and conclusions of these relationships. It aims at uniting and integrating the work of the class. It is carried out by organising, outlining and relating the facts studied. It encourages the students to direct their thinking process towards the solution of a problem and to use their experiences for a further clarification and consolidation of learning material.

Discussion is to be distinguished from debate in which the participants seek to prove a point rather than to discover a truth. Debate may also be marked by uncontrolled exchange to verbalism.

Discussion is very important in stimulating mental activity, developing fluency and ease in expression, clarity of ideas in thinking and training in the presentation of one's ideas and facts. An exchange of ideas and opinions offers valuable training to students in reflective thinking.

Constituents of Discussion

These are as under.

1. The leader – the teacher
2. The group – the students
3. The problem – or the topic
4. The content – body of knowledge
5. Evaluation – change in ideas, attitudes etc.

Organisation of Discussion

Following are the main techniques of organising discussion.

1. Introducing a topic or a problem by the teacher by giving points or explanations to serve as the basis of discussion.
2. Calling upon a pupil by the teacher to give facts, describe a sense or situation, explain an incident, event or happening for getting the discussion started.
3. Preparing an outline of points cooperatively by the teacher and a few students which may become the starting point for discussion.
4. Asking the students to describe their own experiences connected with the subject topic or problem and making them points for discussion.
5. Presenting detailed papers by the teacher and discussions thereon.

6. Presenting detailed papers by the students and discussing them in the class.
7. Showing special works and projects to the class and discussing them.
8. Showing some pictures, charts, diagrams or any audio-visual material and discussion about them.

Merits

Following are the merits of discussion:

1. It helps in clarifying issues.
2. It helps children in crystalising their thinking.
3. It helps students in discovering what they do not know and what they have overlooked.
4. It engenders more reflection. It is very different from rote learning.
5. It represents a type of pooled knowledge, ideas and feelings of several persons.
6. It develops team spirit.
7. It engenders toleration of views which are at variance.
8. It affords opportunities to the students to learn together, make suggestions, share responsibility, comprehend the topic, evaluate the findings and to summarise results.
9. It provides opportunities to the students to speak distinctly, stand and sit correctly, respect the ideas of others, share interests, ask pertinent questions and comprehend the problem before the group.
10. It helps the teacher in discovering talented students who have potential for becoming good leaders.

Demerits

Limitations of discussion are;

1. It is not suitable in all topics.
2. It is likely to be dominated by a few students.
3. It is likely to go off the track.
4. It may lead to unpleasant feelings.
5. It may create emotional tensions.
6. It may involve unnecessary arguments.

Directing Group Discussion

The teacher has to show immense patience and skill to ensure that discussion takes place on right lines and in the appropriate environment. Following points may be considered in this respect:

1. Students should be well acquainted with the significance of the topic, its nature and scope and causes why the class should discuss it.
2. Discussion should be confined to important aspects.
3. Students should be encouraged to participate in the discussion.
4. Ideas may be invited without pressure or embarrassment.
5. Explanations, where needed, should be provided.
6. Personality cult should be avoided.
7. Cooperation rather than competition should be encouraged.
8. Efforts should be made to develop team spirit.
9. Doubts, mistakes and wrong interpretation should be made clear by the teacher.
10. Facts and points should be evaluated.
11. Facts and points should be summarised.
12. Students should be guided to appreciate difference of opinion and views.
13. Goals of discussion should be kept in view.
14. Only a few students should not be allowed to dominate classroom discussion.
15. The students may be given training in discussion in small groups so that their hesitation is removed while participating in bigger groups.

Panel Discussion

In panel discussion three or four speakers discuss various aspects of a single topic in the class. One of them may act as chairperson to monitor discussions. A time schedule is drawn up. When the panel is ready to hold discussions the chairperson may explain the topic briefly. No one makes a speech. Rather, there is interplay back and forth among the panel members. The panel chairperson keeps the discussion to the point and ensures that all panel members participate equally. The panel members interact with each other with a good deal of spontaneity. Once the panel members have made their presentation, students of the class may be invited to ask questions. Being a group activity in which students are directly involved, panel discussion enables them to reflect deeply upon an area of interest.

The teacher is behind the scene, motivating, encouraging and guiding the panel members and other students to derive the optimum benefit from this approach.

A panel discussion may be organised with the Managing Director of a Road Transport Corporation, Railway Zonal Manager, Managing Director of an Air Company, Incharge of a Shipping Company to give views on transport.

Seminar

A seminar is an advanced group technique which is usually used in higher education. It refers to a structured group discussion that usually follows a formal lecture or lectures often in the form of an essay or a paper presentation on a theme.

Individual students also prepare papers or reports and present them before a group of peers as part of the course work.

Duration of the presentation of papers at seminars varies from topic to topic and discipline to discipline.

Papers can be illustrated through projected aids (filmstrips,-slides, transparencies) or non-projected aids (charts, diagrams, maps, etc.).

Presentation of paper or papers is followed by general discussion by the entire group. Considerable student participation is expected.

As a seminar involves student preparation and participation and response from the peer group, it not only breaks the monotony of the lecture method but also motivates the students to probe into topic deeply. Understanding power and questioning ability in a relevant situation are developed. Self-reliance, Self-confidence, sense of cooperation and responsibility are developed. The presenters of papers develop habits of sustained work, learn to collect and organise data in a sequential manner.

We can organise a seminar on business organisation where the presenter can outline his theme followed by questions from the participants. He should keep in view the following points in this regard:-

1. Selection of a meaningful and relevant topic.
2. Selection of students who are effective speakers to take lead.
3. Duration of the seminar-usually two hours.

4. Preparing the participants-providing them suitable guidelines for collecting and arranging the material.
5. Wise selection of the chairperson.
6. Framing suitable rules

Seminar could be arranged by inviting experts on a topic and students asked to listen to their views and also provided opportunities to ask questions. Experts may be requested to keep in view the maturity level of the students. Time schedule for speakers may suitably be framed. Follow-up action on the seminar will enhance its utility.

Symposium

Symposium is a group discussion in which subject experts or speakers holding different points of view about the subject under discussion participate. Each speaker presents his ideas in a short speech. Generally the moderator or the chairperson and speakers discuss the various aspects of a theme in the symposium. The chairperson coordinates the different speakers' presentation. The total number of speakers usually does not exceed five excluding the chairperson. The audience very seldom participates as the chairperson and the speakers anticipate possible questions and incorporate these in their presentation.

The tendency among educators in India is to use the term seminar and symposium synonymously.

We can organise a symposium on business organisation with 3 speakers, each outlining a particular type i.e. the partnership, joint stock company and cooperative organisation, with a moderator coordinating the symposium. We can also have a symposium in which experts on business organisation participate a bank executive, a registrar of cooperative organisation and a leading partner in a business.

Workshop

Workshop procedure is a type of group procedure of teaching learning where 'work' or 'doing' is the essence. In group discussions 'lecturing' or 'talking' is the key-note. A workshop is an activity centred technique. It involves directly the skills of both cognitive and psycho-motor domains.

Making teaching and learning aids, charts and models, etc., preparing assignments, instructional designs, syllabi, manuals and critical reviews are the important activities of a workshop session under the guidance of experts. The participants work collectively and produce plans, solve problems, collect and organise resources, develop tests and find out ways and means of solving classroom problems faced by them. The experts help the participants to draw on their own experience.

Use of Laboratory

Laboratory method is usually associated with the teaching of science subjects. Nevertheless there is a tendency in certain quarters to use the term 'laboratory method' in the teaching of social sciences including Commerce. The method may be explained as, "the greater part of the students will be studying and writing at their work tables. Two or three students may be having a quiet conference on some moot point. Others may be comparing notes or outlines of some phase of the work. One student may be busy at the dictionary, hunting for the explanation of some phrase or term; another may be consulting an atlas; a third may be sharpening a pencil or filling his fountain pen; a fourth may be making a map or preparing a graph; a fifth may be conferring with the teacher about some difficulty or asking for a criticism on his, notes or outlines. Usually one or two students will be browsing among the volumes in the bookcases or going through tables of contents or indexes to find a clue to some obscure item. Now and then an idler or a dawdler will be observed. In general, however, the room is a place of quite, disorderly order, in which ' students are busily engaged in profitable activities of one kind or another."

By Way of Lecture

It is the oldest teaching method given by philosophy of idealism. As used in education, the lecture method refers to the teaching procedure involved in the clarification or explanation to the students of some major idea. This method lays emphasis on the presentation of the content. Teacher is more active and students are passive but he also uses question answer to keep them attentive in the class. It is used to clarify matters, to expand content and motivate the students. By changing his voice, by impersonating characters, by shifting his position and by using simple devices, a teacher can deliver his lesson effectively. While delivering his lecture, a teacher can indicate by his facial expression, gestures and tones the exact shade of meaning that he wishes to convey.

Merits

Following are the merits of the lecture method.

1. It is economical as it needs no apparatus and no laboratory. A large number of students can be taught at a time.
2. It saves time and covers syllabus in a limited time.
3. It is very effective in giving factual information and in relating some of the thrilling anecdotes with historical lessons. The life stories of great adventurers, experimenters, investigators and thinkers can become very interesting and valuable talks by a teacher.
4. Lecturing makes the work of the teacher very simple. He need not make elaborate arrangements.
5. A good lecture not only stimulates the students but also lingers long in their imagination. It motivates students to become good orators.
6. It provides better scope for clarification and for laying stress on significant ideas.
7. It brings a personal contact and touch to impress or influence the pupils.
8. It provides flexibility. As the teacher is in close and intimate contact with his pupils, he can adjust his technique in accordance with their abilities, aptitudes and interests.
9. It gives the students training in listening.
10. It gives the students training in taking notes rapidly.
11. It develops good audience habits.
12. It provides opportunities of correlating events and subjects.
13. It enables the linkage of previous knowledge with the new one.

Demerits

The limitations of this method are as follows:

1. There is very little scope for pupil activity.
2. It does not take into consideration individual differences.
3. Lecturing is against the principle of 'Learning by Doing'.
4. It spoon feeds the students without developing their power of reasoning.
5. Speed of the lecture may be too fast for the learner to grasp the line of thought.

6. An average student may not be able to fix up his attention to a lecture of forty to forty-five minutes.
7. A lecturer is likely to cover more content without realising that little learning takes place.
8. A lecture may become monotonous to the students after a while. Very few teachers can keep the interest of the student upto the end.

Guidelines for the Effective Use

The following points should be kept in view in using this device of teaching:

1. Matter should be arranged in such a way as to leave a single clear impression on the minds of the students.
2. The teacher should have pauses in between the lesson so that the students may learn the new knowledge bit by bit.
3. The rate of exposition should be slow when the class is backward. The teacher should utilise different ways of presenting the same information.
4. There should be abundant repetition but it should be in a new way so that the class may not feel dullness.
5. Children's way to looking at things should be considered in exposition. Language used should be familiar and suitable.
6. The lesson should be divided into sections which have logical sequence. This will enable the students to understand easily and will also train them in systematic thinking besides assisting them to put their own thoughts logically.
7. The rate of exposition and the size of the subject-matter are determined by the individual capacity of children and teacher's natural rate of speech.
8. Proper use of the blackboard should be made.
9. Actual objects, models, diagrams, sketches etc., should be used.
10. The students should be encouraged to ask questions. This will enable them to get their doubts removed.
11. Verbal illustrations such 'as examples, comparisons, etc., should be used to enable the students to grasp the exposition.

12. Pictorial illustrations such as pictures, maps and charts be freely used as these help in motivating the students.
13. The aim of the lesson should be kept in view and the students fully made conversant with the aim.

Dictation of Notes

Reasons for note dictating.

1. Note dictating is resorted to on account of pressure of work upon the teacher and less time available for preparing the lesson.
2. Note dictating is a short-cut to prepare the students for examinations.
3. Note dictating is a short cut to finish the heavy and overcrowded syllabi.
4. Sometime note dictating is done when the teacher does not possess adequate power of expression.
5. Note dictating is done when there is non-availability of suitable textbooks.

Methods of dictating notes.

1. Detailed notes on important topics after discussing the topic in the class.
2. Notes in the question-answer form primarily from examination point of view-guess questions and their answers.
3. Explanatory notes and summaries on the blackboard.

Defects in the method of note dictation.

1. It does not provide training in developing critical approach.
2. Note dictation makes commerce teaching synonymous with memorisation of facts communicated by the teacher.
3. Note dictation fails to develop proper insight into the subject.
4. Note dictation proves to be a great hindrance in developing the habit of consulting reference books and textbooks also.

Instead of dictating notes to the students, they should be encouraged to prepare their own notes.

Playing a Role

Role-playing involves dramatization of a situation by two or three students under the direction of the teacher with the sole purpose of understanding the feelings, action and behaviour of others, especially in a problem situation. Role playing is life-like representations of experience. As the role playing is going on, the rest of the students of the class observe as a group. It gives opportunities to students to express their feelings. Verbalizing the actions, the students get an insight into behaviour patterns. It is an attention-getting device for some students and helps in adjustment behaviour. However, role playing is a time-consuming method. It is not suitable for those students who are not alert and who cannot articulate well.

Based on Sources

Source method implies the use of original material and documents in the teaching of commerce. A source method provides first hand experiences and leads to better understanding of the subject.

Sources may be divided into two categories:

(a) Primary sources
(b) Secondary sources

An act passed by the parliament or a state legislature on the commerce policy is a primary data whereas its extracts published in newspapers come under the secondary data.

The report of the Curriculum Committee or Curriculum Development Centre of the University Grants Commission is a primary source but extracts published in newspapers and journals fall under the category of secondary sources.

Use of the source method. It can be used at the following stages of the lesson.

(a) Pre-lesson use of source. Visits to local markets, banks or exchanges etc. may be arranged before taking up a lesson on these topics. The teacher may also ask the students to read selected passages of an Act connected with the lesson before hand.
(b) Mid-lesson use of the source. Extracts from the act may be read during the course of the lesson. This creates a real situation, provides vividness to the subject-matter and reinforces the impact of teaching.

Post-lesson Use of the Source

Pre-lesson use of a source can also take the form of post-lesson use of the source and vice versa. Students may be given assignments which need to make use of the sources.

Merits

Following are the main merits:-

1. It provides a real situation.
2. It makes the subject-matter vivid.
3. It develops a sense of objectivity.
4. It arouses curiosity among the students.
5. It provides a motivating environment.
6. It develops elementary skills of collecting data, sifting the relevant and organising the same.
7. It provides opportunities for useful mental exercises- right thinking and imagining, comparing and analysing, drawing inferences etc.
8. It promotes interest in the study of the subject.
9. It initiates the students in research.
10. It provides functional knowledge. Even the slow and backward children feel interested when they see original sources. Their learning becomes functional because it is gained in the real context.
11. It supplements class-room lesson.

Demerits

Limitations are given below:

1. It is very difficult for the school teachers to have an easy access to original sources.
2. Utilisation of original sources is a very difficult task for the school students as they lack the requisite training.
3. The method is very complex and technical.
4. Contemporary authors and writers have given their own prejudices, preferences and limitations with the result that it becomes very difficult to sift fact from fiction. The students are, thus, lost in the maze of conflicting views about the same event or movement.
5. Source method of teaching Commerce is very expensive.
6. Source method of teaching Commerce is time consuming.

How to make source method effective. The students should be encouraged to study the resource books in the library. Educational tours to places of importance may be arranged. The students may be asked to write their own impressions and inferences about the places they visit. Copies of important extracts from the relevant records may be pasted on the blackboard for the use of students.

Dr. Keatings thinks that original sources can be used for creating suitable environment in the lower form. Well planned, purposive and well directed efforts have to made by the teacher in the use of this method. By suggesting the use of resource method, we do not aim at making our students research scholars. Use of the method in selected topics is likely to make the study of commerce more meaningful and real.

Story Telling

Story telling as an art. Story telling is one of the most important methods of teaching. It is an art which enables the teacher to come very close to the heart of the students and thereby he attracts their attention. Some teachers are born story tellers and they are very fortunate in this respect. This art of story telling aims at presenting to the pupils, through the medium of speech, clear, vivid, interesting, ordered sequences of events, in such a way that their minds reconstruct these happenings and they live in imagination through the experiences recounted either as spectators or possibly as participators. Story telling enables the teacher to make lesson lively and interesting to the pupils. Stories of great reformers, writers, saints, discoverers etc. must be told to the students. Story telling helps in enhancing the interests of the students in the subject. It goes a long way in firing the imagination of the students.

The art of story telling can be cultivated by:

1. Observing skilful narrators.
2. Studying the work of successful story writers.
3. Practising story telling.
4. Critically evaluating one's own performance and bringing about necessary changes.

In telling a story the teacher should be guided by the following points:

1. Suitable stories for the age of the students should be selected.
2. The stories should be short and the plot easy.
3. The teacher must know the story well that he wants to narrate. If he stops in the middle, it will detract charm from the story.
4. Language employed in telling a story should be very simple and easy.
5. A story should be told and not read. The story loses a great deal of its interest for the children if it is read.

6. The teacher himself should like the story and take interest in story-telling.
7. There should be plenty of action in the stories. Key sentences and phrases should be repeated as the children enjoy this repetition. The stories should be loaded with activities and experiences familiar to the children.
8. Conversation, if any, in the story should be given indirect speech.
9. The method of introducing and developing the story should be thought out before hand.
10. The story should be told in a natural way and very vividly.
11. Humour makes the story more interesting and should not be neglected.
12. To make the story more realistic, the teacher may use pictures and draw diagrams on the blackboard.
13. The story should suggest and inspire the students to action.
14. Ryburn suggests that well-known and familiar stories can be made fresh if they are told as though one of the characters in the story were telling it.
15. The story must have some aim besides mere enjoyment. The teacher must keep in mind the aim while narrating a story. The students too must know the aim.

Study Supervision

Meaning and significance. Arthur C. Bining and David II. Bining describe the meaning of supervised study as, "By supervised study, we mean the supervision by the teacher of a group or class of pupils as they work at their desk or around their tables. In this procedure, we find pupils busy at work that has been assigned to them by the teacher. When they meet a difficulty that they cannot overcome, they ask the teacher for direction and assistance. The teacher, when not called upon, walks up quietly up and down the classroom or remains at his desk watching the pupils do their work continually, alert for any wrong procedures that the pupils may follow. He is always ready to direct and aid them."

Individual attention. Supervised study is an aid in helping to solve the problem of individual differences. Supervised Study aids in preventing failures. The pupil works along his own mental level and at his own capacity. Assignments can be given to meet all levels of ability.

Better pupil teacher relations. Another good feature of supervised study is seen in the better pupil teacher relations that it promotes. In the usual class teaching procedure, the teacher is frequently considered a hard task master and the procedure often produces a "class versus teacher" attitude. Under the supervised study programme; he appears in the role of a helper and guide. There is greater opportunity for the display of sympathy and understanding. The teacher is able to understand the pupil and his difficulties better and is in a position to spurt him on to a greater effort.

Development of skills. There are certain skills which can best be developed under this procedure. A thorough use of the supervised method would reveal weaknesses in the learner. Following skills can be developed easily.

(a) Skills as to how to read commerce material.
(b) Skills as to how to use encyclopedias.
(c) Skills as to how to use dictionaries.
(d) Skills as to how to use maps, atlases, indexes and almanacs.
(e) Skills as to how to read graphs.

Objections to supervised study.

There are some objections such as:

1. Some investigations have concluded that the weak pupil is not helped by this method and in some cases is even hindered.
2. Supervised study requires the lengthened school day and which is not possible due to various pressures of co-curricular activities.
3. Supervised study is a costly method. It would necessitate an increase in the teaching force that would mean an increased cost of education.
4. Supervised study depends too much on the initiative and enthusiasm of the students which they seldom display.
5. Supervised study destroys the supremacy of the teacher as he plays a secondary role in the teaching learning process.

QUESTIONS

1. "True teaching is arousing and directing meaningful learning activities in the pupils." Elucidate the statement and bring out clearly the significance of dynamic methods of teaching Commerce. Explain any such method of teaching.
2. Illustrate the characteristics of dynamic and progressive methods of teaching Commerce. State the merits and demerits of the lecture method.
3. "The teacher is a guide and director, he steers the boat but the energy that propels it must come 'from those who are learning." Comment upon this statement and state the main features of sound methods of teaching Commerce.
4. "It is well to remember one caution-do not do for the student that which he may be led to do for himself." Explain this statement in the context of dynamic methods of teaching.
5. Explain the use of discussion method in the teaching of commerce. What measures would you adopt to make it effective?
6. How would you adopt the approach 'Learning by Doing' in Commerce?
7. What place would you give to the following in the teaching of Commerce?
   (i) Source Method (ii) Note Dictation (iii) Lecture method (iv) Assignment method. (v) Case Study Method.
8. "How we teach is more important than what we teach?" Discuss this with reference to the teaching of Commerce.
9. Explain lecture method of teaching. What steps would you take to make this method really helpful to the pupils?
10. Explain clearly the use of case study approach in commerce teaching.
11. How would you organise a seminar on a topic in commerce for higher secondary pupils?

10

Assignment Method

Among the important methods, following deserve careful attention. However, it may be stated that these methods overlap in their treatment and it is not always possible to draw a clear-cut line.

1. Assignment Method
2. Case study Method
3. Dalton Method
4. Discussion Method
5. Home Assignment or Home Task
6. Laboratory Method
7. Lecture Method
8. Note Dictation
9. Observation Method
10. Problem Method
11. Project Method
12. Questions-Answer Method
13. Quiz Method
14. Review Method
15. Role Playing/Group Dynamics Method
16. Socialised Classroom Recitation Method
17. Source Method
18. Story Method
19. Supervised Study Method

20. Survey Method
21. Textbook Method

(Note: Sometimes some methods of teaching are also called techniques of teaching and vice versa. There is no water-tight compartment between methods and techniques. However, the Dalton Plan, the Problem Method and the Project Method are not used as techniques of teaching.)

N.L. Bossing has observed, "The central position of the assignment in the techniques of teaching has remained unquestioned." G.H. Betts asserts, "Upon the proper assignment of the lesson depends much of the success of the recitation, and also much of the pupil's progress in learning how to study." W.N. Drum suggests, "Teachers generally do not appreciate the importance of the assignment, and the work of the pupils probably suffers as much from hasty or careless assignment as from any other single cause." H.R. Douglass and others are of the view, "The assignment represents one of the most important phases of teaching."

Assignment and Homework

1. Writing of essay type answers to questions arising out of the subject-matter already done in the class.
2. Verbal memorising work pertaining to curricular and co-curricular activities. It may take the form of cramming facts, principles, memorising work in respect of debates etc.
3. Practical work, e.g., preparation of charts, maps and models, advance preparation for the coming lesson.
4. Problem assignment
5. Group assignment

Assignment : Purposes

1. To provide opportunities to students to work independently and thereby to develop in them self-reliance and initiative.
2. To develop habits of reading regularly among the students.
3. To provide opportunities to the students to utilise their leisure time profitably. It is generally seen that our school children waste their precious time in loitering about or making mischief when no such work is given to them.

4. To give them an opportunity to do practice what is done in the school.
5. To finish the prescribed courses in time. The syllabi is too heavy to be finished in the classroom work.
6. To serve as a link in the parent-teacher co-operation. It enables the parents to know that regular work is being done in the school.
7. To develop permanent interests and to train the students in the profitable use of leisure.
8. To enable the child to revise his previous lesson and prepare the next one.
9. To provide remedical measure for backward children.
10. To give chance to every child to progress at his own speed.

Assignment : Essentials

1. The assignment should be clear and definite.
2. The assignment should be concise but sufficiently detailed to enable each student to understand the task assigned.
3. The assignment should anticipate special difficulties and suggest ways to remove them.
4. The assignment should relate the new unit to past experience.
5. Students should understand the imprortance of the assignment.
6. The assignment should arouse an interest in advance work.
7. The assignment should provide for differences in the ability and interest of students.
8. The assignment should be motivated chiefly by the hope of worthwhile achievements, rather than scholastic reward or the fear of punishment.
9. The assignment should stimulate thought.
10. The assignment should provide necessary and specific directions for the study of the lesson.
11. The assignment should be adjusted to the time and opportunity of the class.
12. Materials of the assignment should be varied and adaptable to the needs and interest of the students.

Difficulties in the Preparation

Fleming and Woodring have listed the following difficulties:

1. Insufficient thought and preparation in planning the assignment.
2. Inability to obtain an acceptance by the pupil of a worthy purpose for performance of the task.
3. Simulation of preparation of the assignments by appealing to the interests of adolescents and by providing for real needs growing out of pupil experience.
4. Prevention of loss of interest due to too long phase of time between the assignment and preparation.
5. Avoidance of assignments so long that successful accomplishment is impossible in the time available for preparation, with consequent loss of interest.
6. Guarding against too many and too varied activities, resulting in dividing interests with consequent bad habits of work, and unsatisfactory accomplishments.
7. Difficulty in presenting work to be done so that it is clearly understood by the pupils; also, the difficulty of ascertaining whether every pupil understands.
8. Gauging the difficulty of work so that success is possible for each pupil.
9. Determining essential requirements, and differentiation of assignments to suit the various levels and types of ability existing in the class.
10. Inclusion of challenges to mental exploration by the pupil, thereby simulating real thinking.
11. Provision for continuity of work by presenting new problems as a continuation of previous experience and anticipation of future problems.
12. Correlating with other subjects and outside activities.
13. Focusing attention on important elements in the new problem of task, and directing the attack in such a way as to increase interest rather than lessen it, to stimulate effort, and to overcome seeming obstacles to accomplishment.
14. Providing the necessary tools for preparation, by training in study procedures and techniques, and in selection, organization, and use of materials, thereby developing effective habits of independent work.

15. Giving to pupils devices for checking the mastery and performance of work undertaken.
16. Evaluating the effectiveness of an assignment by the quality of response during the presentation of the assignment, and by the adequacy of pupil preparation.
17. Providing sufficient time for adequate consideration of the assignment and determining the psychological moment for its presentation.

Assignment Procedure

The procedure suggested for the preparation of a good assignment is as follows:

1. Analyse the nature of the learning process required in the advance unit. This is without exception the first step in a good assignment procedure. Much of what follows in any good assignment depends upon this analysis.
2. Study the various types of assignments available and select the one, or modified form of it, that appears to fit best the learning situation. Some assignment types are admirably adapted to one form of learning for teaching but not to others.
3. Provide the essential background for the advance work where uncertainty exists that such background obtains. At this point too many teachers are likely to assume the adequacy of this background when in fact it may not exist. Scarcely can one emphasize too strongly the apperceptive preparation for the new.
4. Whether this is the next step in the assignment procedure or not, it is obvious that very early in the assignment phase the teacher must throw out a challenge to the student that will enlist his interest and maximum effort in the new unit.
5. Outline in sufficient detail the advance unit to be studied.
6. Suggest some plan of attack upon the new unit. It is well to remember one caution-do not do for the student that which he may be led to do for himself. This suggests the desirability of leading the class in a co-operative discovery of desirable leads for the general attack upon the new.
7. Where reference to source material other than the textbook is necessary, this should be made specific. The

most satisfactory plan in the large unit assignment is to provide select list of available sources in mimeographed or hectographed form with chapter or inclusive page references given.

The Controversy

Whether or not homework should be given to the students is a controversial point. Extreme views have been expressed regarding the usefulness of home work. The assignment of home task, has been emphatically denounced by Bray. He writes, "Under normal conditions a reasonable day's work for a child has been done at the close of the afternoon and homework as it is generally organised does more harm than good as a rule in this country except perhaps from the point of view of examination success." On the other hand, P.C. Wren commends the assigning of homework. An average guardian also feels that some work should be given to the student which he should do at home.

The Objections

1. It deprives the children of participating in recreational activities when it imposes heavy demands upon them.
2. It is great hindrance in the way of the students of enjoying family and social life.
3. It deprives children of the opportunity to help their parents in supplementing their income.
4. It imposes a great physical strain on small children and thus endangers their health.
5. It becomes a constant source of fear and worry to the students and therefore it endangers their emotional stability.
6. Children are tempted to copy whenever they find that the home task is difficult to do.
7. Sometimes children are tempted to tell a lie that due to certain reasons they have failed to do home task.
8. Unhealthy home conditions make study more harmful than profitable. There is a lack of adequate light and quietness in a large number of Indian homes and the atmosphere is not congenial for study.
9. Too much of homework develops an attitude of indifference on the part of the pupils and they become careless.

10. Lack of proper correction by the teacher, sometimes, gives rise to carelessness on the part of the pupils. It also develops wrong habits of work if the work is not properly checked.
11. Too much 'work is set by some over-enthusiastic specialist teachers in their subjects completely disregarding what other teachers of the same class might have set for the same day.
12. The task is generally too academic in nature and ignores those activities which are needed most for an all-round development of the personality of the child.
13. It is not properly adjusted to pupils' needs and capacities.

Basic Principles

Following are the principles of assigning homework.

1. The nature of the homework should be such as it does not require any kind of assistance from a private tutor or guardian.
2. It should not be purely mechanical, i.e., requiring no general knowledge on the part of the child.
3. Homework should aim at developing the taste of the individual child. This purpose can be very conveniently realised if homework is in the nature of hobbies.
4. Homework should be very definite:
5. It should be supplementary rather preparatory as far as possible.
6. A single assignment for the whole class may not be considered as appropriate. It should vary according to the mental and physical makeup of the students.
7. Homework in different subjects should be co-ordinated. Homework time table should be framed so as to avoid confusion.
8. Normally home assignment in Commerce should not require more than one hour every day to complete it.
9. Home task should not be set as a punishment.
10. Home task should be properly checked.
11. Library books should be given for reading at homes as a home task.
12. Copies of the homework time tables may be sent to the parents to seek their cooperation which is very important.

13. While assigning homework the teachers should take into consideration the home conditions of the child such as domestic employment, working condition in the home, etc.
14. 15% marks should be reserved for the evaluation of the student's work based on the assignments done throughout the year.

Correction Process

The following methods of correction may be adopted:

1. Correction by the teacher.
2. Correction with the help of the bright students in the class.
3. Correction with the help of the blackboard.
4. Correction by interchanging the exercise books among the students.
5. Glance checking and signing by teachers.

Case Study

The case-study has been described by Harvey Newmen and D.M. Sidney in their book entitled Teaching Management in these words, "The name case study is a blanket term describing a selection of facts, either fictious or drawn from real life, describing a technical or human relation situation usually in an industrial or commercial setting. It is a segment of history or a piece of reporting and like both history and journalism depends on selection and coindensation for its effects." We may think of these case studies. 1. Success stories of Birlas or Tatas. 2. Role of Kurian in the promotion of Dairy cooperative movement in India. 3. Case study of a sick mill or some other institutions.

A case study involves an analysis of data to determine output, price, expenditure or some other aspect of business endeavour of an individual or institution. Analysis may be made through group discussion.

The case study approach has the following merits:-

1. It develops a scientific outlook and the ability to apply the scientific method to areas like business management.
2. It helps the students to apply theoretical principles to on the job situations.
3. It develops in the students management skills from a practical stand point.

4. It provides a 'dramatic touch' to the situation.
5. It provides adequate experience in studying an actual situation.

Case study approach is not without limitations. Some of the important ones are given below:-

1. It is not possible for the teacher to cover the entire course by the use of case method.
2. The use of case method puts heavy demands upon the commerce teacher.
3. Case study method expects too much from the students.
4. Case study method gives the students an exaggerated idea of his own importance.
5. A prolonged exposure to case study method may develop in the students a too critical and negative approach of looking for what is wrong rather than developing a more constructive and positive approach.

11

Dalton Plan

The plan is named not after its originator Miss Helen Parkhurst but after the name of the town in which it was first adopted in a High School in the U.S.A.

Why is it called a Laboratory Plan. Miss Parkhurst attaches importance to the use of the word 'Laboratory'. She writes, "I cling to it in the hope that it may gradually shift the educational point of view away from the atmosphere of prejudice which the word 'school' calls up in our minds. Let us think of school rather as a sociological laboratory where the pupils themselves are the expereimenters, not the victims of an intricate and crystallised system in the evolution of which they have neither part nor lot. Let us think of it as a place where community conditions prevail as they prevail in life itself." Her aim was to create a new type of educational society by putting boys and girls under entirely different conditions of living from those provided in the ordinary class-room and to re-organise the community life of the school.

Plan at Work

Assignment or contracts. The teachers outline the work of the year to be done in their respective subjects to enable the students to know about the scope and the nature of the work they are required to complete in each subject. The work is further subdivided into suitable monthly units by the subject teachers. While preparing the assignment the teachers bear in mind factors like holidays, time available, revision at various stages, co-curricular activities and the demands of other subjects.

Each unit of work is accepted by the pupil as a 'contract' and he promises to complete the work and to satisfy the teacher before going to the next unit.

Each subject has its separate assignment. The child will be given the new assignment only when he has completed his assignments in all the subjects. A pupil is not allowed to do more than the month's work in a single subject unless he finishes the month's contract in every other subject. The child is free to undertake an assignment for a month in any manner he likes, i.e., he may devote one week completely to complete big assignment in one subject and may ignore assignments in other subjects during that particular week and take up assignments in other subjects in the second, third or the fourth week. He may spend his whole day in one assignment of a subject and so on. The only limitation is that he must finish the whole contract, i.e., monthly assignments in each subject for a particular month, before the second contract is entered upon.

Subject teachers. The Dalton Plan does away with class teachers and accepts specialist teachers. Each specialist teacher supervises each child in his subject and guides his work. He renders all possible help to the child to complete his assignment in time.

Subject rooms. The plan scraps classrooms and gives their place to subject-rooms which are called subject-laboratories. Each specialist is the incharge of his room. Each subject-room is adequately equipped with the material required in that subject. It contains books and magazines, charts, maps, models, apparatus and appliances etc., concerning that subject. There is no fixed time-table and no fixed period. Each student is free to devote more time to the subject in which he is weak and less in which he is up to the mark.

Records. Graphs are kept to show the work done by each child and in each subject so that the pupil himself and the teachers may know how he is progressing. Two records are maintained by the pupil himself; one showing his progress in each subject and the other in all subjects. The third record is kept by the subject-teacher himself and is hung in the subject-room. These records serve as a mirror to indicate the work of the pupils and are kept up-to-date. These also serve as a link between the teacher and the pupil and bring them in close co-operation for effective learning. The graph, in fact, is a constant reminder of the 'contract' or 'promise' and helps to make one conscious also of the extent to which progress is made and is to be made.

Conferences. Usually the morning time uptil recess is devoted to individual work by each child or may be devoted for voluntary group work. The afternoon time may be used by the teacher for oral lessons in his subject. Group discussions under the guidance of the teacher may be held. These oral lessons or group discussions are called 'conferences'. These conferences may be devoted to retrieve common difficulties or to explain certain items of common interest and importance.

Responsibilities and Duties

The role of a teacher in the Dalton Plan may be stated as under:

(i) Preparation of assignments and giving them to the pupils as and when required.

(ii) Keeping an atmosphere of study in the room.

(iii) Giving explanation of any details of the assignement and removing the difficulties of the pupils.

(iv) Giving information with regard to the use of relevant equipment and material.

(v) Ensuring that each assignment is finished properly before the new assignment is given to the pupil.

(vi) Keeping full records of the progress made by pupils in different classes.

(vii) Keeping the subject-library and other equipment up-to-date and in proper order.

The teacher, in the Dalton Plan, is 'a helper, not a driver; the pursued not the pursuer.'

Basic Principles

The principle of individual work. John Adams says, "It is the most dramatic and systematic break away from the class-teaching unit." It is now generally accepted that the Students differ in various respects and it is folly to tag them for keeping pace in studies. The plan aims at providing equal opportunities to all pupils to work at their own rate and speed. The time taken is not necessarily equal but a minimum uniform achievement is required. In the words of Miss

Parkhurst, "It is a piece of machinery for putting into operation the principle of individual work."

The principle of freedom. Children work well when they are allowed freedom to do so. There are no arbitrary fixed periods. There are no class-room restrictions or rigidity of discipline. In the Dalton Plan, children are free to move about, to consult one another and to work in any particular subject. In the words of an educationist. It aims to giving to the older child that freedom for self-development which has proved so valuable in the school life of the "infant" while at the same time ensuring that he shall master thoroughly the academic work required by the curriculum of the school."

The principle of self-effort. Learning to be effective must be the product of one's own self-effort. In the Dalton Plan, the child learns through his own efforts.

The principle of co-operation. In a subject laboratory pupils of different age groups not only assist each other when occasions demand but are very much helped in turn, without being distracted in the task of a companion being similar if not identical. According to Miss Parkhurst, the school can only reflect the social experience of the community when all its parts or groups develop the same intimate relations with one another as is found in society as a whole. The schools should be organised in such a way as the pupils and teachers come in close interaction with one another. Miss Parkhurst has used the term 'interaction of group life'. The students live and work together with the same teachers, in the same shared common workshops or laboratories.

The principle of setting goals. The child is enabled to survey the whole field, to see the goal at which he is aiming at and thus a stimulus is provided to him and he takes up the work bit by bit thereby increasing and ensuring better learning.

Merits

Individual teaching. Each pupil is permitted to work at his own rate. The plan approaches teaching and instruction from the point of view of the pupil. The weak are not hurried along at the speed of other pupils and the bright are not kept back because of their slow class-fellows. The teacher pays individual attention to each child.

Continuity of work. There is no waste of time as is usually the case in the conduct of various examinations for promotion or other purposes. There are no failures and the promotions from one grade to another may take place at any time. Absence from school of a child due to ill-health or otherwise does not stand in his way of working smoothly. He can start the work just from where he had stopped and can make up his deficiency at his own speed. There is no danger that some courses have been covered in his absence and he has missed them.

Development of qualities like self-effort and self-confidence. There is absolutely no spoon feeding in the Dalton Plan. Ready-made knowledge is not given to the child. He has to depend upon himself in the solution of his problems. He has to consult suitable books and other reference material. He, himself has to experience difficulties and to solve his problems. All this makes him self-confident.

Purposeful learning. Student's 'contract' or 'assignment' is like a project in front of him and for its completion he tries his best and devotes his heart and soul into the work. Thus learning becomes motivated and purposeful.

Development of desirable study habits. The students have to make use of a variety of material to complete their assignments. They have to study reference books, source books, etc., and all this helps to develop desirable study habits in them.

Development of sense of responsibility. The 'contract' is a constant reminder to the children to complete their work in time. They feel that they must fulfil their responsibility that they have accepted in entering upon the 'assignment'.

Solving the problem of home task. There is no need for giving home task. The child in order to complete his assignment may of his own accord devote extra time in the subject-laboratory. Thus compulsory homework loses its terror in the school.

Solving the problem of discipline. No restrictions are put on children. They work in an atmosphere of freedom. They accept their own responsibility and work for its fulfilment. There is no rigid timetable and the students are not forced to attend to studies according to a set time-table. Problem of truancy, mischief and delirquency are rare.

Simplification of the problem of evaluation. The graph system is a valuable check on the progress of each child. The records show the progress of each pupil and enable him to know where he stands. In a way records can help to give incentives to him. There is no necessity to frequent tests and awarding of marks.

Better pupil-teacher relationships. The plan enables the teacher to know the child individually. Every child is free to seek the teacher's guidance at any point when a difficulty occurs. The teacher is essentially a guide and a helper.

Demerits

Not suitable for the average child and a shirker. The clever and the bright students can derive a lot of benefit from this scheme. It is not possible for the average child to learn new principles without a formal lesson. The shirkers also find opportunities to develop the attitude of 'postponement'.

Development of individualistic tendencies. As a child has his own assignment to do, he may not like to help his other friends if he is required to do so on the plea that he is absorbed in his own work. Pinkevitch observers, "We cannot but express the fear that it will be instrumental in developing individualistic tendencies in children."

A purely intellectual plan. The plan fails to provide for liberal group activities. There is little scope for social service activities. Dr. Cox states, "The Dalton Plan is highly inadequate for social education."

Unsuitable for lessons that require inspirational treatment. There are certain subjects which require collective lessons for appreciation purposes. Physical training, music and drill in languages need group teaching. Therefore, the plan is unsuitable for these subjects.

Lack of suitable teachers. For the successful working of the plan, competent, liberal and progressive teachers are required. The plan puts heavy demands upon the teachers who are expected to prepare good assignment and be able to guide and help the pupils if and when such guidance or help is needed. Teachers must be in a position to inspire students to work hard independently. It is very difficult to get such teachers.

Lack of well-equipped libraries. Most of the libraries of our schools are not adequately equipped and are without trained librarians. But under the Dalton Plan, we acquire a wide variety of suitable text-books, source books and other relevant material so that the children may prepare their assignments.

Unsuitable for junior classes. The plan is more suitable for children above nine years of age.

Very costly. The plan is very expensive. It requires many more teachers and well-equipped libraries and other equipment.

Difficult to change traditional approach. It is very difficult to change the attitude of the teachers who are accustomed to old methods of class teaching. They do not like sweeping changes. Moreover, they do not like to give freedom to pupils.

Summary

A review of the limitations and difficulties of the Dalton Plan shows that it is not possible to introduce this plan in its entirety in our schools. However, there is much that can be introduced in ordinary teaching. We should try to evolve some system in which class teaching may be done in the morning and individual teaching in the afternoon. More individual attention should be given to the students. They should be encouraged to read extra books and a record of that should be kept. Some sort of day-to-day assessment should be made of the work done by each child and the result communicated to them so that they may be motivated to work hard.

QUESTIONS

1. "Garments which fit everybody, fit no body." Explain this statement in the context of individualised instruction in Dalton Plan.
2. Explain the merits and limitations of the use of Dalton Plan in Commerce teaching.
3. Discuss the role of the commerce teacher in the Dalton Plan.
4. Can we combine class teaching method with the Dalton Plan? Give arguments in support of your answer.

12

Significance of Values

In fact, vague terminology is one of the greatest problems in any discussion of teaching as a discipline. Some of this is perhaps inevitable because teaching is concerned with the behaviour and personality of human beings. Several terms like aims, objectives, values and competencies do not lend themselves to clear interpretation. Occasionally they are used to convey the same meaning.

General Aims

Aims are necessary to select meaningful and significant content, teaching methods and techniques. They point to the broad ideals we intend to achieve.

Among the important specific aims of the study of Commerce, following may be mentioned.

1. Vocational aim of the study of Commerce.
2. Consumer efficiency aim of the study of Commerce.
3. Economic efficiency aim of the study of Commerce.
4. Training or a professional career aim of the study of Commerce.

Other aims are (i) Knowledge aim. (ii) Character development aim (iii) Social efficiency aim. (iv) Citizenship development aim. (v) Ethical, moral and spiritual aims. (vi) Hobby development aim.

Vocational Aims

High philosophies apart, the full education for an individual must be both for 'making a living' and 'making for life'. Thus viewed, the full education of an individual involves both 'Vocational education' and 'cultural or liberal education'. The individual must be able to earn a living for leading a civilised life. In such a perspective, business education is to be looked upon as just one phase of education, not inferior or superior to any other phase or branch. Gandhiji has observed, "True education ought to be for them (boys and girls) a kind of insurance against unemployment". The vocational education can train individuals to become socially efficient. Therefore, they will neither be drags nor parasities on the society. They will contribute to increase production and national wealth. The advocates of the vocational aim of teaching Commerce argue that all the knowledge a pupil gains in an educational institution, all the culture he requires will be of no use, if he is not able to make both ends meet when he enters life.

It is true that an individual does not live by bread alone. It is also equally true that without bread an individual cannot live. The 'bread and butter aim' does not mean that an individual will not be trained for higher values of life.

Jawaharlal Nehru has very rightly pointed out, "Education has mainly two aspects, the cultural aspect which makes a person grow, and the productive aspect which makes a person do things. Both are essential. Everybody should be a producer as well as a good citizen and not a sponge on another person even though the other person may be one's own husband or wife."

While favouring the vocational aim of education, it must be borne in mind that it is not restricted to 'money making'. If it happens, education would be deprived of its elevating and inspiring influence which leads to fuller and richer life.

The words of wisdom said by the University Education Commission 1948-49 must also be remembered by all those who advocate vocational aim so that this aim does not remain one-sided and narrow. "If we wish to bring about a savage upheaval in our society, a 'Rakshak Raj', all that we need is to give vocational and technical education to starve the spirit. We will have a number of scientists without conscience, technicians without taste, who find a void within themselves, a moral vaccum and a desperate need to substitute something, anything for their lost endeavour and purpose." The fact is that we neither can starve the body, nor the mind and nor the spirit. A harmonious blend of the three is needed. "There is" as the great philosopher Whitehead puts it, "only one subject matter of education and that is life in all its manifestations." Trade, commerce and industry constitute a vital part of our life activities. These aspects of our life's experiences are extremely important and if we depise them, all our educational efforts will be fruitless toils.

Aims of Studying

Knowledge aim is the most predominant aim of studying theory of Commerce. Here cognitive or intellectual aspect is emphasised. It is believed that human progress consists in the increase of knowledge. Knowledge aim emphasises that the person who develops problem solving ability remains successful in his private as well as official life.

Skill development is the chief aim of studying Accountancy and Auditing. Here stress is on vocational competency.

Lecture method, description method and problem-solving method are the important methods of teaching used in teaching theory of Commerce. On the other hand in teaching Accountancy and Auditing, demonstration and practice play an important role.

Teaching Values

Aims are considered as conscious purposes and goals. Values are the outcomes or results achieved after teaching according to these aims. Aims are ideals which are not based on experiments. Values on the other hand spring as a result of experimentation or after putting aims into practices. Values are based on reality and the aims on philosophical consideration.

Values of the study of Commerce may be divided into the following four categories.

1. Cultural Values
2. Disciplinary Values
3. Practical Values
4. Social Values

Cultural Values : Commerce is an important aspect of the life of a nation. It explains the nature of the society in its special aspect of business and material prosperity. Commerce attempts to relate production with consumption. Fair dealings, good salesmanship, honesty in business and pleasing manners-all go to make up the good cultural tracts of the individual in the commercial field. Several philanthrophists in India from the business community have set up a large number of cultural and educational institutions in the country.

Disciplinary Values: The word 'discipline' has a special connotation in Commerce. It is not in terms of 'order' and 'authority'. It is to be interpreted in terms of intellectual traits only. A study of Commerce helps to develop the powers of knowing, understanding and application. It also develops certain skills how to write good business letters etc.

Practical Values: Practical Values relate more to the needs of various occupations at different levels in the hierarchy of employment-from clerical to management level.

Social Values: The study of Commerce should enable an individual to appreciate that man is a social being and he must play an important role in bringing about social progress. Bad business dealings, corrupt methods, smuggling and tax evasions are examples of anti-social values which should be avoided as outcomes of a study of Commerce. Profit motive should not be the end and-be-all of all business enterprises.

Desired Competence

Although development of vocational competency was and still is the chief objective of Commerce Education, it is no longer the only objective. It must be remembered that much of the growth of Commerce Education is due to our recognition of objectives other than vocational competency.

Far reaching changes are taking place in different areas of life with the result that people change their vocations and professions especially within a few years after entering into them. These occupational changes are generally on account of advances in technology. Inventions make several jobs out of dates and create new jobs. For meeting such situations, suitable competencies need to be developed in the students.

There are several fundamental competencies which are needed in several vocations and these should be suitably looked after.

Several students offer Commerce subjects not because they propose to enter a profession related to business, commerce and industry but because of the use of the subject in their personal life. Competency in book-keeping may be used for a housewife in keeping household accounts. Book-keeping may help a doctor in keeping the accounts of his clinic.

Competency in typewriting helps the students in preparing assignments, helps the authors in preparing their manuscripts of books etc.

A similar analysis of other Commerce subjects would show that most of them may be used personally as well as vocationally.

Consumer-business competency enables all students not only to use more efficient methods of buying goods and services but also to make more efficient use of the goods and services provided by business activities.

There is a need to have an understanding and appreciation of the role of commerce played in our daily lives. Commerce education as a phase of general education can make a significant contribution to the development of socio-economic competency by assisting students to develop a clear understanding of the national economy. The nation needs people who are socially efficient and at the same time economically sound.

Tonne, Pophan and Freeman (1965) hold the view, "Commerce Education is also good general education, in so far as it helps the students to become an intelligent consumer of business goods and services. It also provides him with some understanding of the national economic system and thus helps him to become a more intelligent and more useful member of his community."

Thus the fulfilment of the objectives of teaching Commerce to students who pass out of the senior secondary schools lies in the development of the following competencies:-

1. Competency desired by the employers i.e. reasonable degree of efficiency and skill in a vocation.

2. Competency desired by the institutions of higher learning i.e., adequate background in the subject for enabling a student to undertake studies in the field of Commerce and allied subjects.
3. Competency of occupational/vocational change.
4. Competency to pursue more than one vocation.
5. Competency to use the knowledge of commerce in day-to-day personal life.
6. Competency in consumer business.
7. Competency in undertaking one's own business.
8. Competency to take up responsibility as an active and cooperative member of the society.
9. Competency in participating in business life of the society.
10. Competency in participating intelligently, and rationally in political and social life of the community.

QUESTIONS

1. Explain the Vocational aim of teaching Commerce. Is it possible to reconcile the values of vocational and liberal education?
2. What are the values of the study of Commerce to the pupils of senior secondary/higher secondary schools?
3. How can you differentiate between the aims of studying theory of Commerce from those of Accountancy and Auditing?
4. What competencies are desired of students of Commerce passing out the higher secondary stage? Explain.

13

Importance of Skill

The development of essential skills in every child should be an important outcome of the teaching of Commerce. The skills may pertain to various subject areas. In several topics in Commerce, Accountancy, Auditing, Banking and Book-keeping. The primary aim is the development of some skills and not the acquisition of knowledge.

The importance of skill subjects in the scheme of education is gradually being recognised. In the Basic System of education, learning of skills of different types is very important. L.P. Jacks has stressed this aspect in these words, "The human body is naturally skill-hungry and until that hunger is satisfied, it will be ill-at-ease, craving for something it has not got and seeking its satisfaction in external excitements which exhaust its vitality and diminish its capacity for joy. Short of skill, the perfect health, even of body, is impossible."

James High of the University of California states that a skill is the wherewithal to gain an end.

According to Webster's New Dictionary, skill is "the ability to use one's knowledge effectively and readily in execution or performance, technical expertness; a power or habit of doing any particular thing competently."

The Pre-requisites

It may be stressed that no one course of studies is mutually exclusive. Accountancy, although is primarily a skill subject; here also before a student can use his acquired skills, he must have attained the knowledge, understandings and attitudes acceptable in the business world or in his own circle, depending on where he is planning to use the skill. Similarly typewriting is not entirely a skill building course although most of the operations in typewriting are skill building and they should be taught in accordance with the principles of skill building. The same statement is true in the case of shorthand.

It is also wrong to think that learning is entirely a mental process. All learning is influenced by physiological factors both within and outside the individual who is learning. At the same time all learning is accompanied by these physiological factors. However, when the physical responses of the individual become more important and prominent, we call it skill development. When a secretary receives callers with charm and poise either in person at the desk or over the phone, we call it a skill development. This is true in learning to typewrite, or to take dictation in shorthand or to transcribe from the shorthand outline.

Many persons have the misconception of considering the learning of skills to be entirely a physical operation. Nothing could be farther from truth. A person can be a successful stenographer only when he understands English or Hindi or any other language usage and punctuation, form and arrangement etc.

Intellectual and Social Types

Prof Charles A. Beard has analysed these skills as under:

1. Skill in methods of obtaining access to information (a) use of libraries and institutions, (b) use of encyclopaedias, handbooks, documents, sources, authorities, statistical collections etc.
2. Skill in the sifting of the materials and the discovery and determination of authentic evidence in the use of primary sources.
3. Skill in the observation and description of contemporary occurrences in the school and community.
4. Skill in methods of handling information (a) in analysis breaking down large themes or masses of data into

manageable units and penettating to irreducible elements, (b) in synthesis—combining elements, drawing inferences and conclusions, and comparing with previous conclusions and inference-logical and systematic organisation, (c) in map and chart making and graphic presentation.

5. Skill in memorising results of study with consciousness of application to new situations by exact reference and analogy.
6. Skill in scientific method-inquiring spirit, patience, weighing evidence, tentative and precise conclusions.

Gaining Mastery

Mastery of a skill is said to be achieved when the skill can be performed even if something else was also in the mind of an individual. L.V. Douglass, J.T. Blanford and R.I. Anderson (1965) give the following example of mastery of skill. "A teacher once had in class a girl who was unusually expert in taking dictation on the stenotype. She quite often was hired to record discussions and proceedings at conventions and important board meetings. She had the reputation of never missing a word in her recording. Yet, while she was recording, she habitually also was reading a book or magazine at the same time. She had developed her skill so highly that it was completely automatized; her fingers reached instantly when the sound of the voice reached her ears. She had actually found that her records were more accurate when she deliberately kept her mind off her work."

The mastery formula for learning a skill may be expressed in three letters TA S. T stands for technique, A for accuracy and S for speed. Some teachers prefer to reverse this order and believe in the efficacy of SAT ie. speed, accuracy and technique.

Following are the six steps to achieve mastery:-

(i) Pre-testing (ii) Teaching (iii) Testing the result (iv) Adopting the procedure (v) Re-teaching and (vi) Retesting and continuing the procedure till the mastery is achieved.

Eight Principles for the Achievement of Skills

HePen Mccracken Carpenter and Alice W. Spieseke have suggested the following principles:

1. For the acquisition and improvement of skills, the learning activity must focus on skill development. Skill development will not take place by chance.
2. Experience designed to promote growth in skills must be meaningful to the learner. A certain skill must be accepted as important.
3. Experience used in skill development must be geared to the maturation level of the learner. Just as a five-year-old cannot usually master the flowing script with a fountain pen, neither can a junior high school student be expected to achieve the same degree of skill in synthetic thought as a college professor.
4. For the successful learning and retention of skills, repetitive practice is necessary. Reinforcement of learning is essential.
5. Skills should be developed in connection with on-going activities and not in isolation. Every skill is in the end an integral part of the life equipment of the citizen.
6. Development of different skills should go on simultaneously. There is a gradual and steady growth of all of the parts in the process of education.
7. Evidence of skill development must be sought to changes in behaviour. The whole purpose of education is to induce an improved behaviour pattern.
8. Provision for the systematic development of skills must be made through the school programme. This is merely to re-emphasise the idea that skills begin with mastery of simple uncomplicated steps and, proceed to more complex and various patterns of activity. This principle is a summary of all the other seven.

Psychological Considerations for Building and Developing Skills

Mort and Vincent of the Columbia University have developed and compiled the following 30 psychological rules for building skills.

1. One learns when one feels some urge to learn.
2. What a person learns is influenced directly by his surroundings.

3. A person learns quickly and lastingly what has meaning for him.
4. When an organism is ready to act, it is painful for it not to act; and when an organism is not ready to act, it is painful for it to act.
5. Individuals differ in all sorts of ways.
6. Security and success are the soil and climate for growth.
7. All learning occurs through attempts to satisfy needs.
8. Emotional tension decreases efficiency in learning.
9. Physical defects lower efficiency in learning.
10. Interest is an indicator of growth.
11. Interest is a source of power in motivating learning.
12. What gives satisfaction tends to be repeated; what is annoying tends to be avoided.
13. The best way to learn a part in life is to play that part.
14. Learning is more efficient, longer and lasting when the conditions for it are real and life-like.
15. Piece-meal learning is not efficient.
16. You cannot train the mind like a muscle.
17. A person learns by his own activity.
18. Abundant, realistic practice contributes to learning.
19. Participation enhances learning.
20. First-hand experience makes for lasting and more complete learning.
21. General behaviour is controlled by emotions as well as by intellect.
22. Unused talents contribute to personal maladjustment.
23. You start to grow from where you are and not from some artificial starting point.
24. Growth is a steady, continuous process and different individuals grow at different rates.
25. It is impossible to learn one thing at a time.
26. Learning is reinforced when two or more senses are used at the same time.
27. The average pupil is largely a myth.
28. If you want a certain result, teach it directly.
29. Children develop in terms of all the influences which affect them.

30. It has been said that a person learns more in the first three years of his life than all the years afterward.

Lesson Planning

Steps in Skill Lesson

Preparation. The mind of the children should be prepared to learn the new skill. They must be motivated. The students should be made to feel the necessity of acquiring a skill. The preparation or introduction may take different forms.

(i) The students may be taken to markets or banks etc.
(ii) Skill work of some experts may be exhibited.
(iii) A model of some good work may be shown to the students.

Statement of the Aim. The students must know clearly what they are going to learn; otherwise they will be groping in the dark and their co-operation will be half-hearted.

Presentation. The teacher presents the new form of skill. The teacher should give a few instructions to the students so that they may properly watch and observe the demonstration given by him. Sometimes the students may handle the model for close observation. This stage consists, largely of observation, listening and seeking on the part of the students. The teacher is doing things and explaining things. The teacher may give the statements of the rules to be observed in practising the skill. But they should be brief and should not be many.

Practice. The students will imitate what the teacher has demonstrated before them. This is the most important step and will also take a longer period. The teacher will not remain passive at this stage. He will supervise and guide the practice of each individual student.

Correction. It is a sort of representation. The teacher will point out the defects and show the correct ways of performing the activity.. He may restate the rules.

Re-practice. Then again will come practice and the students may practise the skill and acquire improvement. The two steps 'correction' and 'practice' may be repeated a number of times.

Guidelines

The following guidelines may be considered in teaching and developing skills:-

1. The teacher should possess the skill which he proposes to the students to learn.
2. The teacher should identify the factors which determine the pattern of the skill.
3. The teacher should appeal to as many senses as possible in teaching a skill.
4. Each segment of the class period should have a specific objective and each student and the teacher should have proper awareness of it.
5. Repetition is of great value only when it is with conscious direction.
6. In teaching a skill, practice time should be divided into short practice periods.
7. Practices of the skill should be varied before the law of diminishing return applies.
8. Group practices are useful only for establishing the desirable pattern.
9. Attainable goals should be set for each student.
10. A skill should be developed to the level of automatization.
11. The teacher must lay more stress on the technique rather than the speed.
12. The teacher should not over emphasis testing on skill development.
13. The teacher has to promote a skill through proper demonstration. Mistakes can be avoided not by telling but by demonstrating better ways of working and doing.

Principles and Techniques

In any subject, the method of teaching is a broad concept which includes several techniques of teaching. However, some authors use these terms 'methods' and 'techniques' as synonyms. For instance 'assignment' is used as a method as well as a technique. Techniques are very valuable instruments for making teaching-learning efficient, meaningful and inspirational. Among the important technique following may be mentioned.

1. Assignment
2. Drill
3. Review
4. Narration
5. Explanation
6. Exposition
7. Illustration
8. Questions and answers (Discussed in a separate chapter)
9. Observation.

Drill

This technique is also known as 'practice' or 'habit formation'. This is a favourite device with the teachers. The purpose of drill is to increase proficiency in performance. In the words of Dr. Yoakam and Simpson (1957), "Drill is a serious work activity or the strengthening of association to make skills more permanent." The subject matter which demands drill for mastery exists more or less in all school subjects and has a wide scope in accountancy.

Important principles of effective drill are as under:-

1. The students should understand the significance of the material which they are to repeat.
2. Appeal to the best motive of the students should be made.
3. The work should be of a graded nature. The child should get success in the early stages of practice.
4. Correct response should be secured from the beginning.
5. Drill exercises should be short and distributed over a period of time.
6. The child's attention should be centred on definite improvement and on reasons of failure or lack of improvement.
7. Drill is an individual affair and it is a wrong practice to ask the few to drill at the expense of many.
8. Right practice should be aimed at.
9. Drill should be varied. It should be of different forms, otherwise it is likely to become monotonous.

The Revision

Review or revision is a 'retrospective view' of what has been learned or experienced. According to the literal meaning it means to a view again. In the words of Bossing, "The term review connotes not a mere repetition of facts or fixing them more firmly in mind, but rather a new view of these facts in a different setting that result in new understandings, changed attitudes, or different behaviour patterns." According to Rusk, "Review means getting a new view or renewal of an old view to assure a better view or grasp of relationships studied."

In the words of Dr. Yoakam and Simpson, "The review involves a recall for purposes of renewing the learning already passed and of carrying it on to mastery. It is the reorganisation and integration of experiences."

Scope of Review

1. It helps in the fixation of relationship of facts by providing a restatement and organisation of facts.
2. It helps pupils to have a broader perspective of what is being taught.
3. It helps to reveal weakness in the teaching-learning process.

Types of Review

1. Review of a section of a lesson
2. Daily lesson review
3. Topical review
4. Cooperative review
5. Review by making charts, models etc.
6. Review by practical application.

Narration

Narration is one of the most important methods of communicating knowledge. It is not possible to elicit everything from the students. Narration implies giving account of events to others. According to Prof. I.H. Panton, "Narration is an art in itself which aims at presenting to the pupils, through the medium of speech, clear, vivid, interesting, ordered sequences of events, in such a way that their minds reconstruct these happenings and they live in imagination through the experiences recounted either as spectators or possibly as participators. To be a good narrator, a teacher should know the skilful use of language. He should use appropriate language which should clearly depict situations and happenings. The speech or the language should also be appropriate to the level of the students.

The art of narration can be cultivated through four methods:

1. By observing the work of other skilful narrators.
2. By studying the work of successful writers of children's books.
3. By practising story-telling.
4. By critically observing one's own performance.

The use of homely illustrations such as metaphors and similes relating the experiences with which children are familiar adds to the effectiveness of narration.

The chief form of narration is story-telling.

Description

Description and narration are quite similar and there is not much difference between these two terms. According to the dictionary meaning "to describe" is to set forth, define, depict or portrary in words" and "Description" is defined as "the act of representing a thing by words; account of the properties or appearance of something."

More effective use of language is required in description than in narration.

Description is needed in most of the lessons of almost all the subjects. The following points should be kept in mind while using this devise- of teaching.

1. The teacher should have a clear and strong visual image of the object. His information should not be mere theoretical. As far as possible the teacher should try to see the actual object. Of course, this will not be possible in all cases. Let it be borne in mind that without forming a clear visual picture of the object in mind, it will not be possible to describe the object in an effective manner.

2. Language employed should be very simple and clear.
3. It is better to give first a broad general effect of appearance of the whole and then to fill in the details.
4. Description should be very brief and simple. Too many details at a time should be avoided as these baffle the children's imagination.
5. Important points should be repeated and stressed.
6. Description should be given in some definite arrangement.
7. Reliance should not be used on words alone. Models, pictures or diagrams should also be used.
8. The aim of the description should be clear to the teacher and the taught.
9. The use of homely illustrations such as metaphors and similes help to vivify description.

Explanation

The object of explanation is to enable the children to take an intelligent interest in the proceedings, to grasp the purpose of what is being done, and to develop their understanding of how to do it."

To explain means "to make plain, manifest, or intelligible; to clear of obscurity: to expound; to lay open the meanings; to elucidate."

Panton observes: "Explanation forms a kind of bridge between telling and revealing knowledge to the learners, and it involves a number of other techniques as well as narration and description. Throughout the process the teacher must keep in close touch with the minds of his pupils suggesting lines of thought, questioning them, answering their questions, setting them on practical work, examining the results obtained, discussing significant problems, etc."

The following points may be noted in this connection:-

1. Some definite aim must be kept in mind by the teacher and the students so as to remove obscurity.
2. The theme should be divided into different sections and must have logical sequence and a definite arrangement.

3. The capacity of the students to understand and assimilate the subject-matter should be given due consideration.
4. Too much of telling on the part of the teacher is likely to confuse the child instead of making things clear or intelligible.
5. The teacher should put the essential points on the black-board.
6. The teacher would do well to ask questions from the students at different stages to ascertain whether they have followed him or not.
7. Illustrations both verbal and non-verbal; or audio-visual aids should be made use of.
8. A summary of the whole discussion should be given at the end of the lesson.

Exposition

To expose means to open, to exhibit, to display, to disclose or to subject to light. Exposition is making clear the new information. It is more than explanation. The purpose of exposition is to enable the children to grasp the sense or meanings of the subject-matter presented to them in an intelligible manner.

Effective teaching is based upon a clear exposition. The things must be explained fully to children. Hurried exposition results in faulty assimilation of knowledge.

The following points should be kept in view in using this technique of teaching;

1. Matter should be arranged in such a way as to leave a single clear impression on the minds of the students.
2. The teacher should have pauses in between the lesson so that the students may learn the new knowledge bit by bit.
3. The rate of exposition should be slow when the class is backward. The teacher should utilise different ways of presenting the same information.
4. There should be abundant repetition but should be in a new way so that the class may not feel dullness.
5. Children's way of looking at things should be considered in exposition. Language used should be familiar and suitable.

6. The lesson should be divided into sections which have a logical sequence. This will enable the students to understand easily and will also train them in systematic thinking besides assisting them to put their own thoughts logically.
7. The rate of exposition and the size of the subject-matter are determined by the individual capacity of children and teacher's natural rate of speech.
8. Proper use of the black-board should be made.
9. Actual objects, models, diagrams, sketches etc., should be used.
10. The students should be encouraged to ask questions. They will enable them to get their doubts removed.
11. Verbal illustration such as examples, comparisons, etc., should be used to enable the students to grasp the exposition.
12. Pictorial illustrations such as pictures, maps and charts should be freely used as these help in motivating the students.
13. The aim of the lesson should be kept in view and the students fully made conversant with the aim.

Illustration

To illustrate an idea or an object means to throw light on it. The term illustration is used in educational literature to mean the use of those aids which make various points, statements and arguments clear and vivid to students and assist them to acquire correct knowledge.

Types of Illustrations. There are several types of illustrations but we may divide them into two broad categories.

1. ***Concrete, Non Verbal, Natural or Objective Illustrations:*** Under this head we may include objects, models, exhibits, demonstration, apparatus, pictures, diagrams, charts, maps, graphs, slides, film, radio, black-board, garden, museum, etc.
2. ***Verbal Illustration.*** These include anecdotes, stories, descriptions, incidents, comparisons, analogies, similes, dramatisation.

Merits

1. They help to simplify explanations.
2. They make the instruction concrete.
3. They give vividness of explanations.
4. They assist in overcoming difficulties of understanding.
5. They create interest and curiosity in learning.
6. They help to strengthen the retaining and recollecting power of students.
7. They are valuable in developing the power of observations of students.
8. They help in the formation of good intellectual habits.
9. They are a ready means of fixing the attention of the students.
10. They lessen the knowledge load and set up associations which help in the economy of efforts.
11. They train the senses to greater acuteness of perception.

Relative Importance of these Two Types: Their relative importance depends upon:

(a) The nature of the subjects.
(b) The level of pupils development.

Non-verbal illustrations are more useful and should be frequently employed in the lower classes. Actual objects or their solid representations, models, etc., should be used. Pictures, diagrams, sketches and graphs should be used in abundance in the higher classes. A high level of intelligence is required to understand verbal illustrations, such as analogies and similes etc., and, therefore, these should come at a higher stage.

It may not be possible in many cases to bring the common objects in class-room. Educational excursions may be planned to take the students to see real things.

Illustrations are means and not ends. It must be remembered that illustrations are good servants but bad masters. Their misuse or overuse is likely to spoil the lesson. It is a wrong notion that without a paraphernalia of illustrative material, a lesson cannot be made effective. Following points may be kept in view in the use of illustrations of all types:-

1. Illustrations should be relevant to the topic.
2. Illustrations should be simple and easily comprehensible.
3. Language used in verbal illustrations should be easy and simple.
4. Illustrations should be subordinate to the topic.
5. Illustrations should be accurate and exact.
6. Number of illustrations should be moderate.
7. Illustrations should be homely.

Technique of Observation

It is rightly observed that observation under the careful observation of a Commerce teacher proves very effective in the process of learning facts, skills, and behaviour which are retained for a longer period. Observation or direct experience or visits to actual place of work i.e. banks, insurance companies, stock exchanges and transport enterprises etc. provide ample opportunities to students for 'seeing 'hearing', 'examining, 'gathering data' and 'asking questions'. By visiting transport companies, students learn how people and goods are transported from one place to another. Pupils understand better the working of banks, cooperative stores, factories and markets etc., when they observe their working and this acquaint themselves with the process of production, distribution, exchange and consumption. Several organisational and managerial practices are learnt better through observation. Observation lends 'reality' to the subject-matter of Commerce.

Among the important techniques mention may be made of field trips, educational excursions and community surveys etc.

Motivating Students

"Don't do too much for the students". "Let students think and do" are the maxims that underlie student-motivated techniques. Student motivated techniques stress the value of analysis rather than the acquisition of facts. Group discussions, seminars, symposiums, workshops, individual assignments, surveys, paper reading contests all come under the category of student-motivated techniques.

The Maxims

Following are the important maxims of teaching which are usually used in teaching all subjects including Commerce.

1. Proceeding/teaching from the known to the unknown.
2. Proceeding/teaching from simple to complex.
3. Proceeding/teaching from easy to difficult.
4. Proceeding/teaching from concrete to abstract.
5. Proceeding/teaching from particular to general.
6. Proceeding/teaching from indefinite to definite.
7. Proceeding/teaching from empirical to rational.
8. Proceeding/teaching from psychological to logical.
9. Proceeding/teaching from whole to parts.
10. Proceeding/teaching from near to far.
11. Proceeding/teaching from analysis to synthesis.
12. Proceeding/teaching inductively.

Basic Principles

Following principles form the basis of all methods, techniques, maxims and devices of teaching. Of course all these principles overlap and are interrelated.

1. Principle of activity
2. Principle of learning by doing
3. Principle of motivation
4. Principle of self-education
5. Principle of individual differences
6. Principle of goal setting
7. Principle of stimulation
8. Principle of association
9. Principle of readiness
10. Principle of effect
11. Principle of repetition
12. Principle of variety
13. Principle of feedback and reinforcement
14. Principle of training of senses
15. Principle of group dynamics
16. Principle of creativity
17. Principle of child-centredness
18. Principle of correlation
19. Principle of remedial teaching.
20. Principle of creating conducive environment
21. Principle of flexibility

QUESTIONS

1. Explain the meaning and significance of a skill. What types of skills are needed to be developed in the students studying Commerce, Accountancy, Banking and Book-keeping?
2. Is it possible to isolate a mental skill from a motor skill? Explain.
3. Prepare a list of skills that you would like to develop in the students studying commerce subjects.
4. What is mastery of skills? How can it be attained?
5. Select any topic in commerce and prepare a skill lesson.
6. Explain the various steps of a skill lesson.
7. State the principles and guidelines for developing skills in commerce.
8. Explain the significance of narration, description, explanation and exposition as techniques of commerce teaching.
9. "Illustrations are good servants and bad masters." Comment upon this statement and state their significance in the teaching of Commerce.
10. Discuss the word 'illustration' as it is technically used in educational literature. What are the purposes and the uses of verbal illustrations in teaching of Commerce? What are their limitations?
11. What is the value of drill in teaching Commerce? How will you make this technique effective?
12. Differentiate between a drill lesson and review. What is the purpose of review?
13. "The modern concept of review is to make it new, deeper and broader overview." Explain how a teacher should plan review effectively.
14. What is the significance of the statement that 'one learns best when he practises'. Describe the meaning, nature and functions of this statement.
15. Write a short note on observation as a technique of teaching Commerce.

14

Testing and Evaluation

At present the tendency is to use the term evaluation in place of the term examination. Evaluation is a process by means of which changes in behaviour of children are studied and guided towards goals sought by a school.

According to Wiles, "Evaluation is a process of making judgments that are to be used as a basis for planning. It consists of establishing goals, collecting evidence concerning growth or lack of growth toward goals, making judgments about the evidence, and revising procedures and goals in the light of the judgments. It is a procedure for improving the product, the process, and even the goals themselves."

The Programme

Chester T. McNernly observes, "The purpose of any programme of evaluation is to discover the needs of the individuals being evaluated and then to design learning experiences that will solve these needs.... Evaluation is an important and delicate process not only from the standpoint of determining the needs and growth or programmes of individuals but also from the standpoint of what it does to the individuals being evaluated... An evaluation cannot adequately be made by using a single check list, an isolated anecdotal record, or a battery of examinations; a complete evaluation will require the use of many techniques."

Thomas H. Briggs and Joseph Justman write that evaluation is "a process by which the values of an enterprise are ascertained."

Further they write "Evaluation should be conceived primarily in terms of educational purposes which the programme of supervision is intended to serve."

(i) If the purpose is to stimulate teachers to improve their techniques of classroom instruction, evaluation must concern itself with ascertaining the extent to which such improvement is being effected.

(ii) If the purpose is to enrich and vitalize the course of study, evaluation must seek to determine whether the pupils are really deriving greater educational value from the "enriched" and "vitalized" programme than they did formerly.

(iii) If the purpose is to re-establish faculty *espirt de corps* and school morale, the objectives of evaluation will be as to assess in various ways the degree of improvement in personal and professional attitudes, in human relations, and ultimately, therefore, in efficiency of teaching and learning.

(iv) If an important purpose of the supervisory programme is to promote greater educational attention to individual needs of pupils, evaluation will necessarily concern itself with estimating the success with which guidance procedures, differentiated programme of study, courses and units of learning experience, individualised teaching and learning procedures, and other educational measures designed to achieve greater satisfaction of individual needs are operating.

Shane and McSwain conceive evaluation, "as a process of inquiry based upon criteria cooperatively prepared and concerned with the study, interpretation, and guidance of socially desirable changes in the developmental behaviour of children ... It is a process within the child as a result of which he responds to the psychological interpretation he makes of his school-community environment."

The Definition

One of the best definitions of evaluation is given by Clara M. Brown, "Evaluation is essential in the never-ending cycle of formulating goals, measuring progress towards them and determining the new goals which merge as a result of new warnings. Evaluation involves measurement which means objective quantitative evidence. But it is broader than measurement and implies that considerations have been given to certain values, standards and that interpretation of the evidence has been made in the light of the particular situation."

The Techniques

The concept of evaluation implies a checking or assessment of what goes on. This is done so that actual facts of a situation may be ascertained and remedial action taken where necessary. Since a detailed analysis helps to isolate the factors which may contribute to the malfunctioning of the whole system, evaluation can perform a vital diagnostic role by suggesting corrective action at every stage of preparation, instead of having the system with all its errors proceed blindly to its final end. Evaluation used specifically for this purpose of correcting an ongoing process, rather than only for final product assessment, is one of the most important contributions of systems thinking to programmes in education. Formative or, continuous evaluation, (providing feedback which enables adjustment of the programme to meet intermediate objectives), results in a better chance for the programme to achieve its final objectives.

The Functions

1. To make provision for guiding the growth of individual pupil.
2. To diagnose the weaknesses and strength of pupils.
3. To locate areas where remedial measures are needed.
4. To provide a basis for a modification of the curriculum and courses.
5. To provide a basis for the introduction of experiences to meet the needs of individuals and groups of pupils.
6. To motivate pupils towards better attainment and growth.
7. To test the efficiency of teachers in providing learning experiences and the effectiveness of instruction and classroom activities.

8. To improve instruction.
9. To bring out the inherent capabilities of a pupil, such as attitudes, habits, appreciation, and understanding, manipulative skills in addition to conventional acquisition of knowledge.

Four Aspects

Schemically the concept of educational evaluation may be presented by showing the relationship among objectives, content (subject-matter), learning activities and evaluation procedures (testing)].

The inter-relationships of these four aspects of evaluation clearly indicates that the process of evaluation is a continuous one and involves continual appraisal of objectives of the teaching-learning process and of the testing procedures used by the classroom teacher.

Strategies and Techniques.

The following figure illustrates the various dimensions of evaluation which a teacher must attend to:

A teacher may adopt the following techniques, in the evaluation of students.

Modern Techniques

Fairly exhaustive techniques have been designed by educationists to evaluate the various aspects of a child's growth. Following are the commonly used techniques.

1. Achievements tests.
2. Aptitude tests.
3. Intelligence tests.
4. Personality tests.
5. Test of attitude and behaviour.
6. Rating scales.
7. Questionnaires and check lists.
8. Interview.
9. Anecdotal records.
10. Autobiographical method.
11. Pupil's diary.
12. Case history.

13. Sociometric techniques.
14. Projective techniques.

For the development of an effective evaluation programme the teacher must be acquainted with:

(i) the objectives of Commerce in respect of the subject as a whole and of specific units.
(ii) the relationship between objectives of instruction and evaluation.
(iii) the varied purposes of evaluation i.e., diagnosis, guidance, grading, classification, etc.
(iv) the elementary theory and practice of measurement.
(v) the techniques and tools of evaluation-their preparation and uses.
(vi) the follow-up procedure to utilize the 'feedback' in the classroom.

The above discussion leads us to conclude that formulation of the objectives of teaching commerce at a particular stage of education is the foremost task. Everything that a teacher does must be based upon the kind of behaviour he wishes to result from his teaching.

Formative and Summative Types

Evaluation in Commerce is classified into the following two categories on the basis of their roles.

1. Formative evaluation
2. Summative evaluation

Formative Evaluation: Formative evaluation is described as evaluation used for the on-going improvement of a process. It is designed to enhance the effectiveness of the teaching-learning process. It aims at discovering the strengths and weaknesses of the students in various subjects so that remedial steps may be taken by the teacher to remove their deficiencies. It is not done for 'pass' or 'fail' purposes. Formative evaluation may be done during the course of a daily teaching lesson.

Formative evaluation is done by informal, periodical teacher conducted classroom tests.

Teacher teaching the same subject and same students conducts the formative evaluation.

School promotional examinations and public examinations or tests conducted by external agencies fall under the category of summative evaluation.

Summative evaluation. The summative level of evaluation is described as evaluation of finished product which has been refined by the use of formative evaluation.

Summative evaluation is concerned with making final judgement about the progress of students.

Formative evaluation is a means and summative evaluation is an end. Most of the criticism relating to evaluation is with regard to its summative nature and summative functions.

Improvement and Recent Trends

1. Question papers usually consist of four types of questions : (i) long essay type; (ii) short essay type; (iii) very short essay type and (iv) objective type.
2. Roughly, the division of marks in percentage is as: essay type 60, short answer type 20, very answer type 10 and objective type 10 marks. Of course, there is no watertight compartment in the allocation of marks to different types of questions.
3. Generally there are no overall options in the paper.
4. Alternative questions are given.
5. The Central Board of Secondary Education, Delhi has introduced multiple set of question papers, of course of the same standard. The main objective of this approach is to minimise copying in the examination.
6. For the guidance of the teachers to use suitable questions, question banks have been established at various places.
7. The Association of Indian Universities, New Delhi has published question banks in different areas at the college level. Several universities have also established examination reform units.
8. The NCERT and various School Boards have published a good deal of literature on examination and evaluation.
9. There has been a trend to provide for internal assessment in the scheme of assessment.

10. Sessional marks are taken into consideration in the determination of final results.
11. Some progressive institutions take into account the home assignments also.
12. Credit is given to project work in various institutions.
13. The system of grading has been introduced instead of awarding marks at various places. Grades at various places are given separately for internal assessment, external assessment and aggregate assessment.
14. Students are now permitted to improve their grades.
15. Re-evaluation of answer scripts is also allowed at various places.

Thus we find that attempts are being made to reduce the subjectivity and vagaries of examinations.

The Tests

According to Froehlick and Dailey, three kinds of tests are needed nearly with all the students: tests of scholastic aptitude, achievement and interests. To quote Jane Waiters, "Inclusion of intelligence tests is practically always recommended, that of achievement tests and of interest tests is usually recommended, that of personality tests is not often recommended and that provision for individual tests of intelligence and measures of special aptitudes is recommended for use with special cases when the training of workers and the financial resources of the school make their use practical."

Many labels are attached to tests and lack of clarity in the naming of tests has created a lot of confusion. J. Rothney and B. Rones draw our attention to this fact when they remark, "Certain testing terms have traditionally been used together, thus, testers speak of clerical, mechanical, musical, and (more recently) scholastic aptitude, but they also use the term mental abilities, academic achievement, and subject-field performance or prognosis-frequently -the same instrument is described as both a test of mental ability and a scholastic aptitude." They go on to point out that lack of clarity in definitions of terms makes a very great difference in actual counselling procedure. They stress that the label on the test is derived from the use to which the test is to be put.

Different Types of Tests

Tests may be classified according to form and purpose etc. as under:-

1. ***Form:*** (a) Oral examinations; (b) Written examinations.
2. ***Purposes:*** (a) Prognostic; (b) Diagnostic; (c) Power; (d) Speed; (e) Accuracy; (f) Quality; (g) Range.
3. ***Organization:*** (a) Essay. (b) Objective.
4. ***Period or Time of Administering:*** (a) Daily; (b) Weekly; (c) Monthly; (d) Term; (e) Year.
5. ***Duration:*** (a) Short; (b) Long.
6. ***Method of Scoring and Interpreting Results:*** (a) Non-standardized; (b) Standardized.
7. ***Abilities Involved.*** (a) Speed; (b) Comprehension; (c) Organization; (d) Judgement; (e) Retention; (f) Appreciation; etc.
8. ***Nature of Material Included:*** (a) Arithmetic; (b) Language; (c) Reading; (d) Spelling; (e) Writing; etc.
9. ***Mental Functions Involved:*** (a) Association; (b) Memory; (c) Recall; (d) Recognition; (e) Problem-Solving.
10. ***Types of Response Involved:*** (a) Alternate response: (1) True-false; (2) Yes-no; (3) Plus-minus; (b) Multiple response: (1) Best answer; (2) Correct answer; (c) Completion; (d) Matching; (e) Identification; (f) Enumeration; (g) Essay.

Educational Achievement Tests

(a) *Survey*—comprehensive examinations used to determine general academic standing.

(b) *Subject*—examination in specific fields-for example, English, Mathematics.

(c) *Diagnostic*—cover a wide range of academic skills (in reading or arithmetic, for example) and are designed to reveal specific weaknesses and strengths.

Intelligence Tests

(a) Individual-administered to one examinee at a time.

(b) Group-administered like a school examination, to many examinees at the same time.

(c) Performance-many little or no use of language, in contrast with the paper and pencil tests in (a) and (b).

Aptitude Tests

(a) General-for example of-
    (i) Mechanical ability.
    (ii) Clerical ability.
(b) Special-aptitude for school subjects.

Tests of Various Aspects of Personality

(a) Personal Adjustment Questionnaries-survey of worries, fears, social inadequacies.
(b) Attitude Surveys-upon social, economic and political questions.
(c) Interest Inventories-related to various occupations.
(d) Environmental Facts Related to Personal Questionnaire covering socio-economic background and other variables.
(e) Projective 'Techniques-subtle and direct measures of dominant personality trends.

Broadly speaking, -there are two methods for collecting information:

(a) Standardized tests.
(b) Non-standardized techniques.

Standardized Tests

Standardized tests have assumed such an important role in the guidance programme that the two terms 'Guidance' and 'Tests' have become synonymous terms/

The standardized tests may be classified as:

1. General intelligence or scholastic aptitude tests.
2. Special abilities or aptitude tests.
3. Achievement tests.
4. Interests tests or inventories.
5. Personality tests or personal adjustment tests.

Significance of Standardized Tests.

They are very useful for the following reasons:

1. They give us objective and impartial information about an individual.

2. Since they give us information in an objective manner, it becomes easier to convince the guardians of the assets and limitations of their wards.
3. They provide information in much less time than provided by any other device.
4. Since there is a definite way of expressing the results of these tests in the form of percentiles or standard scores, it has the same significance for all the guidances workers and all of them have the same interpretations.
5. These tests measure those aspects of the behaviour which otherwise could not be obtained.
6. In subjective observation we may overlook shy children but these tests discover such cases also.

Achievement Tests and Intelligence Tests

By an achievement test we mean test of academic achievement such as Commerce, English or Hindi etc. An achievement tests is a measure of learning itself and an intelligence test is a measure of learning capacity. An achievement test attempts to measure education whereas intelligence test attempts to measure educability.

The development of an individual in the future is likely to be along the lines of tests for specific aptitude rather than test of general intelligence. Dunlop writes, "The more 'general' the intelligence tests the less its value. By increasing the specificity, we add to its value."

Achievement tests are used for the following purposes:

1. To diagnose students' strength and weakness.
2. To motivate students.
3. To report to the parents.
4. To predict future progress.
5. To reflect teacher's effectiveness.

Aptitude Tests

According to Bingham and Freeman, aptitude tests are tests that will predict success to some degree. It may be mentioned here that aptitudes are relatively constant.

Aptitude tests help us to measure the probability of success in an activity such as playing at piano, learning a language, etc.

Any definition of aptitude should be in terms of these characteristics: (a) ability to acquire the skill, information, etc., necessary for success, (b) readiness to acquire, (c) constancy, and (d) satisfaction in the job.

In many countries, tests of aptitudes for specific school subjects have been developed.

Tests of clerical aptitude, of mechanical aptitude and dexterity, of aptitude in art and music, aptitudes in professions have also been devised.

Aptitude tests are made by analysing the particular occupation or activity for which aptitude is to be measured and test items are then devised for revealing the component abilities. Tests of aptitude for law will include items which measure accurate recall, reading comprehension of legal material, skill in logic, and reasoning by analogy and by analysis.

Interest Tests

It is not possible to measure interest as an independent entity as it is related to general intelligence and special aptitudes and is determined partly by social environment of an individual and his opportunities to find out different kinds of activities. Interest is not as consistent as aptitude.

Educational interest inventories are intended to help pupils to choose their courses, curricula and co-curricular activities. There are also vocational interest inventories. The names of Kuder and Strong may be mentioned in this field.

Training of the Teacher and Counsellor

The effectiveness of the school's testing programme depends greatly upon the competence of counsellor in the use of various tests. The high level of competence depends upon the following factors:

(a) The commerce teacher should attend several courses in the field of psychological measurements and statistical techniques.

(b) The teacher should be well-versed with different types of tests.

(c) The teacher should know where to find detailed information on specific tests.

(d) The teacher should know how to supplement the test data.

(e) The teacher should be acquainted with the elementary statistical measurement.

(f) The teacher should keep himself in touch with the latest methods of the use of tests.

(g) The teacher should bear in mind that tests are one of the several kinds of techniques that are devised to facilitate understanding of the individual.

The Word of Caution

A word of caution may be said in the use of tests. Tests are tools and should be used as such. It would be a great error to use tests as the sole basis for evaluating pupil needs and abilities. Ross writes, "Guidance is always more than the giving of tests, no matter how extensively or carefully done.

Tests, when correctly used, yield more accurate and speedy information than the subjective techniques, such as the interview, observation and questionnaire. However, these have their own limitations. They fail to provide comprehensive measurement. There are factors like cultural and social background, emotional stability, etc., which play their own role and these tests fail to measure them.

Diagnostic and Prognostic Test

The main purpose of a diagnostic test is to analyse the nature of the difficulties experienced by the students in the learning of commerce and thereafter taking remedial steps for improvement in learning. A diagnostic test can also be used as an inventory test to find out 'how much'. The students know about a particular area of the subject matter. A diagnostic test can be a standardised test as well as a non-standarised test.

While constructing a standardized diagnostic test the teacher has to consider the individual difficulties experienced by students in solving problems. The test items should also give due consideration to the varying abilities of students in solving different types of problems. The age-norm, and the group-norm etc. should also be given their due consideration. Before constructing such a test, a pilot study should be conducted over a given area or unit and its results analysed before finalising the test.

The reliability of co-efficient of the test has to be calculated and then a diagnostic test deemed to be considered fit for administration over a large sample.

Formative type of evaluation is primarily meant for diagnostic purposes. A unit test can be administered for this purpose. We can think of a unit test in production, a unit test in income and expenditure and a unit test in banking etc., depending upon the prescribed syllabi.

A study of wrong answers given by the students is very helpful for purpose of diagnosis. The teacher's informal test in the class is generally meant for the purpose of finding out the difficulties of the students. Teacher made diagnostic tests usually fall under the category of non-standardised tests. Diagnosis is necessarily to be followed up by remedial measures.

A prognostic test is aimed at finding out the future prospects of success of a student is a particular area. This test is very helpful in providing guidance in choosing a career or a vocation.

Aptitude tests help us to measure the probability of success in a subject or an activity.

Tests of aptitudes for specific subjects have been developed in several countries.

An achievement test is used to measure the learning acquired by a student.

Recording and Administration

Following considerations may be kept in view while planning, administering and recording tests.

1. Tests should be given under standardised conditions that permit each testee to perform at his best i.e. physical environment, emotional environment etc.
2. The testers should prepare themselves in advance.
3. The testers should give clear instructions to the testees.
4. The testers should follow verbatim the test instructions contained in the manual.
5. Orientation talks, on the usefulness of testing may be given to the students so that they are motivated to take tests and are convinced that tests are genuinely important.

6. Records should be kept systematically so that they are made use of conveniently by the appropriate agency. Of course, results should be kept confidential.

The Characteristics

A good test in Commerce should have the following characteristics:-

Validity. The validity of a test implies that it should fulfil the objectives for which it is meant. It means that if our aim is to measure the ability of students to understand and apply commercial facts, then language factor should not come in the way.

Reliability. A test is said to be reliable if it gives the same results every time it is used for testing the abilities of the students under same conditions. The reliability of a test is affected by these factors: (i) The whims of the examiner; (ii) The physical and mental state of students; (iii) The language of the questions; (iv) Lack of clear-cut instruction and (v) Inefficient methods of scoring.

Comprehensiveness. A good test should assess various aspects like Knowledge, skills, abilities and attitudes etc.

Administrative ease. It should be easy to administer, economical in time and money, easy to score and interpret.

Diagnostic. It should reveal the difficulties faced by the students so that remedial measures may be adopted.

Utility. A test should be useful in several ways as far as possible i.e. its results may be used for improvement of teaching, for measuring some desired ability/quality etc.

QUESTIONS

1. Explain the concept evaluation. What is its scope in Commerce?
2. What is a good evaluation device in Commerce?
3. What are the various types of tests? What type of test will you prefer for covering maximum topics of Commerce? Give reasons for the choice of your type.
4. Explain formative and summative evaluation.
5. Write notes on:

   (i) Diagnostic tests; (ii) Prognostic tests; (iii) Aptitude test; (iv) Remedial teaching.

15

Training and Guidance

Guidance implies personal help given by the guidance counseller or the Commerce teacher to his students. It is designed to assist the student in deciding, where he wants to do, what he wants to do, or how he can best accomplish his purposes. Guidance does not solve his problems but helps him to solve them. The focus of guidance is the individual or the student, not the problem.

Learning about the individual student, helping him to understand himself, effecting changes in him which will help him to grow and develop as much as possible-these are the elements of guidance.

Guidance seeks to help the student discover his own talents in comparison to the opportunities available in various fields and help him prepare himself so that he can make a rational choice and adjust himself to situations.

Scope and Requirement

The need for guidance is universal. Everyone needs guidance at some time in life; some will need it constantly and throughout in their entire lives, while others need it only at rare intervals at times of great crisis. There always have been and will continue to be people with an occasional need for assistance of the older or more experienced persons in meeting situations.

The need for guidance to students studying commerce has assumed a great importance in view of startling changes in the modes of production, distribution, exchange and consumption etc. The entire structure of business organisation has undergone sea change. Several new courses and careers in commerce and management areas have emerged.

There are two sets of differences which are involved in educational and vocational situation: those among individuals studying commerce subjects and those among courses of actions and activities open to them in commercial, industrial and managerial concerns. Proper adjustment must be made to balance individual differences.

Objectives and Functions of Guidance. The primary objectives and functions of guidance are as under:-

Main Objectives

1. Satisfactory adjustment to academic work, getting the most out of students and school work.
2. Diagnosis of severe learning problem, instructional difficulties and their remedy.
3. Placement in educational experiences in accordance with individual needs and potentialities.
4. Transfer of the student from one course to another or from one programme to another, depending upon need, performance or other circumstances.

Vocational Objectives

Jones states as follows the specific objectives of guidance.

1. To assist the student to acquire such knowledge of the characteristics and functions, the duties and rewards of the group of occupations within which his choice will probably lie as he may need for intelligent choice.
2. To enable him to find what general and specific abilities, skills, etc., are required for the group of occupations under considerations and what are the qualifications of age, preparation, sex, etc., for entering them.
3. To give opportunity for experiences in school (try-out courses) and out of school (after-school and vocation jobs) that will give such information about conditions, of work as will assist the individual to discover his own abilities and help in the development of wider interests.
4. To help the individual develop the point of view that all honest labour is worth and that the most important bases

for choice of an occupation are: (a) the peculiar service that the individual can render to society, (b) personal satisfaction in the occupation, and (c) aptitude for the work required.

5. To assist the individual to acquire a technique of analysis of occupational information and to develop the habit of analysing such information before making a final choice.
6. To assist him to secure such information about himself, his abilities, general and specific, his interests and his powers as he may need for wise choice.
7. To assist economically handicapped children who are above the compulsory attendance age to secure, through public or private funds, scholarships or other financial assistance so that they may have opportunities for further education in accordance with their vocational plans.
8. To assist the student to secure a knowledge of the facilities offered by various educational institutions for vocational training and the requirements for admission to them, the length of training offered and the cost of attendance.
9. To help the worker to adjust himself to the occupation in which he is engaged; to assist him to understand his relationships to workers in his own related occupations and to society us a whole.
10. To enable the student to secure reliable information about the danger of alluring short-cuts to fortune.

Guidance Services

Individual Inventory Service. Compilation of individual inventory giving detailed information about each student concerning his abilities and achievements in different areas is the first essential of every, guidance programme in the school. This information should be kept up-to-date and is to be used for the good of the student. It may be compiled in the form of a cumulative record.

Information Service. Students of higher secondary schools generally need three types of information which is very helpful to them in making decisions about various courses, occupations and institutions such as : (a) Information about colleges and training opportunities, (b) Information about available occupations, and (c) Information about scholarships and other financial help available during the training period, Information may be collected from papers and magazines, government notifications and bulletins and information centres of the Employment Exchanges, etc. The usefulness of this information will be lost if the information is not-up-to-date. This information may be supplemented by talks of people from different occupations.

Counselling Service. Counselling service is regarded as the 'heart' of the guidance programme. This service must assist an individual in identifying, understanding and solving problems that confront him. Counselling can be done by a well-trained counsellor.

Placement Service. This service implies help to the individual in obtaining employment. There are three stages of this service.

(a) Assessing the abilities, aptitudes and interests of the individual student.
(b) Analyzing several occupations, particularly the ones in which the student expresses his interests.
(c) Relating occupations and abilities.

Follow-up Service. Follow up service enables the institutions to check the worthwhileness and effectiveness of the guidance programme.

Information Service

Individual Invent

Guidance Services in the school

Counselling Service

Follow Up Service

Placement service

Fig. : Services in the School

Course Selection

Different subjects require different degree of intelligence. Some call for a higher order of intelligence and the others of a low. A

nationwide study conducted in the United States gave the following
I.Q. of the High School boys in different courses:

Course	Medium
Technical	114
Scientific	108
Academic	106
Commerce	104
Trade	92

Group Techniques

1. Imparting occupational information as a regular subject.
2. Occupational information through career conferences.
3. Occupational information through special subjects.
4. Occupational information through school clubs.
5. Occupational information through home rooms or tutorials.
6. Occupational information through class talks.
7. Occupational talks by specialists in the occupations.
8. Occupational information through work experience projects.
9. Occupational information through visits to places of work.
10. Occupational information through dramatisation.
11. Occupational information through films and film strips.
12. Occupational information through displays or exhibitions.
13. Occupational information through Bulletin Board announcements.
14. Occupational information through library.
15. Occupational information through booklets.
16. Occupational information through co-curricular activities.
17. Occupational information through display Comer.
18. Occupational information through Radio and Television.
19. Occupational information through video cassettes.

Material Sources

1. Directorate-General of Employment and Training, Shram Shakti Bhawan, New Delhi.

2. National Council of Educational Research and Training, Mehrauli Road, New Delhi.
3. Vocational Counselling Bureau, Y.M.C.A., Indore.
4. Y.M.C.A. Publishing House, 5, Russell Street, Calcutta-16.
5. Manovigyan Shala, U.P., Allahabad.
6. Ministry of Scientific Research, Government of India, New Delhi.
7. Directorate-General of Health Services, Ministry of Health, New Delhi.
8. Government of Maharashtra, Institute of Vocational Guidance and Selection, 3, Cruickshank Road, Bombay-1.
9. Ministry of Railways (Railway Board). Government of India, Rail Bhawan, New Delhi-1
10. Bureau of Education Research, Ewing Christian College, Allahabad-3.
11. Rotary International, Rotary Club, Hyderabad (Andhra Pradesh).
12. College of Educational Psychology and Guidance, Jabalpur (M.P.).
13. Faculty of Education and Psychology, Maharaja Sayajirao University of Baroda, Baroda.
14. Offices of the Employment Exchanges in all States.
15. University Employment Bureaus attached to the Universities.
16. Ministry of Human Resource Development Department of Education, Information Section, Shastri Bhawan, New Delhi.
17. Association of Indian Universities, Kotla Road, New Delhi.
18. Public Service Commission of Union Territories and States.
19. Staff Selection Board, CGO Complex, Lodhi Road, New Delhi.
20. State Bureaus of Educational and Vocational Guidance Bureaus.

Teacher's Role

1. Cooperating the school counsellor in forming and organising a guidance committee.

2. Setting up an educational and occupational centre in the Commerce Department/assisting the school counsellor in this regard.
3. Giving orientation talks to commerce students regarding availability of guidance services in the school.
4. Organising guidance talks for commerce students.
5. Orienting class X students and their parents with regard to the subjects available in class XI and XII.
6. Orienting pupils of class X and XII with regard to university and non-University and professional courses along with apprenticeship schemes.
7. Collecting and displaying educational and occupational information.
8. Arranging career talks by experts in the field of Commerce and allied subjects.
9. Arranging visits to commercial and industrial establishments.
10. Cooperating the counsellor in his programmes.

Conference on Career

Career Conference technique has been found to be very valuable as a means of supplementing the information given to a group by the counsellor or the teacher. A number of successful persons explain the vocations in which they work and answer questions about their jobs.

Commerce career conferences serve the following purposes-.

The school is brought directly into contact with the community and the community is made aware of the problems of the youth.

Students get opportunities to hear eminent persons who discuss the actual problems regarding various occupations.

The career conferences help make the parents guidance-minded and make them think about the occupational future of their children.

The career conferences motivate students to seek accurate and realistic information about occupational life.

The career conferences are very helpful in making the trade and industry aware of its responsibilities in assisting the guidance agencies and the school to provide for students reliable information about occupations and training facilities.

The Guidelines

The duration of the conference may be one day or more. In planning a conference, the school counsellor or the commerce teacher will seek the cooperation of other teachers and the students. The students of the higher secondary classes and their parents should be invited to attend such conferences.

Conferences should not be treated merely as a show work.

Sufficient care should be taken in the selection of the speakers who will explain the problems connected with particular occupations.

Speakers selected should be those who can explain very clearly their viewpoints to the students and who place occupations in their true perspective. It is better if they are given certain outline which they should keep in view while preparing their talks.

In between different speeches some occupational or educational films may be shown to the audience.

An exhibition containing charts which throw light on careers and courses may be organised on this occasion.

E.Rocber and others give the following suggestions of holding career conferences:

1. The meeting should last approximately fifty-five minutes. Half of the time should be spent in presenting important facts/ regarding the field of work and the other half in answering questions.
2. The audience should consist of students between the ages of thirteen and eighteen.
3. Conference discussions should usually cover the following topics:
   (a) Importance and history of the work.
   (b) Kinds of tasks involved in the work, tools, materials and
   processes.
   (c) Personal qualifications; the most essential and also the most
   desirable ones.
   (d) Special training required, ways of obtaining the training.

(e) Income compensation, pensions and benefits.
(f) Working conditions, hazards, effects of work on workers.
(g) Possibilities of promotion, usual lines of promotion.
(h) Ways of finding jobs.
(i) Professional and workers organisations to which the worker belongs.
(j) Sources of further information.

QUESTIONS

1. What is the meaning of guidance? Do all students need guidance? Explain.
2. What is the significance of guidance for commerce students? State the role of the Commerce teacher in guidance.
3. Suggest a suitable guidance programme for Commerce students?
4. What type of educational and occupational information is needed for the guidance of Commerce students? How would you make arrangement for the same?
5. Elucidate the concept of vocational guidance. Why is it important for Commerce students?
6. State the various sources for obtaining educational and vocational information.
7. What are the important areas in which a Commerce teacher can cooperate with the school counsellor?
8. List the various types of competencies needed for a Commerce teacher to guide his students.
9. What is the significance of a career conference in guiding Commerce students? How can it be made effective?
10. Prepare a chart showing various careers and courses available after class XII.

16

Curriculum in Vogue

In modern terms, curriculum consists of all the educative experiences under the conscious guidance of the school. This concept differs from the older idea of the curriculum as a body of subject matter to be learned. Just as the assigned lesson was the basic unit in the old definition, so an experience is the unit of the new. In the overall context, it means a rounded programme of learning, doing and living for every child as opposed to the curriculum as a series of lessons or a collection of courses. Finally in this modern view, the curriculum is not confined to the classroom but flows out into the life of the school and beyond school hours. As observed by the Secondary Education Commission 1952-53, "It must be clearly understood that according to modern educational thought, curriculum does not mean only the academic subjects traditionally taught in the school but it includes the totality of experiences that a pupil receives through the manifold activities that go in the school in the classroom, library, laboratory, workshops, playgrounds and in the numerous informal contracts between teachers and pupils. In this case, the whole life of the school becomes the curriculum which can touch the life of the students at all points and help in the evolution of balanced personality." Similarly the Education Commission 1964-66 observed, "We conceive of the school curriculum as the totality of learning experience that the school provides for the pupils through all the manifold activities in the school or outside, that are carried under its supervision. From this point of view, the distinction between curricular and extra-curricular work ceases to exist, and a school camp and games and sports are curricular rather than co-curricular activities."

Seen in the above light, Commerce curriculum includes the academic subject matter of topics and experiences provided through debates, discussions, case studies, surveys, community resources and visits also.

Inclusion as a Subject

Commerce or Business Studies as a discipline has been included in the curriculum on account of its cultural, disciplinary, practical and social values. It also develops certain competencies which are found to be of great value in our day-to-day life.

Following are the main reasons for the inclusion of Commerce Education in the curriculum:-

1. It enables students to understand the flow of goods and services from the producer to the consumer.
2. It enables the students to understand how prices of different products are determined.
3. It enables the students to understand how markets for commodities are developed.
4. It enables the students to understand how improvement in the quality of production of goods takes place through competition.
5. It enables the students to understand how a variety of consumer interests are developed.
6. It enables the students to understand how commerce in a country is the index of its prosperity.
7. It enables the students to understand the economic structure of a society.
8. It enables the students to choose further courses of study.
9. It enables the students to prepare for entry in a vocation.
10. It enables the students to make several types of commercial transactions in their day-to-day life.
11. It enables the students to understand their role as enlightened citizens.

The Construction

Following are the important principles which should be given their due consideration in the selection of Commerce Curriculum:-

1. Principle of preservation and transmission of traditional values.
2. Principle of forward-looking-feature-oriented curriculum.
3. Principle of preparation for life.
4. Principle of linking with life.
5. Principle of individual differences of students.
6. Principle of maturity of the students.
7. Principle of child-centredness, activity and experience.
8. Principle of comprehensiveness and balance.
9. Principle of flexibility.
10. Principle of core-areas.

Factors and Principles

H.A. Tonne, in Principles of Illusions Education (1955) suggested the following considerations in the building of Commerce Curriculum:-

1. Commerce Education Curriculum to be in consistent with the needs of community in which the school is located.
2. The interests of the students influencing their ability and willingness to learn and their capacity to use Commerce Education.
3. The state of business of the community which manages and controls the school.
4. Facilities available in the school for teaching Commerce Education.
5. Availability of Commerce Education teachers in the school.
6. Availability of facilities like libraries, machines and other equipment for the teaching of Commerce in the school.
7. Support of the community to the school in carrying out programmes in Commerce Education.
8. Facilities available in the school for the selection of students for Commerce Education course.
9. Resources of the school for meeting the requirements and regulations of the Board of Education.
10. Availability of local experts in formulating the curriculum.

11. Availability of teaching material.
12. Allied subjects offered in the other departments of the school.
13. Local practices and vested interests.
14. Attitude of the officers of the State Departments of Education towards Commerce Education.
15. Size of the School.
16. Students of each sex who want to take up Commerce Education.
17. Aptitude and intelligence of the students desiring to take up Commerce Education.
18. Level of general education of the students who want to study Commerce.
19. Latest trends in Commerce Education.
20. Subjects offered in other departments of the school that may realize same or all of the special aims of certain Commerce subjects.

The Syllabi

The two terms curriculum and courses of study are not synonymous. The term curriculum includes courses of study and other experiences relating to Commerce Education. Courses of studies is a selection of topics and it excludes other experiences. Usually curriculum is concerned with various disciplines taught in the school or various courses of study and experiences. Curriculum is a broader terms. Courses of study or syllabi of a subject is divided into terms of the academic session. They are also taken up to be covered daily or weekly.

The Procedure

All the States and Union Territories in India have their own mechanism of curriculum developement. Usually State Boards of Education function through course committees, academic councils and the governing bodies. These committees generally comprise principals, teachers, teacher educators and experts in the field of commerce and business.

The National Council of Educational Research and Training prepares model curriculum which may be adapted/adopted by State Boards.

The members of the Commerce Committee meet from time to time to lay down the course of study in different branches of Commerce. These are then sent for approval to the governing body of the State Board. Thereafter these courses are circulated to the schools affiliated to the Boards.

The Central Board of Secondary Education, Delhi prescribes courses of study for schools affiliated to it. This Board is considered to be the pace setter board in the country.

Courses Prescribed in Commerce by the Central Board of Secondary Education, Delhi

At the outset, it may be noted that the CBSE has used the terms 'Business Studies' and 'Accountancy' and not 'Commerce'.

Studies in Business

During the first 10 years of schooling, students are not given formal instructions in Commerce and Accountancy subjects. Against this baekground, it becomes necessary that at this stage, instructions in these two subjects be given in such a manner that students have a good understanding of the principles and practices bearing on business, trade and industry and their relationship to society. They need to be exposed to the realities of the business world as a part of the economic, legal and social environment. This will enable them to understand and appreciate the functions and scope of business activities in the economic set up.

The increasing complexity of business organisation in the present day world makes it obligatory for students to be conversant with the principles and practices of management. A study of these principles will make the students aware of the functions of management in general and the purpose of management in particular activities.

The syallabus for Class XII in Business Studies comprises of two parts-Part I "Principles and Functions of Management" is compulsory for all students while Part 11 is optional. The students are required to choose any one out of the three optional parts depending on their interest and aptitude. The optional course on Functional Management specifies application of management principles in different spheres of business activities such as Personnel, Finance and Marketing. This topic is expected to be helpful to those who wish to pursue Commerce at higher level of studies.

Organising a Factory

The course on Factory Organisation provides invaluable information and practical hints to such students who aspire to start their own small manufacturing unit in near future or they have a family business involving factory operations. A study of this topic will orient them on different aspects of setting up and organising a small scale factory unit and in handling factory routines in a small scale factory business.

The third optional course is on office administration which lays down specific aspects relating to an office Organisation and the techniques involved in efficient handling of paper work. A study of this topic is expected to provide basic foundation knowledge to students who wish to take up a career in a business office in future. A student offering this course is expected to be fit into routine office job with greater expertise and confidence. The topics included in the syllabus will also assist students in their higher studies.

Since women are coming in a big way for wage employment and self-employment the last two optional courses are expected to be of equal interest to girls students.

Main Objectives

The major objectives of teaching Business Studies at the Senior Secondary Stage are as follows:

To develop in the student an interest in the theory and practice in business, trade and industry.

To acquaint students with the theoretical foundations and practice of organising, managing and handling routine operations of a, business firm;

To inculcate attitudes and values leading to the integration of business with the social system with a positive approach.

Option I: To enable them to apply the principles and functions of management to specific aspects of business.

Option II: To equip them with essential fundamental knowledge for setting up, organising and handling routine operations of a small scale factory.

Option III: To equip them with basic information on modern methods of office operations for effectively carrying out paper work in a business office.

ACCOUNTANCY

Introduction

Accounting is an important vehicle for communicating business information of financial nature. It enables a businessman to measure the results of his business activities effectively. It also provides useful information to parties interested in the working of a business organisation such as management, employees, creditors, investors, Government etc. Accounting also offers a variety of career avenues in the field of wage employment and self-employment. The three optional areas are expected to provide knowledge and understanding in the fields of analysis of financial statements, costing and auditing. Depending on their interest and aptitude, students can choose any one out of the three optional topics.

Option I: Analysis of financial statements can be viewed as an application of the basic accounting principles for better understanding of financial statements. Its knowledge is of extreme importance to managers in arriving at important decisions relating to financial health of a business unit.

Option II: Costing as a branch of accounting provides vital information to businessmen on different aspects of cost computation. Those who intend to run a small scale factory unit will find study of costing useful to them.

Option III: Auditing provides fundamental information on detection and correction of errors and frauds in financial accounting. Its knowledge is useful to those students who wish to engage in financial aspects of business activities.

To impart knowledge of methods considered useful in maintaining records of proprietary and partnership firms, companies and nontrading organisations.

To generate and promote awareness of students in modern techniques of maintaining accounting records with the help of computers.

Option I: To enable students prepare financial statements and interpret results for decision making.

Option II: To acquaint the students with practice and procedure of determination of cost from the view point of its elements.

Option III: To create an awareness of the necessity of auditing for detection/rectification of errors/frauds in the process of accounting.

CLASS XI BUSINESS STUDIES

One Paper **3 hours**
100 Marks

Unitwise Weightage

Unit		*Marks*
Business Studies-I. (Foundations of Business)		50 Marks
1.	Economic Activities and Business	5
2.	Nature and Purpose of Business	5
3.	Structure of Business	5
4.	Service Sector and Business	10
5.	Forms of Business Enterprises	15
6.	Corporate Organisation	10
Business Studies-II (Corporate Organisation)		50 Marks
7.	Formation of a Company	10
8.	Sources of Business Finance	15
9.	Stock Exchange	8
10.	Internal Trade	10
11.	External Trade	7

FOUNDATIONS OF BUSINESS

Unit 1: Economic Activities and Business **10 Periods**

Meaning of economic activities and distinction between economic and non-economic activities, types of economic activities. Business, Profession and Employment: their meaning and comparison.

Business as an economic activity. Range of business activities.

Unit 2: Nature and Purpose of Business 12 Pds.
Characteristics of Business, Business-risks, nature and causes, Objectives of Business-Economic and Social. Role of profit in Business. Concept of social obligations. Case for social- obligations. Responsibilities towards different interest groups eg. shareholders, employers, consumers, government and society.

Unit 3: Structure of Business 12 Pds.
Business environment-economic, political and social. Classification of business activities, Industry and its types. Meaning and functions of Commerce Trade and its types. Auxiliaries of Business activity.

Unit 4: Service Sector and Business 22 Pds.
Need and classification of service sector. Meaning and importance of Transport-modes. Banking-Types and functions of Commercial Banks. Insurance-Principles and types-life, fire and marine. Others (warehousing, packaging, advertising and promotion).

Unit 5: Forms of Business Enterprises 40 Pds.
Types of Business undertaking-Private sector and public sector. Characteristics of public, private and joint sector enterprises. Forms of private sector enterprises-General characteristics. Meaning, features, merits and limitation of following forms-Sole proprietorship including expansion. Joint Hindu Family business-Features. Partnership, including types of partners, formation and registration, partnership deed (main clauses), and type of partnership formation. Co-operative societies. Company.

Unit 6: Corporate Organization 24 Pds.
Types of companies-Private and Public

Privileges of private company
Rationale of public sector
Forms of organising public sector enterprises
(a) Departmental undertakings; (b) Statutory corporation
(c) Government company; Multinational companies (examples).

CORPORATE ORGANIZATION, FINANCE AND TRADE

Unit 7: Formation of a Company **24 Pds.**

Promotion: meaning and role of promoters.
Incorporation of Company:
(a) Memorandum of Association, Articles of Associations
and distinction between the two documents;
(b) Filling of documents and registration;
(c) Certificate of incorporation;
Commencement of business
Floatation-Propectus, its nature and importance.

Unit 8: Sources of Business Finance **36 Pds.**

Nature and significance.
Types of Business finance and their uses-long term, medium term and short term. Sources of finance – owners funds and borrowed funds-meaning and characteristics of the following sources.
(a) Equity and preferences shares;
(b) Debentures-types (secured and unsecured, convertible and nonconvertible);
(c) Institutional finance – objectives, types of assistancee, names of national level institutions;
(d) Retained profits-meaning and characteristics; (e) Public deposits-meaning and characterisitcs; (f) Bank Finance.

Unit 9: Stock Exchange **18 Pds.**

Meaning and importance: Functions and Service.
Location
of Stock Exchanges in India. Types of operators-

Brokers, Jobbers (Tarawaniwala), Bull and Bears. Terms in stock exchange quotationsex dividend cum-dividend, spot delivery, forward delivery.

Unit 10: Internal Trade **24 Pds.**

Meaning and Types. Wholesale Trade-functions and services. Types of retail organization: (a) Itinerant and fixed shops: (b) Departmental store, chain store, mail order house, consumers cooperative store (including super bazar). Their meaning, features, merits and limitations.

Unit 11: External Trade **18 Pds.**

Nature and importance. Import procedure (Brief outline) Export procedure (Brief outline) Document used in foreign trade-Indent. Letter of Credit. Bill of Lading. Charter Party Financing of trade (Elementary Treatment)

One Paper Class XII 3 Hours
100 Marks

BUSINESS STUDIES

Principles and Functions of Management

1. Nature and Significance of Management
2. Principles of Management
3. Planning
4. Organising
5. Staffing
6. Directing
7. Controlling

A. Functional Management

1. Personal Management
2. Financial Management
3. Marketing Management

Or

B. Factory Organisation **50 Marks**

1. Nature of factory and its characteristic features 5

2.	Setting up a Factory	12
3.	Factory Design and Layout	10
4.	Internal Organisation of a Factory	5
5	Factory Materials and Stores	8
6.	Factory Labour and Employment Conditions	10

C. Office Administration **50 Marks**

1.	Nature and functions of Office	5
2.	Office Layout and Working Conditions	6
3.	Work Flow in Office	3
4.	Office Organization	5
5.	Office Communication	5
6.	Office Mechanisation	6
7.	Handling Inward and Outward Mail	10
8.	Filing and Indexing	10

Or

PRINCIPLES AND FUNCTIONS OF MANAGEMENT

Unit 1: Nature and Significance of Management **16 Pds.**

Management as an activity, a process, a discipline and as a group.

Nature of management-management as a science and an art.

Management as a profession.

Objectives and importance of management.

Distinction between management and administration.

Levels of management-top level, middle level and lower level (supervisory).

Management function-Planning, organising, staffing, directing and controlling. Coordination-nature and meaning.

Unit 2: Principles of Management **16 Pds.**

Nature of and need for management principles.

Fayol's principles of management.

Scientific management: principles and techniques.

Unit 3: Planning **15 Pds.**

Meaning, features, importance and limitations of planning. Steps in planning.

Unit 4: Organising **24 Pds.**

Meaning, process and structure of organization.
Importance of organisation.
Formal and informal organisation.
Principles of organisation.
Types of administrative organisation-line, line and staff,
and functional-meaning, features and distinction.
Delegation of authority, authority, responsibility and accountability.
Importance of delegation.
Difference between delegation and decentralisation.

Unit 5: Staffing **12 Pds.**

Meaning, need and importance of staffing.
Staffing Process-estimating staff requirements, role of managers in recruitment and selection process.
Remuneration to workers-concepts of time rate and piece rate.

Unit 6: Directing **25 Pds.**

Meaning and importance of directing.
Elements of directing:
- Supervision-functions of supervisors.
- Motivation-need and incentives (monetary and non-monetary incentives).
- Leadership-importance, qualities of a good leader.
- Communication importance-types of communication (formal and informal), channels of communication (oral, written).

Unit 7: Controlling **12 Pds.**

Meaning and importance.
Steps in the process of control.
Features of a good control system.

BUSINESS STUDIES

Note: One of the following three parts is to be selected for study: Functional Management or Factory Organisation or Office Administration.

FUNCTIONAL MANAGEMENT

Unit 1: Personnel Management **36 Pds.**

Meaning and nature of personnel management.
Role and responsibilities of Personnel manager.
Manpower planning, estimating manpower requirements.
Job analysis, Job description and job specification.
Recruitment-meaning and sources, Selection.
Process-Employment tests and Interviews.
Training and Development-Purpose and Methods.
Job Evaluation-concept and methods. Methods of wage payment including incentive bonus plans.
Performance appraisal and its importance, compensation. Personnel records-Uses and Types.

Unit 2: Financial Management **48 Pds.**

Meaning and objects of Financial Management.
Functions of Financial Manager.
Financial Planning-meaning and importance.
Capital structure-meaning, factors governing capital structure. Capitalisation-Over and Under.
Sources of business finance: scope and importance of capital market.
Management of fixed capital. Capital budgeting-nature and scope.
Management of working capital. Factors determining working capital.

Unit 3: Marketing Management **36 Pds.**

Marketing Management-meaning and objectives
Marketing concept and selling.
Marketing functions

Marketing mix-elements
Sales promotion-methods
Advertising-features; benefits to manufacturers and society. Media of advertising. Choice of media. Features of personal selling. Qualities of a good salesman. Consumer rights, Means of consumer protection.

FACTORY ORGANISATION

Unit 1: Nature of Factory and its Characteristic Features12 Pds.

Nature of manufacturing activity (seasonal and perennial); concept of factory and workshop. Definition of factory under the Factories Act. Characteristic features of small and large factories (small scale units and large-scale establishments).

Unit 2: Setting up a Factory 28 Pds.

Setting up a small-scale unit:

(a) Deciding on the nature of product and volume of production with reference to products reserved for small-scale sector.
(b) Availability and source of raw materials, fuel, power, water, transport and banking facilities.
(c) Estimation of capital: long term funds and working capital (factors to be considered).
(d) Selection of factory site (location) consideration in selection.
(e) Placing orders for machinery and equipments: Sources, methods and procedures.
(f) Major provisions in local laws and rules; permission from local authorities; procedure.
(g) Registration of factory under Factories Act or other appropriate laws (Shop and Establishment Act.): Procedure

Unit 3: Factory Design and Layout: 24 Pds.

Factory design: meaning, importance, factors to be considered.

Types of factory building (horizontal, vertical/single storey & multistorey)-relative needs and advantages.

Factory layout: meaning, types, considerations: heating, lighting, ventilation, service facilities. Rules of law regulating factory layout (main requirements).

Unit 4: Internal Organisation of a Factory 12 Pds.

Departmentation in a factory-operating departments (workshops) and service departments.

Status, authority and responsibilities of the factory manager. Factory manual-meaning and broad outline of contents.

Organisation chart of a typical factory.

Unit 5: Factory Materials and Stores 20 Pds.

Raw materials, work in process, finished goods, spare parts, stores and supplies-their meaning.

Materials procurement procedure.

Storage-need, importance and methods.

Materials control: issue and replenishment of materials, safety stock, ordering levels, order quantities.

Unit 6: Factory Labour and Employment Conditions. 24 Pds

Types of factory workers-skilled, semiskilled, unskilled, seasonal, casual, regular.

Recruitment of factory workers-sources.

Methods of wage payment: time rate and piece rate; their relative advantages and suitability.

Employment conditions.

Safety, health and welfare amenities.

Or

OFFICE ADMINISTRATION

Unit 1: Nature and Functions of Office 12 Pds.

Meaning and importance of office. Relationship of

office with other departments. Functions-basic and auxiliary. Position and role of an office manager in an organisation.

Unit 2: Office Layout and Working Conditions **16 Pds.**

Location of office-factors, importance, Office building-Need, characteristics of a suitable office building. Office layout-nature – principles, types. Open and private offices. Office environment-Meaning and elements: lighting, ventilation, temperature and interior decoration (general outline).

Unit 3: Work Flow in Office **6 Pds.**

Concept of work flow and flow charts.
Difficulties in work flow.

Unit 4: Office Organization **12 Pds.**

Principles.
Types-line, line and staff and service organization.
Office charts and manuals, meaning and usefulness.

Unit 5: Office Communication **12 Pds.**

Basic principles,
Methods of internal and external communication.

Unit 6: Office mechanisation **14 Pds.**

Need for mechanisation. Considerations in mechanisation.
Types of office machines and equipments including the use
of computers.

Unit 7: Handling Inward and Outward Mail **24 Pds.**

Organisation of the mailing section.
Arrangements with post offices for receipt and despatch of mail.
Inward mail routine.
Dealing with correspondence.
Mechanising mail service.

Unit 8: Filing and Indexing **24 Pds.**

Indexing.

(a) Meaning and Importance
(b) Bases of Indexing
(c) Types of Indexing

Filing

(a) Meaning and importance
(b) Basis of Classification of papers for filing,
(c) Methods of filing: horizontal and vertical.

The Evaluation

There is no doubt that while constructing the curriculum, efforts are made from time to time to take into consideration the changing demands and needs of the trade, industry and commerce. Still it is felt that the commerce curriculum is by and large, theory-oriented. At the school stage, it is geared to the requirements of higher education. It is still narrowly conceived, bookish and theoretical. It is overcrowd. There is little provision for practical work. It is examination ridden. Most of the experts in Commerce Curriculum Committees are usually drawn from colleges and universities with the result that they hardly take into account the maturity level of the school students.

Representatives of business and trade need to be associated in the development of the Commerce Curriculum.

The Commerce Curriculum should be need-based. It should be vocation-oriented.

It may be observed that most of the criticism relates to the general Commerce Curriculum and not to the Vocational Commerce Curriculum (Vocational Courses).

Before finalising Commerce Curriculum, there should be wider consultation with teachers of Commerce in schools.

Commerce Course Prescribed for Indian Certificate of Secondary Education Examination (ICSE)

Aims

(i) To create an awareness of the environment within business activity takes place.
(ii) To develop knowledge and understanding of the meaning and importance of Commerce.
(iii) To expose the students to certain technical terms in Commerce.

(iv) To understand the various hindrances of trade and to appreciate the aids that remove these hindrances.

(v) To understand the way in which changes in the environment influence business activities.

SYLLABUS FOR CLASS IX

There will be one paper of two hours.

1. ***Meaning and scope of Commerce:*** Business activities – Types of industries-Trade and aids to trade-Importance of Commerce-Stages in the evolution of Commerce.
2. ***Economic basis of Commerce :*** Human wants – Characteristics of human wants and their satisfaction.
3. ***Organisation of Commercial Activities:***
   (a) Public and private sectors-Concepts-Difference between public and private sectors.
   (b) Meaning, features, merits and demerits of sole proprietorship.
   (c) Meaning, features, merits and demerits of partnership – Kinds of partners-Meaning of partnership deed.
   (d) Meaning, features, merits and demerits of joint stock companies-Types of companies.
   (e) Public utilities-features.
   (f) Co-operative undertakings-meaning-feature-difference between co-operative and joint stock companies.
4. ***Trade:***
   (a) Meaning-Types of trade.
   (b) Home trade and international trade-meaning and types of home trade–meaning of import and export and entrepot trade.
   (c) Retail trade:- Meaning of retailer-His function–types of retail trade-features of small scale and large scale retailers.
   (d) Wholesale trade:- Meaning and functions of a wholesaler.
   (e) Documents used in home trade only–meaning and definitions-Inquiry, Quotation, Order, debit Note, Credit Note, Despatch Note, Delivery Note, Invoice and statement account.

SYLLABUS FOR CLASS X

Part 1: External Examination-100 Marks

There will be one written paper of two hours.

The paper will be divided into two sections A and B.

Section A will consist of questions requiring only short answers and will cover the whole of the syllabus. There will be no choice of questions.

Section B will consist of essay-type questions. There will be a choice of questions and candidates will be required to answer four.

1. ***Commercial Office:*** Importance of commercial office departments of a commercial office-only concepts.
2. ***Aids to trade:***
   - (a) Money:- Barter system-meaning-functions-kinds Evolution.
   - (b) Banking-meaning-types-functions of Commercial Banks and Central Banks. Types of deposit accounts-meaning and features of cheque and pass book.
   - (c) Transport:- meaning-types-merits and demerits of road, rail, air and sea transport—comparative study of the above.
   - (d) Capital.
   - (e) Warehousing:- Necessity for storage-functions-types of warehouses.
   - (f) Insurance:- General principles-types-meaning and importance of insurance.
   - (g) Advertising:- Purpose-methods or media of appeal benefits and damages.

Part II: External Examination -100 Marks

Project/Practical work

(a) Internal Assessment:- The course work undertaken by the pupils may be on any one aspect of the syllabus or may be based on any one or more of the topics given below.
   - (i) Three charts based on the syllabuses or
   - (ii) Open a savings account in the bank and prepare a report on the procedure followed by him or
   - (iii) any other type of work deemed fit by the teacher concerned. Note:- This is to be valued by the concerned teacher.

(b) External Assessment:- Project work to be complied by the pupils as suggested by the teacher. This is prepared under the guidance and supervision of the concerned teacher but will be valued by the external examiner.

QUESTIONS

1. Explain the term 'curriculum'. Why should Commerce Education be introduced in the curriculum?
2. What is the scope of Commerce Education Curriculum? Evaluate the prevalent Commerce Education Curriculum in your state. What suggestions would you like to make it more effective and meaningful?.
3. What considerations should be kept in view while constructing the Commerce Curriculum? What is the role of the teachers in curriculum construction?
4. Do you think Commerce academic stream is over-loaded? Give arguments in support of your answer.

17

Book-keeping

Accountancy is an important vehicle for communicating business information of financial nature. It enables a businessman to measure the results of his business activities effectively. It also provides useful information to parties interested in the work of a business organisation such as management, employees, creditors, investors, government etc. Accountancy also offers a variety of career avenues in the field of wage employment and self-employment.

Objectives of Teaching Bookkeeping and Accountancy. The Central Board of Secondary Education, New Delhi has specified the following objectives:

1. To impart knowledge of methods considered useful in maintaining records of propriety and partnership firms, companies and non-trading organisations.
2. To generate and promote awareness of students in modern techniques of maintaining accounting records with the help of the computers.
3. To enable the students to analyse financial statements and interpret the result for decision-making.
4. To acquaint the students with practice and procedure of determination of cost from the view-point of its elements.
5. To create an awareness of the necessity of auditing for detection/rectification of errors/frauds in the process of accounting.

Aims and Objectives

A publication of NCERT, entitled Instructional Objectives of School Subjects (1989) lists the following instructional objectives:

1. To acquire the knowledge of facts, concepts, terms, principles and procedures, forms and statements related to Book-keeping.
2. To develop an understanding of facts, concepts, terms principles and procedures, forms and statements related to Book- keeping.
3. To apply the acquired knowledge and understanding of concepts and principles of Book-keeping in new situations.
4. To acquire the skills in maintaining books of accounts and presentation of Bookkeeping data properly.
5. To develop desirable interests in Bookkeeping and in the acquisition of further knowledge of Bookkeeping and accountancy.
6. To develop positive attitudes towards Bookkeeping practices, and related aspects.

Objective to Acquire the Knowledge of Facts

Specifications of the Objective:

To demonstrate the achievement of the above objective, the pupil:

1. recalls items constituting different forms;
2. recognises items in various proformas;
3. reproduces, principles and concepts, etc. in Bookkeeping as mentioned above.

Objective to Develop an Understanding of Facts

Specifications of the Objective:

To demonstrate the achievement of the above objective, the pupil:

1. distinguishes between facts, terms, etc;
2. discriminates between various forms and proformas;
3. classifies facts related to various forms and proformas;
4. compares and contrasts;
5. gives examples;
6. identifies relationships;
7. arranges steps in proper sequence;
8. gives reasons for the occurrence of problems related to Bookkeeping;

9. interprets data;
10. locates errors and rectifies them.

Objective to Apply the Acquired Knowledge

Specifications of the Objective:

To demonstrate the achievement of the above objective, the pupil:

1. analyses the given situations and problems;
2. selects facts, relevant to a given problem;
3. judges adequacy of data for studying a particular situation;
4. establishes relationships;
5. suggests innovations for improving procedures;
6. formulates hypothesis and verifies them;
7. draws inferences;
8. predicts probabilities in a given set of situations.

Acquiring Necessary Skills

Specifications of the Objective:

To demonstrate the achievement of the above objective, the pupil:

1. calculates and computes quickly and correctly;
2. handles and maintains calculating machines;
3. fills in proformas, statements and account correctly, proportionately and neatly;
4. writes entries and figures in the appropriate manner;
5. writes in a good and legible hand;
6. preserves and maintains the Books of Accounts properly.

Developing Desirable Interests

Specifications of the Objective:

To demonstrate the achievement of the above objective, the pupil voluntarily:

1. collects information about new developments in accounting systems;
2. reads literature on Bookkeeping and accounting;
3. studies Final Accounts and statements published by different business concerns, corporations, etc.

Objective to Develop Positive Attitudes Towards Bookkeeping Practices

Specifications of the Objective:

To demonstrate the achievement of the above objective, the pupil:

1. shows receptivity to scientific and modern ideas;
2. assumes responsibility in assigned tasks and volunteers to do more;
3. possesses integrity and honesty of purpose;
4. respects and follows laws and rules relating to Accountancy;
5. develops a habit of hard work and perseverance.

SYLLABI IN ACCOUNTANCY

Class XI

One Paper **3 hours**
100 Marks
Unit wise Weightage

Units	*Marks*
ACCOUNTING-I	
1. Accounting-Meaning, Objectives and Basic Accounting Terms	
2. Theory Base of Accounting	
3. Origin and Recording of Transactions	
4. Trial Balance and Errors	
5. Financial Statements-Trading Account, Profit and Loss account and Balance Sheet	
6. Computer Awareness	
ACCOUNTING-II	
7. Depreciation, Reserves and Provisions	
8. Bills of Exchange	
9. Accounts of Non-profit Organisation	
10. Accounts from Incomplete Records	

ACCOUNTING-1

Unit 1. Accounting-Meaning, Objectives and Basic Accounting Terms **14 Pds.**

Meaning: (summarisation of accounting process in simple words): (a) Financial transaction; (b) Recording; (c) Classification and summarisation; (d) Analysis and interpretation.

Objectives: (a) To maintain records of business; (b) Calculation of profit or loss; (c) Depiction of financial position; (d) To make the information available to various groups and users.
Basic Terms: (a) Capital; (b) Liability; (c) Asset; (d) Revenue; (e) Expense; (f) Purchase; (g) Sales; (h) Stock; (i) Debtors; (j) Creditors.

Unit 2: Theory Base of Accounting **12 Pds.**

Basic assumptions: (a) Accounting entity; (b) Going concern; (c) Money measurement; (d) Verifiable objective; (e) Accounting period.
Basic Principles: (a) Revenue realisation; (b) Expense; (c) Matching; (d) Full disclosure; (e) Verifiable objective; and dual aspect.
Modifying Principles: (a) Materiality; (b) Consistency; (c) Conservatism (prudence); (d) Timelines; (e) Practice in Industries.

Unit 3: **Origin and Recording of Transactions** **24 Pds.**

Origin of transactions –
Accounting equation-meaning and computation.
Rules of debit and credit: (a) for assets; (b) for liabilities; (c) for capital; (d) for revenue; (e) for expense.
Double entry Book Keeping. Source documents and Accounting Vouchers (format only).
Books of original entry-meaning, format and entries: (a) Journal; (b) Cash Book-Single column (cash and bank) and petty cash book; (c) Day Books-purchases, sales, purchase returns and sales returns.
Ledger: (a) Meaning, utility, format, distinction between books of original entry and ledger; (b) Classification of ledger accounts; (c) Posting from journal, cash book and day books; (d) Balancing of accounts.
Bank Reconciliation statement: (a) Meaning; (b) Need and importance; (c) Preparation-simple exercises.

Unit 4: Trial Balance and Errors **20 Pds.**

Meaning of trial balance.

Meaning and Objectives of Balance Errors: (a) Errors of Commission; (b) Errors of Omission; (c) Errors of Principle; (d) Compensating errors. Rectification of Errors. Suspense account-Meaning, utility, preparation and disposal.

Unit 5: Financial Statements—Trading Account, Profit and Loss Account and Balance Sheet **36 Pds.**

Trading account-Meaning, need and preparation. Profit and loss account-Meaning, need and preparation. Balance sheet-Meaning, need and preparation.

Additional information for adjustments in preparation of final accounts:

(a) Depreciation; (b) Provision for doubtful debts;
(c) Outstanding expenses; (d) Prepaid expenses;
(e) Income received in advance and accrued incomes;
(f) Allocation of items between capital and revenue;
(g) Closing stock; (h) Provision for discount on debtors and creditors.

Methods of presenting final accounts: (a) Horizontal form-meaning and presentation; (b) Vertical form meaning and presentation.

Unit 6: Computer Awareness **14 Pds.**

Introduction of computers-meaning and features
Role of computer in accounting
Concept of flow chart
Type of process in relation to accounting system such as spread sheet, data base and word processor
The student should be exposed to the software packages relevant to elementary accounting applications.

ACCOUNTING-2

Unit 7: Depreciation, Reserves and Provisions **4 Pds.**

(a) Meaning of depreciation; (b) Need for charging

depreciation; (c) Methods of depreciation-straight line method, written down value method.
Reserves and Provisions: (a) Importance; (b) Difference between reserves and provisions; (c) Types of reserves: revenue reserves, general reserves and specific reserves for replacement of assets, capital reserves (example); (d) Need for provision for doubtful debts, provision for discount on debtors, provision for taxation; (e) Accounting for reserves and provisions.

Unit 8: Bills of Exchange:

Definition Features. Parties to a bill of exchange. Specimen of a bill of exchange. Difference between Bill of exchange and Promissory Note.
Important terms: Terms of bill, days of grace, date of maturity, negotiation, endorsement, discounting of bill, dishonour of bill, nothing charges, retirement and renewal of a bill Journal entries.
Necessary accounts in the books of drawer and drawee.

Unit 9: Accounts of Non-Profit Organisations 36 Pds.

Meaning of non-profit organisation with examples
Receipts and payments account (a) Meaning and relevant items. Income and expenditure account and balance sheet. (a) Meaning and relevant items;
(b) Preparation of Income and expenditure A/c from Receipt and Payment A/c with additional information. Distinction between receipt and payment account and income and expenditure account; Preparation of receipt and payments account from income and expenditure account with additional information (simple exercises).

Unit 10: Accounts from Incomplete Records 36 Pds.

Meaning
Ascertainment of profit/loss by statement of affairs method. Preparation of trading and profit and loss

account and balance sheet (with reference to missing figures in debtors accounts, creditor accounts. B/R. B/P and cash).

Class XII

One Paper	**3 Hours**	**100 Marks**

Unit wise Weightage

	Unit	*Marks*
ACCOUNTING-III		**50**
1.	Accounting for Partnership Firms	27
2.	Company Accounts	18
3.	Final Accounts of Companies	05
ACCOUNTING IV		**50**

Note: One of the following three to be offered from Accounting IV

A. Analysis of Financial statements

Or

B. Elements of Costing

Or

C. Auditing.

ACCOUNTING-3

Unit 1: Accounting for Partnership Firms **65 Pds.**

Nature of partnership firm.

Partnership deed (meaning, impact on accounting treatment).

Special aspects of partnership accounts: (a) Fixed vs Fluctuating capital; (b) Division of profit among partners; (c) Past adjustments and guarantees; (d) Change in the profit-sharing ratios of existing partners.

Admission of a partner: (a) Effects of admission of a partner. (b) Change in profit-sharing ratio-sacrificing ratio to be emphasised; (c) Goodwill: Nature, methods of calculation: Average profit, Super profit, Capitalisation, Accounting treatment; (d) Need for revaluation of assets and liabilities-Accounting treatment (excluding memorandum revaluation account).

Retirement/Death of a partner: (a) Change in profit sharing ratio (emphasis on gaining ratio); (b) Share of capital; (c) Share of goodwill and accumulated profits/ reserves; (d) Joint life policy.

Dissolution of partnership firm: (a) Meaning; (b) Settlement of accounts: Preparation of realization account and related accounts (excluding piecemeal distribution, sale to a company and insolvency of a partner).

Unit 2: Company Accounts **43 Pds.**

Nature of a company

Accounting for share capital: (a) Issue and allotment of shares: entries to be passed for application, allotment and call; (b) Over-subscription and under-subscription; (c) Issue at par, at a premium and at a discount; (d) Calls in advance-permissibility and accounting entries; (e) Calls in arrears.

Forfeiture of shares due to non-payment of calls: (a) Accounting treatment; (b) Re-issue of forfeited shares at par, at a premium, and at a discount-accounting treatment. Issue of debentures:
(a) Meaning of debentures; (b) Nature of debenture capital (loan capital); (c) Issue of debentures at par, at a discount and at a premium; (d) Debentures as a collateral security; (e) Debentures interest-concept of periodic payment.

Redemption of debentures: (a) Meaning; (b) Accounting entries-issue at par and redeemable at par, issue at discount and redeemable at par, issue at premium and redeemable at par, issue at par and redeemable at premium, issue at discount and redeemable at premium; (c) Treatment of discount/ loss on the issue of debentures; (d) Sources of redemption of debentures:

– from the proceeds of fresh issue of share-capital and debentures,

– out of accumulated profit, including sinking fund;
– out of current resources.

Methods of redemption of debentures: (a) In lump-sum at the end of stipulated period; (b) By draw of lots; (c) By purchasing in the open market; (d) By conversion into new debentures or shares.

Unit 3: Final Accounts of Companies **12 Pds.**

Balance sheet in the prescribed form with major headings only (Schedule VI, Part one only)

ACCOUNTING-4
ANALYSIS OF FINANCIAL STATEMENTS

Unit 1: Analysis of Financial statements **14 Pds.**

Meaning, Significance and Purpose, Limitations.

Unit 2: Ratio Analysis **36 Pds.**

Meaning of ratio analysis.

Meaning, objectives & computation of: (a) Liquidity ratios: Current ratio, quick ratio; (b) Solvency ratio: Debt equity ratio, Interest coverage ratio; Debt to total funds ratio; Proprietary ratio; (c) Activity ratios: Capital turnover ratio, fixed asset turnover ratio, Net working capital turnover ratio, Stock turnover ratio, Debtors' turnover ratio; Debt collection period; (d) Profitability ratios: Gross profit ratio (GP), Net profit ratio (PR), Return on Investment (ROI), Return on Equity (ROE), Operating ratio.

Unit 3: Statement of Changes in Financial Position (SCFF) 48 Pds.

Meaning and objectives of SCFP

Preparation of: (a) Funds flow statement (net working capital basis); (b) Cash flow statement (statement on cash basis); Adjustments related to depreciation and amortization of intangible assets with reference to (a) and (b). Difference between the two types of statements.

Unit 4: Comparison of Financial Statements **12 Pds.**

Meaning and purpose. Changes in absolute figures for not more than 3 years to be commented upon (Intrafirm only)

Unit 5: Cash Budget **10 Pds.**

Meaning of Budget: Cash Budget: (a) Concept; (b) Utility; (c) Preparation of simple cash budget with 10- 15 variables and with no missing figure.

Or

ELEMENTS OF COSTING

Unit 1: Meaning and Objectives of Costing and Cost Concepts **17 Pds.**

Meaning, distinction between cost accounting and financial accounting. **Objectives:** (a) Ascertainment of cost; (b) cost control.

Cost Concepts-meaning with illustrations: (a) Fixed Cost; (b) Variable cost; (c) Semi-variable cost; (d) Direct cost; (e) Indirect cost (overheads).

Unit 2: Elements of Cost-Naute, Characteristics and Examples 17 Pds.

Direct material; Direct labour; Direct expenses; Factory overheads; General office and administrative overheads: Selling and distribution overheads.

Unit 3: Costing for Raw Materials and Stores **28 Pds**

Meaning and types of raw materials and stores.

Stores records: (a) Bin card-meaning and proforma preparation; (b) Stores ledger-meaning and proforma.

Pricing of materials issued-methods: (a) First-in-first out (FIFO)-meaning and advantages; (b) Last in first out (LIFO) – meaning and advantages; (c) Simple average meaning and advantages; (d) Weighted average-meaning and advantages; (e) Preparation of stores ledger on the basis of FIFO and LIFO resulting in valuation of closing stock.

Material losses – meaning and illustration:

(a) Wastage, (b) Scrap, (c) Spoilage, (d) Defectives, (e) Normal loss, (f) abnormal loss.

Stock-Levels – meaning and computation:
(a) Minimum level, (b) Maximum level, (c) Average stock level, (d) Reorder level.

Reorder quantity: (a) Meaning; (b) Application of economic order quantity (EOQ) formula.

Unit 4: Costing for Labour **24 Pds.**

Time Keeping: (a) Meaning; (b) Methods-Attendance register and card-punching machine.

Time Booking: (a) Meaning; (b) Job-card-Meaning and preparation, (c) Idle time-concept.

Methods of wage payment: (a) Piece basis-Meaning and simple calculation; (b) Time basis-Meaning and simple calculation; Incentives wages plans (discussion of specific incentive plans not required): (a) Meaning and forms; (b) Importance.

Unit 5: Costing for Overheads **17 Pds.**

Classificaiton of overheads. Factory overheads-meaning and example. General and administration - overheads meaning and example.

Allocation-Meaning.

Apportionment-Meaning and method.

Absorption (Labour-hour rate and Machine-hour rate methods).

Unit 6: Cost Sheet **17 Pds.**

Meaning and importance.

Components of cost sheet: (a) Prime Cost; (b) Works cost or cost of production; (c) Cost of goods sold; (d) Cost of sales; Preparation of cost sheet.

Or

AUDITING

Unit 1 : Auditing: **12 Pds.**

Meaning and definition; Nature; Objectives.

Unit 2 : Auditor: 12 Pds.
Attributes; Qualifications as per Companies Act.

Unit 3 : Types of Auditing: 12 Pds.
Statutory audit; statutory and internal audit-meaning, purpose and difference.

Unit 4 : Modes of Auditing: 20 Pds.
Continuous audit, periodic audit, interim audit-meaning, advantages and limitations.

Unit 5 : Audit Process: 28 Pds.
Steps: Audit Programme-meaning and purpose.
Review of internal control and internal check: (a) Meaning; (b) Form; (c) Difference between these two systems.
Audit notebook and working papers: (a) Meaning of audit notebook; (b) Forms of audit notebook; (c) Preparation of audit notebook; (d) Meaning of working papers; (e) Manner of maintenance of working papers; Permanent file; Current file.
Errors and trial balance: (a) Meaning of error and fraud; (b) Difference between error and fraud; (c) Types of errors—Errors of omission;-Errors of principles; Compensating errors; (d) Trial balance and errors affecting and those not affecting agreement of trial balance.

Unit 6: Evidence, Vouching and Verification: 24 Pds.
Meaning of Evidence; Relevance of Evidence in auditing; Meaning of Vouching; Vouching of normal trading transactions of general type of business; Vouching of transactions of assets and liabilities of common types; Verification of assets and liabilities of common types (only physical and documentary verification).

Unit 7: Audit Report: 12 Pds.
Meaning; Scope; General Features; Purpose.

Teaching Approaches to Bookkeeping and Accountancy. Following are the important approaches:-

1. The Journal Approach;
2. The Ledger Approach;
3. The Balance Sheet Approach;
4. The Equation Approach;
5. The Spiral Development Approach;
6. The Complete Cycle Approach;
7. The Single Entry Approach.

Journal Approach. In this approach, steps in book-keeping cycle are taught in the order they are used in different offices. The student first learns how to journalise and to record business transactions in a book of original entry i.e. journal. Important steps in this approach are:

(i) Defining debit and credit;
(ii) Analysis of transactions in terms of debt and credit;
(iii) Writing of debits and credits in the journal;
(iv) Posting;
(v) Balancing and ledger account;
(vi) Profit and Loss account;
(vii) Balance-Sheet;
(viii) Closing entries.

This approach has certain limitations. Students are required to labour hard for learning how to journalise and how to post into the ledger. They do not very clearly know where they are heading to. On the whole, this approach is considered very dull.

Ledger Approach. In this approach, the basic and fundamental concepts of book-keeping are stated i.e. the accounts, the book of second entry, the why and how of accounts balance and their debits and credits. According to this approach, the most common order of presentation is to move ahead to prove the equality of debits and credits by taking a trial balance, the journalising, posting and proceeding to the preparation of final accounts. This approach is criticised on the ground that it is a mechanical process which fails to share with the students the purpose and the use to which the routine work of keeping the accounts will be put. This approach starts in the middle of the book-keeping cycle and lends confusion by moving back to the journal and then ahead to the culminating steps in the cycle. This approach does not present the subject-matter in a systematic manner. From the third cycle (i.e. preparation of final accounts), the students have to go to the second and the first cycle.

Balance-Sheet Approach. This approach is based on the maxim of teaching 'from whole to parts'. It first of all acquaints the students with the important objectives and the important reasons for keeping records. The order of presentation is the balance-sheet (the end product) and it is followed by profit and loss statement. 'Proceeding from 'whole to parts' gives a ' logical and sequential development of ideas, concepts and principles.

Following procedure needs to be followed in this approach:

(i) Introducing the students with the book-keeping cycle on the first day.

(ii) Presenting a summary of closing the income and expense account on the next day.

(iii) Repeating the above summary and adding some adjustment of inventory account.

(iv) Introducing the liabilities account after the review of the previous work.

(v) Taking up assets accounts after the review of previous work.

(vi) Inclusion of some more adjustment work after the review of the previous work.

(vii) Introducing more formal statements of accounts.

(viii) Introducing finally the scrutiny of accounts and thereafter journalising.

This approach is objected to on the ground that it violates the teaching 'simple to complex' and on the contrary follows the maxim &complex to simple'.

Equation Approach. In this approach, students are introduced with the following three concepts:

(a) Assets: These refer to anything owned by the owner.

(b) Liabilities: These refer to anything owed or outsider's interests.

(c) Capital: It refers to owner's interest in the business.

With every transaction, there occurs a change in assets or liabilities or capital. This is made on the following equation:-

Assets = Liability + Capital

Liability = Assets - Capital

Capital = Assets -Liability.

Following rules are observed in this equation

(i) To indicate increase in assets, + (plus) sign is used and for decrease in assets - (minus) sign is used.

(ii) Assets are increased on debit side and decreased on credit side.

(iii) Liability and capital are increased on credit side and decreased on the debt side.

Spiral Development Approach. In this approach a concept is developed by adding some new learning while repeating the bookkeeping cycle. Part of the cycle is retaught and part of it is expanded each time. Following steps are adopted under this approach:-

(i) Developing the concept of journals;

(ii) Developing the concept of subsidiary books;

(iii) Developing the concept of ledger;

(iv) Developing the concept of trial-balance;

(v) Developing the concept of work-sheet balance;

(vi) Developing the concept of profit and loss account and balance sheet;

(vii) Developing the concept of closing entries.

Complete Cycle Approach. Under this approach, the whole cycle of book keeping is introduced to the students, namely journalising, posting, trial balance, balance sheet and the adjusting entries. It is a good review device. It is very suitable in remedial teaching. The entire exercise on the complete cycle should be done on one sheet of the paper on one -side. This may be repeated for several days on different exercises. This approach enables the students to have a thorough knowledge of accounting practices. For making the maximum use of this approach, following suggestions are offered:

1. Students maybe asked to make journal entries without giving explanation for debits and credits.
2. Posting references are omitted and simple check marks are used.

3. Cyclostyled forms are used by students.
4. Account headings of assets, liabilities and capital are supplied to students on which they work upon.
5. Transactions with simple figures and round numbers are used.
6. Detailed discussion on 'Why' aspects are kept in abeyance.
7. A new concept is introduced only when the basic cycle is mastered.
8. To start with instead of mentioning debt and credit, it is better to mention left side and right side.
9. Books are allowed on the very first day.

Following advantages are claimed by the use of this approach:-

(i) Students get a glimpse of the complete cycle on a single look.

(ii) All entries are done on a single sheet and nothing is kept blank.

(iii) Use of journal and ledger accounts gives students a realistic picture.

(iv) The concept of 'whole' is developed easily under this approach.

Single Entry Approach. In this approach, records of assets, liabilities and capital are maintained but no account of the sources of profits and losses is maintained. An incoming asset is debited and an outgoing asset is credited. An entry is made either for credit or for debit. The journal in this approach does not make any distinction between debit and credit. This approach provides data and everything is entered in a single book.

This approach is seldom used in popular houses but is still in use in small establishments. This system provides only the position of debitors and creditors and does not depict the picture of financial position of the business as and when required by the businessman.

Of the various approaches to bookkeeping, which approach should be followed , is to be decided by the teacher. It is advisable for the teacher to follow the approach introduced by the textbook. Indian conditions favour the journal approach. Adequate journalising exercises and then posting to ledger accounts, closing of accounts and extracting of trial-balance may be taught in the sequence.

Procedures and Scope

We have discussed in detail the various methods of teaching in an earlier chapter. It may be emphasised that a balanced, judicious, rational and scientific combination of various methods will go a long way in teaching bookkeeping and accountancy effectively. Students will also learn the subject joyfully, involving themselves wholeheartedly. No single method can be recommended. Use of a method also depends on the availability of requisite material in the school. Lecturing in bookkeeping should be of a different nature than lecturing in other subjects because here the lecture is to explain certain points which are to be applied in the problem. While lecturing key words and technical points involved may be written on the blackboard so that what the students hear can also be seen on the blackboard and they can connect them and keep in their memory. The teacher should explain each step.

Skill Requirement

Bookkeeping and accountancy is by and large a skill subject. However it must be remembered that no course in mutually exclusive. Even in the skill-building courses, before a student can use his acquired skills, he must have attained the knowledge, understanding and attitude accepted in the business world.

In skill lesson 'TAS' i.e. technique, accuracy and speed-is very important. Demonstration and drill are the two most important methods or techniques in teaching skills.

Following points need consideration in demonstration:

1. Get the attention of the students before demonstration.
2. Explain the purpose of demonstration.
3. Explain briefly what is to be demonstrated.
4. Hold the attention of the students throughout.
5. Ensure that all the students in the class can observe clearly what is demonstrated.
6. Give suitable explanation during demonstration.
7. Let the students try to imitate the procedure immediately.
8. Observe the students while they imitate the demonstration so that to give help where needed.
9. Ensure that the students' books 'are closed and that full attention is given to demonstration and presentation.
10. Use a pointer.

Teaching Techniques

Following are the three stages in the teaching of accountancy or bookkeeping. These stages may be compared to a pyramid with the base, the middle layer and the apex.

1. Recording of original entry in subsidiary books.
2. Posting the entries into the appropriate accounts in the main books called ledger.
3. Preparing the profit and loss account and balance sheet.
   (i) Journal is one of the subsidiary books. It means 'daily record'. A sound graph of the principles behind the use of journal and the construction of journal entries will enable the students to master the general theory of double entry system in accountancy.
   (ii) The ledger occupies the middle of the pyramid and is the main book of account. Journal is a subsidiary book. The balance sheet and profit and loss statements can be prepared from the ledger. Recording the business transactions under the head of debits and credits is known as journalising. Posting implies processing these transactions further and taking them to appropriate accounts.
   (iii) The balance sheet is the apex in the pyramid. The balance sheet can be the starting point for teaching accountancy. This leads to the profit and loss account which is the ultimate aim of accountancy and book-keeping process.

Basic Problems

1. Accountancy is a technical skill comprising a number of terms. These terms will have to be comprehended.
2. Quite a large number of students who take commerce lack calculative and mathematical skills which need to be taken note of by the teacher.
3. Students differ in their ability to understand the subject matter.
4. Poor handwriting of some of the students may cause difficulties for them and their teachers.

5. The skill aspect of accountancy puts heavy demands upon the commerce teacher who is required to check several asssignments.

Effective Teaching

1. Pupils should be involved in the development of the lesson.
2. Emphasis on neatness in making entries should be laid.
3. Individual attention should be paid to the difficulties of the students.
4. Exercises of the students should be checked when they are working upon them.
5. Home work should be very definite and checked regularly.

The Guidelines

1. The use of the 'why' approach rather than the 'how' approach. It is more important to know 'why' rather than to make the correct entry.
2. Urge students to think in terms of the rules of journalising. This will help than in making any bookkeeping entry in any book of accounts at any level of knowledge.
3. Teach a new unit before you ask students to read the textbook for the unit. It may be kept in view that only a few students can learn bookkeeping and accountancy by reading the textbook.
4. Illustrate the rules of debit and credit graphically by drawing connecting lines to tie up debit and credit entries.
5. Insist on legible, fair and correct homework or classwork.
6. Present headings of the journal, ledger, trial balance, subsidiary book and final account on cardboards which can be Put on the blackboard very quickly.
7. If possible, make permanent ruling on the black-board.
8. Use portable blackboard when needed.
9. Superwise the work of the students when they are doing exercises by taking round of the class.
10. Penalise a student only once for an error that is carried over and evaluate future recording on the basis of that error.

11. Give definite home assignments.
12. Give assignments relating to principles, besides practice and procedure.

Other Objectives

(Determined by NCERT)

1. To acquire the knowledge of facts, terms, concepts, principles, trends, etc. in Money and Banking.
2. To develop the understanding of facts, terms, concepts, principles etc. in Money and Banking.
3. To develop the ability to apply the knowledge of facts, concepts, principles, etc., in Money and Banking in unfamiliar situations.
4. To develop the practical skills related to the elementary banking functions.
5. To develop desirable interests in banking procedures and currency functions.
6. To develop healthy attitude, expected of a good banker.

Objective to Acquire the Knowledge of Facts

Specification of the Objective:

To demonstrate the achievement of the above objective, the pupil:

1. recalls facts, concepts etc. in Money and Banking;
2. recognises facts, concepts, proformas, etc. in Elements of Banking;
3. fills up and uses various proformas and banking documents.

Objective to Develop Understanding of Facts

Specifications of the Objective:

To demonstrate the achievement of the above objective, the pupil:

1. distinguishes between relevant and irrelevant, essential and incidental data;
2. discriminates between different facts, concepts, etc. in Money and Banking;
3. classifies;
4. compares and contrasts;
5. cites illustrations;
6. detects errors and rectifies them;

7. identifies relationships between cause and effect;
8. interprets data presented in various forms.

Objective to Develop the Ability to Apply the Knowledge

Specifications of the Objective:

To demonstrate the achievement of the above objective, the pupil:

1. analyses a new problem to identify the issues involved in it;
2. selects facts relevant to a new situation;
3. establishes relevant relationship between different facts, concepts, etc.;
4. judges the adequacy of data, arguments, etc.;
5. draws inferences and generalisations;
6. predicts events, trends, etc.

Objective to Develop the Practical Skills

Specifications of the Objective:

To demonstrate the achievement of the above objective, the pupil:

1. draws cheques, B/Es, Hundies, etc. neatly and accurately;
2. prepares various proformas neatly and correctly;
3. collects relevant information, preserves and displays it;
4. conducts simple banking surveys.

Objective to Develop Desirable Interests

Specifications of the Objective:

To demonstrate the achievement of the above objective, the pupil voluntarily:

1. reads periodicals, related books, newspapers, etc. giving information about banking;
2. collects specimens, pictures, charts, data and other such materials related to areas of his interest in banking and currency;
3. discusses problems related to banking and currency with his colleagues, teachers and parents;
4. participates in banking transactions in and outside the school;
5. visits places of banking importance;

6. prepares exhibits related to the subject matter of Elements of Banking for display in schools and elsewhere;
7. maintains and operates bank accounts.

Objective to Develop Healthy Attitudes

Specifications of the Objective:

To demonstrate the achievement of the above objective, the pupil:

1. assumes responsibility;
2. is open minded towards new ideas;
3. behaves courteously and politely;
4. respects law;
5. develops thrifty habits.

QUESTIONS

1. State briefly the objectives of bookkeeping.
2. What approaches are employed in the teaching of bookkeeping? Which approach do you like most? Support your answer with reasons.
3. State the instructional objectives of bookkeeping. Specify anyone of them.
4. Evaluate the bookkeeping curriculum prescribed in your state in classes XI and XII. Do you agree with it? Give arguments in support of your answer.
5. Write brief notes on:
   (i) History of teaching of bookkeeping and accountancy.
   (ii) Vocational objective of the study of bookkeeping and accountancy.
6. State instructional objectives of banking.
7. What is demonstration. State its importance in skill lesson of Bookkeeping and Accountancy?
8. Explain the significance of TAS in a skill lesson.
9. State the important techniques of Teaching Accountancy and Bookkeeping. What are the problems of teaching these subjects? Suggest suitable guidelines.

18

Reference Books and Textbooks

A textbook may be described as being an aid to teaching and learning which is specially prepared by experts for the use of pupils and teachers, presenting a course of study usually in a single subject. It is a manual of instruction, a book containing a presentation of the principles of the subject used as a basis of instruction. It is equipped with the usual teaching devices. It includes exercises at the end of each chapter for the students. All students are expected to study a textbook thoroughly. Questions in the examination are normally set on the basis of the contents of a textbook.

Meaning and Definition

Following are the important definitions of a textbook:

According to Francis Bacon (1561-1625), an English philosopher, a textbook is "a book designed for classroom use, carefully prepared by experts in the field and equipped with the usual teaching devices."

Andrew Lang (1844-1912), a Scottish author, states that a textbook is "a standard work for any branch of study.

Encyclopedia of Educational Research, edited by B.R. Buckinghan (1960) explains the term a textbook as, "in the modern sense and as commonly understood, the textbook is a learning instrument usually employed in schools and colleges to support a programme of instruction."

In the words of J.A. Lauwerys and H.C. Barnard, authors of *A Handbook of British Educational Terms* (1963), a textbook is "a book prepared specially to assist learners in mastering a subject or a part of a subject."

The Encyclopedia of Education (1971) by Lee C. Deighton (Editor-in Chief) notes, "The essential and definite characteristics of textbooks are that they are designed for students as written guides to the subject content of a course of study. The physical form of the textbook is not significant. It may be hardback or soft back. It may be Printed, mimeographed or Photographed."

The Encyclopedia Britanica (1972) edited by Bu. L.R. defines textbooks in these words, "standard works or manuals of instruction in a subject of study".

Cart V. Good. (Ed.). in Dictionary of Education 0973) explains textbook as "(1) Any manual of instruction (2) A book dealing with a definite subject of study, systematically arranged, intended for use at a specified level of instruction, and used as a principal source of study material for a given course."

Page, G. Terry and Thomas, J.B. in International Dictionary of Education (1978) consider a textbook as a "basic book used in a particular course of study."

Tillin and Quinly in Educational Technology: A Glossary of Terms (1979) state that a textbook is "a book used in instruction which contains the basic principles of a subject."

The International Encyclopedia of Educational Technology (1989) reads as, "Textbooks are books that are designed to present the basic principles or aspects of a given subject for use as the basis of instruction; they can, in fact, be considered as an entire course of instruction. They are highly organised."

The Oxford English Dictionary (1989) explains the term textbook in these words, "A book used as a standard work for the study of a particular subject, now usually one written specifically for this purpose, a manual of instruction in any science or branch of study, especially a work recognised as authority."

Functions

Text book is an 'assistant master in print'. A text book is content plus instructional technique. This technique is aimed at enabling the content understandable to the pupils even in situations where they are not helped by the teacher.

A text book has a structured framework. A text book clearly spells out and interprets the syllabus both for the students and teachers.

A text book is an instrument of some instructional objectives. As an important tool of instruction, a text book is an instrument for the achievement of pre-determined objectives.

A text book is an important tool for the teacher. A text book assists the teacher to plan his daily lesson, prepare assignments and organise class activities.

A text book is a constant companion of a student. A text book guides the students in learning-in the school and at home. A student uses it continuously and constantly. This feature distinguishes it from a general and reference book which a student consults once a while. Each word of the text book has not only to be read by every student but he is also expected to understand it.

A text book is a self-teaching device. A text book enables a student to learn through his own efforts. A text book provides an opportunity to a student to reflect and evaluate. A student can find the specific information he needs in a book without listening to extraneous material that comes before and after it. He can review material he has read from time to time to clear up uncertainties. He can move ahead as quickly or as methodically as his individual capacities for comprehension permit.

A text book provides logical and comprehensive material. A good text book by providing in a systematic and comprehensive form, sets a standard of minimum essential to be achieved by students of all categories. For a teacher, it provides essential knowledge at one place. All teachers are not in a position to dig up facts. A text book, therefore, can be a constant standby of the commerce teacher.

A text book is a transmitter of culture. It serves as potential media of mass communication. It has a positive role to play in bringing about desirable cultural change by discarding certain outdated values and customs and introducing radical changes.

A text book helps to revolutionise society. A text book is used not only for preserving the cultural heritage but also revolutionising a society, its values, beliefs and social systems.

A text book serves as a rallying point. By providing a common ground for both the teachers and the students, it focuses attention on the same issues, events, sequences and circumstances.

A text book serves as a laboratory. A text book enables a student to reinforce the learning, to do assignments at home, to prepare for the examination and to seek guidance and reference for further studies. It provides a common basis on which the process of reading, analysing, outlining and summarising can be mastered.

A text book serves as a basis for almost all the methods. Almost all the methods of teaching like the Assignment, Unit Method, Discussion and the Project Method can be used with advantage with the help of a text book.

A text book gives definite information. A text book is a storehouse of basic and definite information needed for learning experiences of different kinds. The use of the text book can help the pupils to sum up all the ideas of the unit, acquaint them with the vocabulary, help them learn enough about the topic to be able to proceed intelligently.

A text book generates educational interaction. A text book plays a crucial role in generating educational interaction in the classroom between the teacher and the learner, and also between the learner and other co-learners as a result of which learning occurs in a group.

A text book serves as a syllabus 'de facto'. A teacher defines and delimits his content of teaching: He uses the text book as a prime instructional aid to generate a variety of educative experiences through group-work and individual assignments.

Limitations

Limitations of text books are stated below:

1. They tend to dominate the educative process. They have influenced the purpose, character and scope of the curriculum. They have dominated the method of instruction and the evaluating process. They have narrowed down the scope of the curriculum.
2. They do not provide for direct experience. The students get readymade knowledge and, therefore may fail to assimilate it properly.
3. They introduce uniformity and rigidity for definite achievements and may kill initiative and spirit of both the pupil and the teacher.

4. Text books are great hindrance in the new methods of teaching like the Heuristic and the Inductive. The students get ready-made answers and this defeats the very purpose of introducing new methods.
5. There is every danger that the text books may be used for the purpose of indoctrination of the ideas and beliefs of the party in power. In fact, text books have been used in many countries for the propagation of Fascist and Communistic ideas. They are a potent instrument in the hands of the party in power to inculcate narrow nationalism and racial prejudices.

How to use text books. A text book should be treated as a means and not an end in itself. It should be borne in mind that it is a useful means to help study. The students should never have the impression that a text book constitutes a boundary and their task is simply to learn what it contains and no more. A text book should serve as a basis of learning. A text book does not provide the last word on the subject. A text book is not to usurp the functions of a teacher. It is to supplement his work and not supplant it.

Can we do away with text books? We may not accept the sovereignty of a text book but it must be admitted that a good text book is an indispensable means or tool in the teaching-learning process, whatever scheme is adopted. It is neither desirable nor feasible for most of the teachers to do without text books. The only point is that a text book should be used very skilfully and intelligently. It should be treated as 'an obedient slave' and not 'a commanding master'.

The Education Commission 1964-66 described the value of the text book as an effective tool of learning and of diffusion of improved teaching methods in these words, "A good text book written by a qualified and competent specialist in the subject, and produced with due regard to quality of printing illustrations and general getup, stimulates the pupil's interest and helps the teacher considerably in his work. The provision of quality text books, and other teaching and learning materials, can thus be an effective programme for raising standards. The need to emphasise it is all the greater because it requires only a relatively small investment of resources. Moreover, a quality book need not cost appreciably more than one that is indifferently produced."

Characteristics

These may broadly be classified under two heads:

A. Academic B. Physical

Academic

I. Selection of content.
II. Organisation of content.
III. Presentation of content.
IV. Verbal communication (Language).
V. Visual communication (Illustrations).
VI. Assignments, exercises etc.
VII. Prelims and back pages.

Physical

VIII. Size and format of the text books.
IX. Printing lay-out.
X. Durability.
XI. Price.

Content Selection

Relevant content: The content should be relevant to the instructional objectives of Commerce.

Coverage of the course: The content should cover the topics given in the syllabus.

Adequate content: The content should be adequate in respect of each topic.

Authentic content: The content should be accurate and authentic.

Up-to-date content: The content should be up-to-date.

Continuity and balance: The continuity and balance among- the various topics covered in the book should be maintained.

Integrated content: The selected topics should be properly integrated from the preceding to the succeeding class or stage.

Linking with life. Considerable material drawn from practical life situations and day-to-day life of the community should be included in the book.

Content Organisation

Division into units. The subject-matter should be divided into proper chapters and units.

Division into sections. The matter should be properly divided into sections and paragraphs.

Psychological approach. The approach followed in the book should be suitable to the needs of the students.

Coherence in the subject-matter. There should be sufficient coherence and sequence in the organisation of the subject matter.

Flexible organisation. The organisation should be flexible enough to submit to changes in accordance with the change in the instructional plans.

Content Presentation

Attractive and appropriate title. The titles of the chapters should be appropriate.

Motivating presentation. The presentation should motivate children for further study.

Interesting and creative approach. The matter should be presented in a creative and interesting manner to sustain interest.

Adequate terminology. The presentation should provide an adequate coverage of the terminology relevant to the syllabus.

Adequate provision for replication. It should provide adequate reinforcement of new items of learning through replication and application.

Provision for suitable suggestions for teachers. The presentation should provide some suggestions and implications for adoption of effective teaching methods and instructional strategies by the classroom teacher.

Communication

Appropriate vocabulary. The vocabulary should be appropriate for the class level.

Short and simple sentences. The sentences should be simple and short.

Correct spellings. The spellings should be correct.

Correct punctuation. Punctuation should be done correctly.

Grammatically correct language. The language used should be grammatically correct.

Proper use of technical terms. The technical terms should be used properly, and suitably explained wherever necessary.

Visual Communication

Clear illustrations. The illustrations should be correct and authentic.

Purposeful presentation of illustrations. The illustrations should be purposeful and appropriately placed in the text book.

Adequate illustrations. The illustrations should be adequate, proper in size and suitably captioned.

Supplementation of text. The illustration should supplement the text.

Variety of illustrations. There should be variety in illustrations.

Assignments for Learning

Adequate exercises. The exercises should be adequate to test the various purposes like recapitulation, consolidation, etc.

Wide coverage. The exercises should cover the significant content.

Scope for projects. The projects provided should help in achieving various purposes of teaching commerce.

Real projects. The projects should have a close resemblance to actual life situations.

Challenging exercises. The exercises should promote the spirit of enquiry and motive the students for further study.

Graded exercises. These exercises should suit the special needs of the gifted as well as slow learners.

The Prelims

Appropriate title page. The title page should give the necessary information, i.e., suitable title, author's name, publisher's name, place of publication and year of publication etc.

Suitable preface. Preface should give an idea about the scope and central theme of the book.

Effective introduction. Introduction should explain the scheme and purpose of the book.

Correct table of contents. The table of contents should be given correctly.

Bibliography. Bibliography should be given correctly and according to the uniform system.

Suitable glossary. Glossary should be given in proper language.

Index. Index should be given where possible.

The Size of the Book

Suitable size. The size should be suitable from the viewpoint of age group of students.

Suitable volume. The size should be suitable in relation to the volume of the book.

Layout and Printing

Suitable length. The length of the line should be such as can be conveniently read by the students.

Suitable type. The type size used for chapter title, subtitles, footnotes, exercises etc. should be suitable for the age-group of the students.

Appropriate margin. The left-hand, right-hand, top and bottom margins should be appropriate.

Aesthetic outlook. The margins should provide an aesthetic look to the page of the book.

Appropriate spacing. Spacing between lines and paragraphs should be appropriate.

Durability

Durable paper. The paper should be durable enough in view of the age-group.

Life of the book. The paper should be durable enough in accordance with the expected life of the book.

Suitable price of paper. The quality of the paper should be in accordance with the cost of the book.

Importance of Supplementary Material. Supplementary material is of potential value for commerce teaching. Text books cannot satisfy all aspects of critical and inspirational knowledge and may be even lacking details with regard to current contemporary affairs. Text books cannot cope with the material of fast changing events. Text books, with rare exceptions, are not self-explanatory and the students stand in need of elaboration. Elaboration is possible through advanced works, reference books and source books, etc. Similarly, autobiographies and biographies serve as inspirational sources. Well written speeches on related subjects are very helpful.

Pamphlets prepared by local, state and national societies provide admirable material for students.

Supplementary material is intended to achieve the following objectives:

1. It aims at helping the students acquire additional information.
2. It aims at widening the horizons of the students.
3. It aims at enriching the knowledge already acquired through the text book.
4. It aims at enabling the students to develop study habits.
5. It aims at motivating them to write articles and speeches, etc.
6. It aims at serving as a means of bringing out the relationship between the present and the past.
7. It aims at enabling the students to form an acquaintance with literature pertaining to commerce.
8. It aims at making the teaching of commerce more inspiring and interesting.
9. It aims at enabling the students to make the best use of their leisure time.
10. It incidentally helps the students form the conception of how material is built up; if used effectively, not only utilises instruction but also provides a new meaning of teaching and learning.

Merits

Bining and Bining point out the merits of supplementary material as "During the period of adolescence, when interest can readily be aroused, when good habits can be developed, when attitudes can easily be built up, when the capacity for forming ideals is strong, and when the mind is wide open to impressions, the natural desire for reading should be skilfully directed and the foundations laid for the wise use of books."

Types of reading

These are as given below:

1. Reading for understanding.
2. Reading for memorisation.
3. Reading for the purpose of locating specific information.
4. Rapid reading for expanding general knowledge.
5. Reading for pleasure.

Most supplementary reading can be classified under the last three categories; major share going to fourth category of rapid reading.

Various Types

Following are the different types of instructional material:-

1. Journals and periodicals in commerce and allied disciplines.
2. Government documents and reports-Reserve Bank Bulletins, Reports of the Planning Commission, Reports of the Finance Commission, etc.
3. Budget discussions in Parliament and State Assemblies.
4. Special issues brought out by newspapers on commerce and allied subjects.
5. Reports by Chairman of public and private companies.
6. Book reviews.
7. Reference books and encyclopaedias on commerce.
8. Survey reports.
9. Special pages/or news of commercial importance—of newspapers for instance bullion market, share prices etc.
10. Teaching aids like films, filmstrips, Video-tape recordings, charts, graphs, cartoons etc.
11. Technical documents of the following types:
    - (i) Bank documents
    - (ii) Business documents
    - (iii) Company documents
    - (iv) Income tax laws and documents
    - (v) Inward and outward registers
    - (vi) Posters
    - (vii) Post-office documents
    - (viii) Proforma of invoice, cheques, bills etc.
    - (ix) Proformas of journal, ledger, trial balance and final accounts, etc.
    - (x) Proforma of shipping documents
    - (xi) Telegraph guide

Magazines and Journals. Many magazines contain interesting and latest material on different matters relating to commerce which can supplement classroom information. They enable the students to keep themselves abreast of the latest developments in various fields. Current events are to be correlated with the teaching of Commerce. Price trends, debates in Parliament and State

Legislatures regarding commerce policy, share-markets and budget discussions etc. which find an important place in journals are very helpful in enhancing knowledge of commerce.

Newspapers. Newspapers help in bridging the gap between information contained in the books and changing developments in movements, trends, ideas and changes in politics, international relations and economic and civil life. Special and Sunday issues such as Republic Day and independence Day are full of important events. Articles on new researches in various fields can enlighten the students. It is, therefore, very essential that from the very beginning of their school career, students are made newspaper-minded.

Travel stories. Travel accounts of the Buddhist Chinese travellers like Fahien, Hieun Tsang and Itsing who visited India provide a comprehensive account of the social and cultural life of the people living during that period. Their accounts are considered a great valuable source of information as they spent a few years in India and travelled widely. Similarly, travel accounts of the Arab sailors, merchants and the visitors who visited India during the medieval period provide interesting accounts. Alberuni and Ibn Batuta have furnished valuable descriptions of the period. Achievements of the rulers of the Vijayanagar Empire have found an important place in the travel accounts given by the Portuguese and the Indian travellers having bearing on trade and commerce.

Work books. Work books are based on the principle of 'Learning by Doing'. They play a vital role in leading to the concretisation of the concepts presented in text books. Work books provide opportunities to the students to apply knowledge gained through text books.

The Guidelines

1. While suggesting supplementary material, the teacher should bear in mind the mental capacity of his students. Only those materials should be suggested which the students can grasp.
2. As far as possible, only those materials should be suggested which the students can get easily from the school library or local sources.
3. Suggested supplementary material should be within the easy reach of the pocket of the students if it is not available in the school library.

4. There should be no element of compulsion in supplementary reading. The teacher would do well to keep in mind the suggestion of Johnson in this regard, "There should be no set questions to answers, no problems to solve, no looking forward to any report, but complete freedom to read because he likes it or to stop reading because he dislikes it."
5. Language of the supplementary material should be simple so that it may maintain the interest of the students.
6. For motivating the students, the teacher should maintain a small library in the classroom or a reserved shelf in the library or hall so as to make it easily available to students.
7. The students may be motivated to keep their own record of supplementary reading done as, (a) Name of the book, (b) Author's name, (c) Publisher's name, (d) Newspaper or the magazine read by them, (e) Extracts taken.
8. Supplementary material should be well illustrated.
9. Supplementary material as the name implies should only supplement the text book and not replace it.
10. Supplementary material should be scientifically and systematically classified and arranged in a proper sequence.
11. Supplementary material should be authentic and not a distortion of facts or politically motivated.

The Significance

As opposed to a text book a reference book is not designed to cover a prescribed course of study for a particular examination conducted by a Board, or a University or any other examining body. It is not meant for a compulsory study by all the students undergoing a course. It is not prescribed by any institution or organisation. It is a book of consultation. It provides a wider exposure to the students and teachers. It is very helpful in providing career guidance also. It has different formats. It may include just the meaning of a difficult word like a dictionary of Commerce. It may deal with a particular topic only, say banking and may include articles on the same topic by experts. It may cover several topics. Usually a book of this type is called an encyclopaedia. Bibliographies also come under the category of reference books. Rules and regulations pertaining to trade, banking, foreign exchange etc., made by the Central Government are also termed as reference material. Government Gazetteers including government notifications fall under this category. Commercial atlases are also referred to as reference publications. Government documents and reports also supply the needed information.

Bulletins issued by the Reserve Bank, Reports of the Planning Commission, and Reports of the Financial Commission etc. have to be constantly referred to keep one in the know of things.

Ready recknors relating to income tax calculation and payment of wages etc. are also needed for reference purposes.

Reference books should be selected very carefully. They should be up-to-date. They should indicate careers to be pursued. They should cover key areas in commerce. They should be in the context of one's country as far as possible. Usually one copy each of these reference publications is kept in the library and is not issued to students or teachers for use at home. Reference material can be consulted in the library.

QUESTIONS

1. "A textbook of Commerce serves as a syllabus 'de facto'. Explain this statement and point out the significance of a textbook for students and teachers.
2. Explain the essential characteristics of a good textbook.
3. "A textbook should be used as a servant and not master." Explain this statement.
4. Explain the need for supplementary material in the teaching of Commerce. How can we make the best use of this material?
5. In what way a textbook is different from a reference book? Explain the importance of commerce reference books at school stage.
6. Describe the criteria for the selection of textbooks and reference books for the teaching of commerce.

19

Planning the Lessons

R.L. Stevenson has very aptly said, To every teacher I would say, 'Always plan out your lesson before-hand but do not be slave to it'. Bagley has put it thus, "However, able and experienced the teacher, he could do never without his preliminary preparation." I.K. Davis is perfectly right when he says, "Lesson must be prepared for there is nothing so fatal to a teacher's progress as unpreparedness." To be effective, every intelligent worker plans out his work. A surgeon diagnoses the case, prepares his surgical instruments before he puts the patient on the operation table; a lawyer makes attempts to anticipate and prepare for every move in the court, and engineer prepares his blue print before he actually starts the construction work of a bridge or a building, the house mistress plans the details of the daily meals; the sales manager gives careful attention to every step in a proposed selling campaign. So must a teacher must plan and prepare his work.

A lesson plan indicates the aims to be realised by teaching a lesson, the methods to be employed and the activities to be undertaken in the class so that it is kept engaged for the realisation of the aim. A lesson plan is actually a plan of action. It includes:

(i) The working philosophy of the teacher.
(ii) His information and understanding of his pupils.
(iii) His comprehension of the objectives of education.
(iv) His knowledge of the material to be taught.
(v) His ability to use effective methods of education.

The Concept

Following definitions deserve careful attention for understanding the broad meaning of a lesson plan.

Bining and Bining: Daily lesson planning involves defining the objectives, selecting and arranging the subject matter and determining the method and procedure.

Lester B. Stands: A lesson plan is actually a plan of action. It, therefore, includes the working philosophy of the teacher, his knowledge of philosophy, his information about and understanding of his pupils, his comprehension of the objective of education, his knowledge of the material to be taught, and his ability to utilize effective methods.

N.L. Bossing: Lesson Plan is the title given to a statement of the achievements to be realized and the specific means by which these are to be attained as a result of the activities engaged in day-by-day under the guidance of the teacher." This definition tends to focus the teacher's attention upon:

1. Outcomes or results in terms of the pupil.
2. Definite processes and procedures with a recognition of activity as the basis of learning.
3. The pupil in the foreground and the teacher in the background as guide and director only of the learning activity.

From above it is concluded that lesson plan

is a blue print.

is a guide map for action.

is a creative piece of work.

is a comprehensive chart of classroom teaching.

is an elastic but systematic approach for the teaching of concepts, skills and understandings etc.

is the teachers' mental and emotional visualisation of the classroom experiences as he plans to occur.

Nature of Lesson Planning

According to Bossing, "Lesson planning is essentially an experience in anticipatory teaching. It is living through in advance, mentally and emotionally, the classroom experience as the teacher visualizes it. The eager faces, the questions that will arise, the difficulties the pupils will encounter, the way these difficulties are to be met all these the teacher will experience in imagination. This is the first essential of good planning. It is here that the teacher can bring into play to subtle power of well-developed imagination. The more vivid, the better, so long as it is fully tinged with realism.

Merits

1. It delimits the field of work of the teacher as well as of the students and provides a definite objective for each day's work.
2. As the goal is determined, the teacher gets impetus to realise his goal.
3. It tends to prevent wandering from the subject and going off the way. It serves as a check on the possible wastage of time and energy of the teachers and students. It makes teaching systematic, orderly and economical.
4. Planning helps the teacher to organise and systematise the learning process. The activities in the lesson are well-knit, interconnected and associated. The continuity of the educative process is ensured.
5. Planning helps to avoid needless repetition.
6. Planning helps the teacher to overcome the feeling of nervousness and insecurity. It gives him confidence to face the class.
7. Lesson planning gives opportunities to the teacher to think out new ways and means of making the lesson interesting and to introduce thought-provoking questions.
8. Lesson plan availability of adequate materials for the lesson.
9. Lesson planning enables the teacher to link the new knowledge with the previous knowledge acquired by students.
10. Lesson planning ensures a proper connection of the new lesson with the previous lesson.
11. Lesson planning enables the teacher to prepare a suitable scheme of selection and organisation of subject-matter, materials and activities.

12. Lesson planning enables the teacher to prepare pivotal questions and illustrations.
13. Lesson planning makes it possible to provide for individual differences in pupils.
14. Lesson planning enables the teacher to provide for suitable summaries.
15. Lesson, planning provides for an adequate checking of the outcomes of instruction.
16. Lesson planning helps the teacher as well as the taught in fixing new learning by making adequate provision for drill work, practice and revision.

Basic Principles

R. Schorling in 'Student Teaching' suggests the following principles and steps in planning a good lesson plan.

1. Select the most appropriate aims.
2. Provide the illustrative materials available.
3. Include crucial questions.
4. Consider the level of the ability and interests of the pupils.
5. Consult courses of study and grade requirement.
6. Select the best procedures.
7. Tie the lesson with previous ones.
8. Take into consideration the knowledge already possessed by pupils.
9. Include an appropriate assignment.
10. Consider supplementary materials in making the assignment.
11. Emphasise the main points of interest.
12. Give a logical, order to activities that would lead towards a realization of the aim of the lesson.
13. Provide for adequate summaries.
14. Make the plan flexible enough to allow the teacher to leave it temporarily and follow pupil interests.
15. Budget the time devoted to phases of the lesson.
16. Provide a means-for evaluating the results of the lesson and the teaching.

A Good Lesson Plan

Generally speaking the following are the characteristics of a good lesson plan:

1. *It should be written.* A lesson plan preferably be written and should not remain at the oral or mental stage. Panton writes, "The teacher is strongly advised, at least in the early stages, to make a written note of his preparation. Memory sometimes proves a treacherous servant, especially when his attention is divided." It is advisable, however, not to teach from notes, "Excessive reliance upon these may undermine the teacher's confidence so that he can never do without them. If, however, the teacher has occasion while teaching to refer to his notes, it is better, for him to do so openly than to take a suspicious look at them. He loses nothing in the eye of the children by the former method whereas by the second he is likely to be misjudged by his pupils." Writing helps in clarifying thoughts and concentration."
2. *It should have clear aims.* The lesson plan should clearly state the objectives, general and specific to be achieved.
3. *It should be linked with the previous knowledge.* The plan should not let the lesson remain as isolated one. It should have its basis on the background of the class. It should grow out of what the pupils have already learnt.
4. *It should show techniques of teaching.* It should state clearly the various steps that the teacher is going to take, and also various questions that he will ask.
5. *It should show the illustrate aids.* The illustrative aids to be used should be shown in the lesson plan.
6. *It should contain suitable subject matter.* The materials of instruction or subject matter should be carefully selected or organised.
7. *It should be divided into sections or units.* The plan should be divided into units; but care should be taken to see that the lesson remains an integrated whole and every unit develops from the previous and submerges into the next one.

8. *It should provide for activity.* The children must be given enough scope to be active. It should not make them mere passive listeners.
9. *It should provide for individual differences.* The plan should be prepared in such a way as it does full justice to all the students of varied abilities.
10. *It should show certain routine -things.* The plan should indicate the duration of the period, the period itself, average age of the students, subject and the class.
11. *It should be flexible.* The plan is a means and not an end. It is wrong to follow it slavishly. It is an instrument and should be used as such. The teacher should be prepared to change his teaching methods from those as referred to in the plan, if need be.
12. *It should include the summary.* The lesson plan should include the summary of the whole lesson which is to be developed on the blackboard with the help of students.
13. *It should refer to reference material.* The plan becomes more useful if it refers to other reading material. This will motivate the bright students to do extra reading. Care should be taken to suggest only that material which is available in the school library.
14. *It should include assignments for students.* A good lesson plan cannot be thought of without appropriate assignments for the students. Assignments can take different forms.
15. *It should provide for self-evaluation.* A good lesson plan must have a suitable plan for self-criticism. The, teacher should put some questions to himself and find out the answer and thereby judge the effectiveness of the lesson or otherwise.

Different Approaches

Following are the main approaches to lesson planning:

1. The Herbartian Approach or Five Steps Approach.
2. Gloverian Approach.
3. The Evaluation Approach.
4. Unit Approach or Morrisonian Approach.

5. Project Approach.
6. RCEM Approach.

Herbartian Approach

J.F. Herbart (1776-1841) and his followers developed the Five Steps Approach to lesson planning. To a great extent these steps are being followed with some modifications even today, Herbart propounded four steps: (1) Clearness, (2) Association, (3) System, (4) Method.

These names were changed by his disciples as given below:

1.	Clearness	to	Preparation
2.	Association	to	Presentation
3.	System	to	Abstract (Comparison and generalisation)
4.	Method	to	Application.

These were further modified as:

1. Preparation
2. Presentation
3. Association and Comparison
4. Generalisation.
5. Application.

Lesson Preparation

This step is concerned with the preparation of the mind of the students so that they may receive new knowledge. This is very essential both for the teacher as well the children. The teacher must know what the children have already learnt and assimilated. He must have an accurate idea of what the children already know. The children must be made to realize what they do not know so that they may have a desire to know more. Preparation is just like 'preparing the ground before sowing the seed in it'. Nothing is to be imparted in vacuum. The 'Apperceptive masses' must be brought to the forefront. J. Welton writes, "Let the teacher then as briefly and concisely as possible, pick up the thread of knowledge and get the pupils into the line of thought which lead from their present requirements to the new end. The better the teacher knows his class, the more accurately and quickly can he do this. This starting point must be known before the planning of the lesson can be profitably begun. It is this determination of the starting-point, this power of putting oneself in the mental place and attitude of the pupils, that marks off the true artist in teaching from the mere mechanical grinder of facts and formulae. To know where the pupils are and, where they should try to be are the two essentials of good teaching."

This step of preparation is also known as introduction.

Preparation means preparation on the part of the teacher as well as on the part of the students.

In preparation the 'will to learn' is arosed to some extent, whereas in motiviation, it is reinforced to a high degree.

Main Features

1. It should contain no new knowledge.
2. It should stimulate curiosity.
3. It should be as brief as possible.
4. Much time should not be devoted to this step.

How to start a Lesson

(a) We may start our lesson with the help of two or three interesting questions.
(b) We may start with the help of some aids, i.e., pictures, charts or models.
(c) We may put some questions on the subject-matter previously taught.
(d) We may start with the help of a situation. For examples in some topics we may take the situation of a co-operative store for profit and loss.
(e) We may start with the help of a relevant story.

The Statement

Announcement of the statement of the aim of the lesson in a clear, concise and specific form is very essential. It is necessary both for the teacher and pupils to know the general and specific aims of the lesson.

The form of the statement of the aim may be a brief question or a statement like this: "Today we shall study the role of the Reserve Bank of India."

Development of Lesson

It is here that the actual lesson is commenced. This step should involve a good deal of activity on the part of the students. The teacher will take the aid of various devices, e.g., questions, illustrations, explanations, exposition, demonstration and sensory aids etc. Information and knowledge may be given, explained, revealed or suggested.

The teacher should bear in mind the following principles at the presentation stage:

(i) *Principle of selection and division.* The material to be presented should be wisely and judiciously selected. It should be divided into different sections. The teacher should also decide as to how much he is to tell and how much the pupils are to find out for themselves.

(ii) *Principle of successive sequence.* The different sections should be well connected and should maintain a proper sequence. The teacher should ensure that the succeeding as well as the preceding knowledge is clear to the students.

(iii) *Principle of absorption and integration.* In the end separation of parts must be followed by the combination of the understanding of the whole.

Sometimes the word development is used in place of presentation as the term presentation smells of passivity. The term development of the lesson indicates the facts that there is pupil-teacher activity.

Association and Comparison

This step is related to the task of strengthening the acquisition of new material. New knowledge is to be presented to the children in such a way as it becomes associated with their previous knowledge or facts. The students are presented with new knowledge and are asked to observe it very carefully and to compare it with another set of facts and knowledge they already know. This helps to associate it with the old and thus to turn it into something new.

Generalisation

This step is concerned with the systematising of the knowledge learnt. Comparison and contrast lead to generalisation. In the inductive type of lessons the students are often required to establish some generalisations, rules or formulae. As far as possible, the teacher should see that the students draw out the conclusion themselves. If the generalisation is not the product of the student's own thinking, reflection or experience, it is of little value to them. The teacher should remain in the background. In the words of Ryburn, "It is bad teaching to give children ready-made general conclusions, concepts as we call them in psychology, which are founded on experiences of the child himself, on his own precepts... The child, with the teacher's help and guidance must be led to make his generalisations for himself ".

Application

Knowledge is power only when it is used and tested. T. Raymont writes, "The mere acquisition of rules, precepts, principles, definitions and laws makes directly for pedantry rather than for healthy mental development." The fundamental law of psychology regarding learning is that the consolidation of knowledge takes place only when the knowledge learnt is applied to similar situations. Knowledge when it is put to use and verified becomes clear and a part and parcel of the mental make-up.

The application also serves the purpose of revision and recapitulation of the principles learnt.

There is a difference between application and recapitulation. Recapitulation merely denotes revision or repetition of the knowledge learnt in the lesson whereas application requires a good deal of mental activity to think and apply the principles learnt to new situations.

Forms of Application

Following are the important forms of application:

1. Solving problems.
2. Drawing of maps, charts or models.
3. Writing of an essay.
4. Doing some practical work.
5. Setting of New Type Tests.

The Concept of Herbartian Steps

Merits

1. It assists in making teaching systematic. The teacher proceeds on well thought-out and definite lines.

2. It helps in avoiding unnecessary repetition in teaching.
3. It is useful in achieving the cognitive objective of teaching.
4. It makes use of the previous knowledge of the students for imparting new knowledge.
5. It employs the deductive and inductive methods of teaching.
6. It provides a useful framework, confidence and self-reliance by following these steps and thus makes teaching effective.

Demerits

1. The scheme being very much intellectual in character is suited to knowledge lesson only. The scheme is not so useful in the case of skill and appreciation lessons.
2. There is more stress on teaching rather than learning.
3. The term preparation has been used in a vague manner. Preparation may be concerned with both teachers as well as learners.
4. Generalisation is not so simple a process as is envisaged by Herbart. It is not possible to have this step in many cases.
5. The plan is rigid, stereotyped and mechanical in nature. This scheme does not provide for much thinking on the part of the students.
6. The term presentation has also been criticized as it speaks of inactivity on the part of the pupils.
7. Herbart was wrong to think that association was a distinct phase of the learning process. The fact is that this process of association and comparison in present from the very start of presentation.

Summary

After considering both pros and cons of the Herbartian steps, one tends to conclude that there is no doubt that the steps as suggested by Herbart are of great value. They present us an attempt to point out the need of an orderly and systematic arrangement of instruction based on sound psychological laws. Steps of preparation and application have been recognised as universally valid. Regarding the value of general rules relating to the teaching process, T. Raymont writes, "The young teacher cannot be too earnestly warned that for him the great thing is to appreciate the 'spirit' of the formal steps and how much does this mean. It means that, though all the steps and how much does this mean? It means that, though all the steps are not necessarily gone through in the treatment of any one section or unit of teaching, yet the 'order' in which steps occur cannot be departed from without disadvantage. That the acquisition of knowledge or of skill is a process of assimilation of new matter in the context of the old, that the relevant parts of the pupil's previously acquired stock of ideas should, therefore, first be recalled, that there should be a progress from the concrete and particular to the abstract and general, that ideas must be possessed before they can be applied, and that application in its turn makes for effective and permanent possession-these are truths as sure as the law of gravitation because they embody the plain facts of the working of a child's mind."

At another place Raymont writes, "Like the rules of any other art, however, the rules of the teaching art will not always be overtly employed. As soon as the teacher has thoroughly imbibed their spirit he may be left quite free to dispense with a formal array of preparation, presentation and the rest. Though the steps may no longer be explicitly stated or even thought of, they will always remain implicit in his best efforts, and he will be wise enough not to despise them because he has learnt to practise his art without conscious need of their help."

Gloverian View

A.H.T. Glover, in his book New Teaching for a New Age criticised Herbartain steps on the ground that these are stereotyped, gives less scope for pupil activity and fail to motivate students. If at all suitable, the Herbartian pattern is suitable in the case of academic subjects, and the 'verbal child'.

Glover's scheme is based on four points:

(a) Questioning,
(b) Discussion,
(c) Investigation,
(d) Pupil-activity.

Questioning. By a conscious process of good questioning, an intelligent teacher can lead his pupil through unfamiliar regions to a desired destination. The teacher should ask questions at different stages of the lesson. He should also encourage students to ask question.

Discussion. The next step is discussion. For this purpose it is better to divide the class into groups. The discussion should be directed in such a way as students are encouraged to express their ideas freely. Discussion should help the students to remove their difficulties.

Investigation. Investigation may be individual or group investigation. The students are required to investigate on the topics selected.

Pupil-Expression. This will be the last step. This should be in the form of practical activities. Glover classifies these as:

1. *Passive.* Here emphasis is on observing and listening.
2. *Active.* Activities may take the form of handwork, craft work, gardening, drawing etc.
3. *Artistic or Recreative.* This includes activities like dancing, music and acting.
4. *Organisational.* This aspect may be present in the above activities.

Morrison's View

This approach is associated with the name of Professor H.C. Morrison (1871-1945) of the University of Chicago. Morrison has explained the Unit Method in detail in his book The Practice of Teaching in Secondary Schools (1926). The unit method is very popular, and frequently used in the U.S.A. The unit approach is based on the growing acceptance of the Gestalt-Organismic-Field Theories of learning which emphasise the 'wholeness' nature of learning. This approach is contrary to the older atomistic conception of learning according to which learning was a matter of adding one small item of knowledge to another bit by bit. The new approach is based upon the assumption that effective learning takes places in an environment in which the goals are clearly perceived and every phase of the operational procedure is viewed as a relational part of the total learner situation. The underlying assumption is that the learner reacts to the situation as a whole and not to parts in isolation.

Definition

A unit may be defined "as a means of organising materials for instructional purposes which utilises significant subject matter content, involves pupils in learning activities through active participation intellectually and physically and modifies the pupil's behaviour to the extent that he is able to cope with new problems and situations more competently."

Major Elements

A good teaching unit has nine elements but the sequence of those elements is not fixed. Following sequences is generally followed:

1. ***Overview.*** This implies the consideration of the needs of the students while formulating the objectives of teaching unit.
2. ***Inventory or background or exploration.*** This element is concerned with exploring the entering behaviour of the students. The teacher is required to establish the behaviour repertoire by linking the new knowledge with the previous knowledge of the students.
3. ***Presentation.*** This element is concerned with providing new experiences to the learners. It includes an analysis and presentation of the elements of teaching units in a logical sequence so that they are helpful to the students. With a view to encourage students participation in teaching, question-answer strategy is employed.
4. ***Motivation.*** This element of the teaching unit is concerned with the creation of motivational situations to facilitate learning.
5. ***Summarization.*** This element of the unit is concerned with providing a summary of the unit.
6. ***Drill.*** This element provides an opportunity to the students for drill or practice which enables them to retain longer what is learnt.
7. ***Review.*** This implies giving the salient features of the unit orally.

8. ***Organisation.*** This element involves giving assignments to the students to organise their learning experiences of their own.
9. ***Evaluation.*** This element of the teaching unit consists of ascertaining how far the teacher has been successful in achieving the objectives of the lesson, i.e., to what extent students have grasped the content and developed meaningful behaviour.

Merits

1. It is based on Gestalt Psychology which emphasises the 'Wholeness' nature of learning.
2. Since the subject matter is divided into small units, it leads to easy comprehension. .
3. In the unit approach, learning does not remain just 'memorisation'. It develops understanding.
4. On account of the delimitation of the learning contents and specification of the unit objectives, teaching and learning becomes more objective.
5. Division of the learning material into small units and subunits makes the task of teaching- learning easy, interesting and simple.
6. All the steps in the unit approach are directed to achieve the desired mastery.
7. This approach encourages the habit of independent and self-study among the students.
8. By providing adequate opportunities to the students to remain active, this approach leads to healthy interaction between the students and teachers.
9. Learning process becomes organised, systematic and sequenced.

Demerits

1. Unit approach is time consuming.
2. This approach is more suitable in the case of intelligent students.
3. This approach puts heavy demands upon teachers.
4. The present day syllabus is very heavy and with this approach it is very difficult to complete the entire syllabus in time.

The Evaluation

B.S. Bloom of the U.S.A. is the orginator of this approach. According to this approach, teaching activities must be objective centred. Bloom considers education as a tripolar process, educational objectives; learning experiences and change of behaviour. This approach is 'objective-centred' rather than 'content-centred'. It is diagrammatically represented as under:

EDUCATIONAL
OBJECTIVES

LEARNING
EXPERIENCE

BEHAVIOUR
CHANGES

Steps in Lesson Planning:

This approach involves the following points:

1. *Formulation of objectives in behavioural terms.* (Discussed separately)
2. *Providing learning experiences.* It includes teachers' activities, pupils' activities and teaching aids.
3. *Evaluating the learning outcomes.* It is concerned with the evaluation devices or techniques used in finding out the extent to which stipulated objectives have been realised.

Bloom's View

1. It provides for specific objectives in behavioural terms.
2. It mentions separately the activities of the teachers and the students.
3. It appropriately presents the contents or learning experiences through the teaching points.
4. The specific aid material, methods, and strategies used for the realization of the pre-determined objectives are properly mentioned.
5. It lays due stress on the evaluation of the desired behavioural changes.
6. It is based on sound psychological principles and theories of teaching and learning.

The Criticism

The task of integration among behavioural objectives, learning experiences and evaluation devices puts heavy demands on teachers and the students.

This approach does not take into account the mental processes or mental abilities for writing out the educational objectives.

This is a highly structured approach and dominated by the role of the teacher in the teaching learning process.

This approach makes the task of lesson planning quite rigid and mechanical.

Project Approach

This approach developed by John Dewey and W.H. Kilpatrick stresses self-activity, social activities and real life activities.

RCEM Approach

This approach to lesson planning has been developed at the Regional College of Education, Mysore and accordingly it is known as RECM Approach.

This approach makes use of the concept of systems approach to education. The three main steps involved in this approach are: Input, Process and Output. The three aspects are as under:

Expected Behaviour Outcomes-EBOS

Communication Strategy—CS

Real Learning Outcomes-RLOS

Input step is concerned with the identification and specification of the educational objectives. It also includes the identification of the entering behaviour of the students. The objectives are written in behaviour terms. Input step resembles the 'introduction' step.

Process resembles the 'presentation' step of Herbartian approach. It represents the interaction process of the classroom. It includes activities of the teachers as well students and teaching strategies.

Demerits

1. It is more suitable to Indian schools as it has been developed in this country.

2. Objectives are stated in terms of measurable abilities and mental process.
3. Teaching-learning situations, strategies, aids and materials are properly stated.
4. Evaluation aspect is properly taken care of.

Limitations of RCEM Approach

1. It is very tedious to write lesson plan of this type.
2. It is time consuming.
3. Very little literature is available on this approach.

Eclectic Approach

Herbartian approach is limited to the realization of the congnitive objective and is hardly feasible in skill and appreciation lesson. Evaluation approach has a wider scope. Both approaches are highly structured, and teacher-dominated.

Evaluation approach is based upon sound psychological principles of learning but it is very difficult to follow in the normal classroom set-up. It needs more expertise on the part of the teachers. Herbartian approach, on the other hand, is simple and can be easily followed.

We should be practical in our approach and try to pick-up the good points of every approach and apply them suiting our classroom environment. We need a harmonious blending of all the approaches, as far as possible. The crucial point in that we follow an approach which makes our students active participants in the teaching-learning process and makes it effective and meaningful.

Notes.

1. Student-teachers are advised to follow the guidelines and the formal of the lesson plan recommended by their supervisors and teachers.
2. In very rare circumstances to meet the extraordinary situation in the class, the pupil-teacher may make a total departure from the lesson plan.
3. A lesson plan based on instructional behavioural objectives will be quite different.

4. A revision lesson will have a different lesson plan.
5. As far as possible, at the presentation or development stage of the lesson, it should be avoided to ask questions from the students from the subject-matter which is yet to be taught.

Steps in Daily Lesson Plan and their Significance

Steps	*Significance*
1. Title of the topic	For taking up the lesson in a definite framework.
2. Objectives of the lesson	For pin-pointing the learning outcomes so that these could be measured after teaching the lesson.
3. Teaching aids	For making teaching-learning more effective and at the same time making enjoyable.
4. Previous knowledge	For serving as a base for the lesson.
5. Statement of the aim (Preparation)	For preparing students for new learning and focusing their attention on a specific aim.
6. Presentation	For teaching the topic and giving new knowledge and understanding. It is infact the heart of the lesson.
7. Application	For providing opportunities to apply the newly acquired knowledge and understanding.
8. Recapitulation	For finding out whether learning has taken place or not. This is also necessary for feedback.
9. Blackboard summary	For focusing attention on fundamentals of the lesson.
10. Home assignment	For reinforcement, practice and evaluation.

QUESTIONS

1. State the significance of lesson planning. Explain the general principles of planning a lesson.

2. Why should a teacher prepare his lesson? What main points should be considered in this regard?
3. State in brief various approaches to lesson planning. Which of these approaches do you like most? Give reasons.
4. Explain the meaning of a lesson plan. Prepare a lesson plan in Commerce on any topic of your choice.

20

Lesson Plans Suggested

LESSON PLAN NO. 1

Roll No. of the Student-teacher	Name
School	Class XI Period
Strength of the Class	Duration of the Period
Subject	Commerce (Business Studies)
Topic	Economic Activities and Business
Date	

Teaching Aids Chart showing different kinds of activities.

Common Objectives

1. To develop in the students an interest in the theory and practice in business, trade and industry.
2. To acquaint students with the theoretical foundations and practices of organising, managing and handling routine operations of a business firm.
3. To inculcate attitudes and values leading to the integration of business with the social system with a positive approach.
4. To enable students to apply the principles and functions of management to specific aspects of business.
5. To equip the students with essential fundamental knowledge for setting up organising and handling routine operations of a small scale factory.
6. To equip the students with basic information on modern methods of office operations for effectively carrying out paper work in a business office.

7. To impart knowledge of methods considered useful in maintaining records of proprietory and partnership firms, companies and non-trading organisations.
8. To generate and promote awareness of students in modern techniques of maintaining accounting records with the help of computers.

Significant Objectives

To enable the students to understand the meaning and types of economic activities.

Previous Knowledge assumed

The students are aware of the day-to-day activities of the people living in a community.

Introduction

1. State the main activity of a carpenter.
2. State the main activity of a mother who is not working anywhere.

Statement of the aim

Well, students today we shall learn about economic activities.

Recapitulation

1. Define an economic activity.
2. State the difference between and economic and non-economic activity.

Blackboard Summary

A chart showing different types of activities divided into business, profession, and service will be drawn on the black-board.

Assignments

1. Write down the difference between economic and non-economic activities.
2. Differentiate between a profession and service.

Project Work

1. Prepare a list of 10 economic activities carried on in your locality.
2. List 5 professions.
3. List three activities which can be categorised as economic or non-economic activity depending upon their nature in different situations.

Development of the Lesson

Matter	*Method*
Meaning of human activities. Human activities are activities in which human beings are engaged to satisfy material and social needs. Economic activities are undertaken by human beings for earning wealth and money for the satisfaction of their day-to-day needs.	Lesson will be developed with the help of the following questions put to students. Find out the difference in the activities of the following: (a) A cricket player plays a friendly cricket match. (b) A cricket player plays a test match at Sharjah.
Human activities Economic Non-Economic	(c) Jawaharlal Nehru fought for the freedom of the country.
In an economic activity, main thrust is on wealth and satisfaction of material needs.	(d) Jawaharlal Nehru worked as the Prime Minister and got some salary. (e) A mother looks after her baby. as economic or non-economic.
Broad Classification of Economic *Activities* 1. Business 2. Employment 3. Profession	(f) A maid-servant looks after the baby. (g) A school where fee is charged. (h) A school without fee. Methodology of Teaching
1. A business activity creates utility by producing goods or services to satisfy human wants.	1. Use of deductive method. Students will be asked to name a few activities and thereafter economic activities will be broadly classified.
2. In employment (Service) a person undertakes to work for another according to the terms of an agreement in return for salary, or wage or commission.	2. An element of play-way will be introduced in the lesson. 3. Teacher will explain the term economic activity on the basis of the replies of the students.
3. Profession is an occupation which renders specialised, expert and personal service to the members of society in return of reasonable remuneration.	Students will be asked to classify the given activities on the blackboard into business, profession and service. 4. A chart showing economic and non-economic activities will be shown or drawn on the blackboard.

LESSON -PLAN NO. 2

Roll No. of the Student-teacher	Name
School	Class XI Period
Strength of the Class	Duration of the Period
Subject	Commerce (Business Studies)
Topic	Meaning and Definition of Business
Teaching Aids	Copy of a Business Deed.

General Objectives

1. To develop in the students an interest in the theory and practice in business, trade and industry.
2. To acquaint students with the theoretical foundations and practices of organising, managing and handling routine operations of a business firm.
3. To inculcate attitudes and values leading to the integration of business with the social system with a positive approach.
4. To enable students to apply the principles and functions of management to specific aspects of business.
5. To equip the students with essential fundamental knowledge for setting up, organising and handling routine operations of a small scale factory.
6. To equip the students with basic information on modern methods of office operations for effectively carrying out paper work in a business office.
7. To impart knowledge of methods considered useful in maintaining records of proprietory and partnership firms, companies and non-trading organisations.
8. To generate and promote awareness of students in modern techniques of maintaining accounting records with the help of computers.

Instructional Objectives

1. To acquire the knowledge of facts, terms, concepts, conventions, trends, principles, generalisations, assumptions, hypothesis, processes etc. in commerce.
2. To develop understanding of facts, terms, concepts, conventions, trends, principles, generalisations, assumptions, hypotheses, processes, etc. in commerce.

3. To apply the acquired knowledge of business and its understanding to familiar situations.
4. To acquire practical skills essential for the study of commerce.
5. To develop interest in the subject and problems related to commerce and commercial life of the people of one's country and of those of the world.
6. To develop desirable positive attitudes necessary for developing a broader outlook as a commerce entrepreneur and as a citizen.

Specifications of Instructional Objectives

The pupils:

1. Recalls the meaning of business;
2. Understands the meaning of business;
3. Defines the term business;
4. Lists the features of business activity;
5. Analyses the features of a business activity;
6. Illustrates the term business;
7. Compares business with profession;
8. Draws a chart on the characteristics of business;
9. Visits business organisations;
10. Read articles or books on business organisations.

Presentation Development of the Lesson

Specifications	*Content/Matter*	*Method/Learning Experiences*
Recalls	Meaning of an economic activity-an activity in which man is engaged to earn wealth.	Q. Name any two activities. With the help of the answer given by the students, the teacher will explain the meaning of a business activity.
Recognises	Business is an economic activity which involves the use of resources. Resources are scarce. Business activity is concerned with transfer, purchase, production and distribution of goods and services with the object of earning profits for the satisfaction of human wants.	Lesson will be developed with the help of the following questions: 1. Name two economic activities. 2. Name the economic activities carried on in your locality. 3. State the categories of persons involved in economic activities.

Specifications	*Content/Matter*	*Method/Learning Experiences*
Table Cond.		
Defines	The term business activity may be defined as a human activity directed towards producing or acquiring wealth through buying and selling of goods.	Explanation will be furnished by the teacher. 1. State the features of a person who is engaged in service.
Lists	**Features of Business** 1. It is an economic activity. 2. It involves the transfer, production or purchase and distribution. 3. It deals in goods and services. 4. It implies regularity of transactions 5. It involves risk taking. 6. It involves profit making. 7. People are important and crucial part of business.	2. Is there any risk of loss of income in service? 3. Is there any major increase in income?
Analyses	1. It is an economic activity as earning wealth is involved. 2. In order to effect sale or transfer, the seller must possess required goods and services. 3. Professional services do not form part of business goods. 4. Profit is the reward of time, money and effort invested in the business. 5. 'No risk', 'no gain 6. Business is conducted through the efforts of human beings.	1. Is a teacher a businessman? 2. Is a chartered accountant a business man? 3. If I purchase a house, sell it for a profit, is it a business? Give reasons for your answer.
	Recapitulation 1. Explain the term business 2. Mention any three features of business.	
Illustrates	Examples taken of sole traders, Business House, Pan shop etc.	
Compares	**Business** 1. No formal educational qualification. 2. No special expertise needed. 3. Generally no code of ethics.	Tata's example Birla's example

Specifications	*Content/Matter*	*Method/Learning Experiences*
Table Cond.		
	Profession	
	1. Usually formal qualification are needed.	1. Does a trader need any educational qualification
	2. Special knowledge and expertise is needed.	2. Does a doctor need any educational qualification?
	3. Generally code of ethics is needed.	3. Does a trader get a fixed salary?
Draws a chart	The students draw a chart on the features of business.	
Visits	The teacher arranges a visit to a big business house.	
Reads	Students are asked to collect and reads deeds on business.	

Recapitulation

1. Define business.
2. Differentiate between business and profession.

Assignments

1. Collect articles from business magazines.
2. Visit a business organisation and observe its functioning.

Blackboard summary

With the help of these two questions, the teacher prepares the black-board summary.

LESSON PLAN NO. 3

Date	R.No.	Name
School		Class XI
Strength of the Class		Duration of the Period
Subject		Commerce (Business Studies)
Topic		Difference between Business and other Activities
Teaching aids.		A chart showing comparison of business and other economic activities

General Objectives of Teaching

1. To develop in the students an interest in the theory and practice in business, trade and industry.

2. To acquaint students with the theoretical foundations and practices of organising, managing and handling routine operations of a business firm.
3. To inculcate attitudes and values leading to the integration of business with the social system with a positive approach.

Instructional Objectives

1. To acquire the knowledge of facts, terms, concepts, hypotheses, trends, principles, generalisations, assumptions, hypothesis, processes etc. regarding between business and other economic activities.
2. To develop understanding of facts, terms, concepts, conventions,, trends, principles, generalisations,, assumptions, hypotheses, processes, etc. regarding business and other activities.
3. To apply the 'acquired knowledge of economic activities, business activities in practical life and its understanding to familiar situations.
4. To acquire practical skills essential for the study of business activities.
5. To develop interest in the subject and problems related to business activities of life of the people of our country and those of the world.
6. To develop desirable positive attitudes necessary for developing a broader outlook as a businessman and as a citizen.

Specifications of Instructional Objectives

Their pupil :

1. Recalls the meaning of business and other economic activities;
2. Understands the meaning of business and other activities;
3. Defines the term business and other economic activities;
4. Lists the features of business activities;
5. Illustrates the term business activities;
6. Analyses business and other economic activities;
7. Compares business and other economic activities;
8. Draws a chart on the characteristics of business and economic activities;

9. Visits business concerns;
10. Reads articles or books relating to the topic.

LESSON PLAN NO. 4

Enrolment No:

Name:	Class: XI	
Period:	Date	
Time: 40 minutes	Subject:	Commerce
Topic:	History of Development of Commerce	

General Aim: To make the pupils aware of the stages of development of Commerce.

Specific Aim: To enable the students understand how Commerce started, developed and reached the present stage.

Teaching Aids:

1. Chart depicting stages of commerce development.
2. Pictures of old machines.

Previous Knowledge Assumed: Students are acquainted with the concept and meaning of Commerce.

Introduction: (i) What is meant by Commerce?

(ii) What is the significance of Commerce?

Statement of the Aim: Today we will take up the various stages of development of Commerce.

Presentation: Lesson will be developed as under.

Matter	*Method*
Section I	
Stage of self-suffiency Man as a wanderer and hunter. Very few needs lived a very simple life. No trade or exchange of goods and services.	1. How did the primitive man live? 2. What did he do for his living?
Agricultural stage Gradually man learnt how to grow crops-settled at a certain place. Occupations like carpenters, weavers and blacksmiths etc. developed. Division of labour among members of society grew.	1. What are the chief characteristics of modern agriculture? 2. Can an individual meet all his own needs by producing everything that he needs. 3. Why does he depends upon others?
Section II	
Barter stage One family had to depend for various needs upon other families.	1. Why do we use money only? 2. Why can't we exchange goods for goods?

Matter	Method
Contd. Exchange of goods-barter system. However barter system was subject to several difficulties. 1. Lack of double coincidence of wants. 2. Lack of common measure of value. 3. Non-subdivision of certain commodities.	3. How can we determine the value of a commodity in terms of another? (These points will be explained to the students with the help of the above-mentioned questions).
Storage and transportation It was not possible to store all commodities for a long time at one place. It was also difficult to transport. Hence the scope of commerce remained limited.	1. What were the earlier means of storage of commodites? 2. What were the earlier means of transportation? 1. Why was the scope of commerce limited in earlier times ?
Discovery of money With a view to overcoming the difficulties of barter, some commonly acceptable medium of exchange came to be introduced. This was money. In the beginning things like stone, cattle, pieces of metals etc. were used as money. With the passage of time metal coins were introduced. Then paper currency beagan to used.	2. What the various types of money used these days? Recapitulation 1. What did the primitive man do for his living? 2. What is barter system? 3. What are the difficulties in the barter system?
Section III	
Industrial Revolution England is the starting point of Industrial Revolution. New dimensions to Commerce. Drastic changes. Increased production. Factory system. Increased use of machinery. Increased importance of industry in place of agriculture. New products in the markets. Need for new markets. Need for quick means of transport. International trade. Colonial rule.	1. What is the difference between a cottage industry and large scale industry? 2. What is the result of increased production on Commerce? (Pictures of early machines will be shown to the students.)

Recapitulation

1. Explain the stages of the development of Commerce.
2. What is industrial revolution? What changes were brought about by Industrial Revolution?

3. Why was Industrial Revolution also called as Commercial Revolution?

Blackboard summary

This will be prepared on the following bases:

1. Stages of the development of Commerce.
2. Effects of Industrial Revolution on Commerce.

Home Assignment

1. Describe the various stages of the development of Commerce.

LESSON PLAN NO. 5

Date	Enrolment No.	
Name	School	Class XI
Strength	Period	Duration 40 minutes
Subject	Commerce (Business Studies)	
Topic	Nature and Causes of Business Risk.	
Teaching aid	Chart will be drawn on the Blackboard illustrating the causes.	

General Objectives of Teaching. As in previous lesson plans.

Instructional Objectives

1. Acquires knowledge about the terms and concept of business risks
2. Understands the terms and concepts of business risks
3. Applies the knowledge in practical life.
4. Develops skill in drawing a chart.
5. Develops interest in business.

Specifications

The pupil:

1. Recalls the term business.
2. Recognises the meaning of business risks.
3. Lists the characteristics of business risks.
4. Enumerate the causes of business risk.
5. Explains the types of business risk.
6. Illustrates business risk.
7. Suggests measures to avoid business risks.
8. Draws a chart showing causes of business risk.

Recapitulation

1. Define the term business risks and its characteristics.
2. Enumerate the causes of business risk.

Assignment

1. What measures would you take to minimise business risks?

Development of the Lesson

Specifications	*Content*	*Method/Learning Experiences*
Recalls	The term business. It is an economic activity which is concerned with the transfer, production, purchase and distribution of goods and services with the object of learning profit.	What do you understand by business? With the help of the following questions, the teacher will explain the term business risks.
Recognises	Business risk refers to the possibility of inadequate profits or losses due to uncertainties or unexpected events which are beyond control.	1. Why is there not always a surety of profit in a business?
Lists down	The characteristics of business risk an essential element of business-uncertainty due to action of human beings lock outs, strikes-profit is the reward for risk bearing-higher the risk, higher the profit-variability degree of risk varies with a) size of firm. b) nature of business c) time.	2. Cite some examples with the help of the following questions, the teacher will explain the term business risks. Lecture Method will be followed to explain. Suppose you are a businessman manufacturing woolen clothes, enumerate the risks involved.
Enumerates	Causes of business risks. – Uncertainties relating to demand for goods, prices, exchange rates affecting costs of imports & exports, govt. control, change in technology. – Unforseen losses due to theft, fire and natural calamities. – Unexpected events like stoppage of work due to power failure strike etc. – Factors affecting availability of funds like changes in interest rates taxes. – Risks regarding political situation – Loss of property on account of misappropriation or embezzlement – Risk of bad debt.	

Project/Practical work

Contact any shopkeeper/businessman and find out if he has undergone any business losses and the reasons thereof.

LESSON PLAN NO. 6

Enrolment No.	Name
School	Class
Strength of the class	Date
Period	Time
Subject	Commerce (Business Studies)
Topic	Social Responsibility
Teaching aid	A chart on for and against social responsibility.

Instructional Objectives

The pupil:

1. Acquires knowledge about the terms and concept of social responsibility.
2. Understands the terms and concepts relating to social responsibility.
3. Applies the knowledge in practical life.
4. Develops skill in drawing a chart.
5. Develops interest in social responsibility.

Specifications

The pupil:

Recalls the meaning of business objectives.

Recognises the meaning of social responsibility.

Defines the term social responsibility.

Analyses the case for assumption of social responsibility.

Recapitulation

1. Define the term social responsibility.
2. What kind of regulations can be enforced by the government on business concerns?
3. Is it in the interest of the business itself to undertake social responsibility? Explain.
4. What do you understand by public image?

Blackboard Summary. Teacher will draw the chart illustrating reasons for the assumption of social responsibility by a business concern.

Assignment. Explain the term social responsibility of business. Why should a business assume social responsibility?

Project/Practical Work

1. Visit a big business firm and find out if it has undertaken some welfare measures.

Development of the Lesson

Specifications	*Content*	*Learning Experiences/Methods to be adopted in the development of the lessons*
Recalls	Objectives of business activities can be classified under three heads: economic, social and human. A balance has to be struck among them.	With the help of the following questions, the teacher will develop the lesson. 1. Why should we have ?
Recalls	Objectives of business activties can be classified under three heads: economic, social and human. A balance has to be struck among them.	With the help of the following questions, the teacher will develop the lesson. 1. Why should we have objectives in life ?
Recognises	Meaning of social responsibility. It implies the responsibility of business to act in the manner which will best serve the interests of society. society? adopted in the development of the lesson	2. What are your objectives? 3. Can a person live alone? If not why? 4. Do we have any responsibility towards
Defines	In the real sense, social responsibility implies the recognition and understanding of the aspirations of a society and determination to contribute in its achievement.	5. Why should business have responsibility towards society? 6. State the circumstances under which a business can flouish.
Analyses	Case for assumption of social responsibility. 1. Long term interest of the business-every business is a part of the society and must consider the needs of the society before using profits for its own benefit.	7. How is business affected by instability? 8. Which is the most popular shop of provisions in your locality? 9. When does the government interfere in the affairs of business firm?

2. Public image-a business firm or company having goodwill will always the and help in increasing its earnings.
3. Avoidance of governmental interference.
4. Moral justification.
5. Consumer's consciousness.
6. Interdependence of various factors involved in running a business.

10. What does happen to a business of the consumers are not satisfied?
11. Why do business concerns adopt charitable measures?

LESSON PLAN NO. 7

Enrolment No.	Name	
School	Class XI	Strength
Date	Time 40 minutes ·	Period
Subject	Commerce (Business Studies)	
Topic	Objectives of Business	

Teaching aids. Chart to be drawn on the blackboard.

General objectives of Teaching Commerce. Same as in previous lesson plans.

Specific Objectives. To enable the students understand the objectives of carrying on a business. Previous knowledge:

1. The students have studied the meaning of business.
2. The students understand the meaning of business activities.

Introduction

1. Explain the term business.
2. Differentiate between economic and non-economic activities.

Presentation

Matter	*Method*
Broadly speaking objectives of business may be classified under three heads: 1. Economic objectives 2. Social objectives 3. Human objectives *Economic objectives of business* 1. Earning profits. 2. Expansion or growth of business.	1. Why should we have some objective in undertaking an activity? 2. Why do we undertake some economic activity? 3. What do you understand by social responsibility? 4. Why does a person take up any business?

Matter	*Method*
Contd.	
3. Creation of customers.	5. Do you think that apart from
4. Facing competition.	profit, there are other
5. Innovation introducing new products	objectives of business?
or making existing products more useful.	6. If so, what are the other
6. Making the 'best' possible use of	objectives?
economic resources.	
Social objectives	7. Why should a business
1. Generating employment.	concern not charge
2. Producing better quality goods.	unreasonable prices?
3. Availability of goods at reasonable	8. How is business helpful to
prices.	generate employment?
4. Enabling people to have a better	9. Why should a business
standard of living.	concern produce quality
5. Helping in reducing concentration of	goods?
wealth.	10. What happens if employees
6. Practising fair trade practices.	do not enjoy job satisfaction?
7. Worker's participation in management.	11. What will be the
	consequences if the workers
Human objectives	are not paid reasonable
1. Job satisfaction	wages ?
2. Fair wages to workers	12. What can be the effects of
3. Better working conditions.	unhygienic conditions of
4. Humane treatment with workers.	work ?

Recapitulation

1. Explain the difference between economic and social objectives of business.
2. Why should a business concern look after the human aspects of workers?

Home Assignment

Write an essay on objectives of business.

Project/Practical work

Visit any business concern and find out the welfare amenities provided to its workers.

LESSON PLAN NO. 8

Enrolment No. Name
School Class
Strength Period
Duration

Date	Time
Subject	Commerce
Topic	Auxiliaries to Business Activity

General Objectives of Teaching

1. To develop in the students an interest in the theory and practice in business, trade and industry.
2. To acquaint students with the theoretical foundations and practices of organising, managing and handling routine operations of a business firm.
3. To inculcate, attitudes and values leading to the integration of business with the social system with a positive approach.
4. To enable students to apply the principles and functions of management to specific aspects of business.
5. To equip the students with essential fundamental knowledge for setting up, organising and handling routine operations of a small scale factory.
6. To equip the students with basic information on modern methods of office operations for effectively carrying out paper work in a business office.
7. To impart knowledge of methods considered useful in maintaining records of proprietory and partnership firms, companies and non-trading organisations.
8. To generate and promote awareness of students in modern techniques of maintaining accounting records with the help of computers.

Assumption of Previous Knowledge

Students have learnt the nature and meaning of an economic and business activity.

Instructional Objectives of Teaching

1. To acquire the knowledge of facts, terms concepts, conventions, trends, principles, generalisations, assumptions, hypothesis, processes etc. regarding auxiliaries to business activity.
2. To develop understanding of facts, terms, concepts, conventions, trends, principles, generalisations, assumptions, hypotheses, processes, etc. regarding auxiliaries to business activity.

3. To apply the acquired knowledge to business auxiliaries activity and its understanding to familiar situations.
4. To acquire practical skills essential for the study of auxiliaries to business activity.
5. To develop interest in the subject and problems related to auxiliaries to business activity in the life of the people of our country and those of the world.
6. To develop desirable positive attitudes necessary for developing a broader outlook as an entrepreneur and as a citizen.

Specification of Instructional Objectives

1. Recalls the meaning of auxiliaries to business activity.
2. Understands the meaning of auxiliaries to business activity.
3. Defines the term auxiliaries to business activity.
4. Lists the features of auxiliaries to business activity.
5. Analyses the features of auxiliaries to business activity.
6. Illustrates the term auxiliaries to business activity.
7. Compares economic activity and auxiliaries to business activity.
8. Draws a chart on the characteristics of auxiliaries to business activity.
9. Visits some concerns/firms relating to auxiliaries to business activity.
10. Reads articles or books on auxiliaries to business activity.

Presentation

Matter	*Method*
1. Auxiliaries to business activity are those activities which assist business. They play a supporting role. Without them, business can hardly take place in the modern world in which business activities have become very complex.	Lesson will be developed with the help of following questions: 1. What is the source of sugar you use everyday? 2. How does the agriculturist send the sugarcane to the mill?
2. Auxiliaries to business activity are. 1. Warehouses; 2. Insurance;	3. Where is sugarcane stored? 4. What are the risks involved in the production of sugarcane

3. Banking; 4. Transport; 5. Advertising.	and sugar? 5. How can such risks be minimised?
Warehouses. Storage of goods help price stabilisation and prevent damage of goods.	6. From where does the farmer get finance? 7. From where does the mill owner get finances?
Insurance. It protects against business risks, weather risks.	8. Why do manufacturers or dealers advertises ?
Banking. Helps business activities by providing financial assistance.	How does transport help in trade?
Transport. It helps in the movement of goods and passengers from one place to another. Internal and external trade.	9. How does advertisement promote business?
Advertising. It provides information to the customers about the availability, uses and quality of goods to induce them to buy particular goods.	10. What are the various forms of advertisements? 11. What are the auxiliaries to learning activity?

Recapitulation

1. How do warehouses help?
2. Why do we insure goods?
3. What facilities are provided by the bankers which help business?
4. What is the purpose of advertisement?

Blackboard Summary. The teacher draws a chart on the blackboard showing auxiliaries to business activity.

Home Assignment. Discuss the importance of auxiliaries to trade.

Project/Practical Work. Visit an advertising/ insurance or transport company and find out how it helps business.

LESSON PLAN NO. 9

Enrolment No.	Name
School	Class
Strength	Period
Time	Date
Subject	Commerce (Business Studies)
Topic	Trade and its Classification

Teaching Aids. Chart showing classification of Trades.

Objectives of Teaching Commerce—As in other lessons.

Previous Knowledge Assumed—Students understand the meaning of business and business activities.

Instructional Objectives

1. To acquire the knowledge of facts, terms, concepts, conventions, trends, principles, generalisations, assumptions, hypotheses, processes etc. in trade.
2. To develop understanding of facts, terms, concepts, conventions, trends, principles, generalisations, assumptions, hypotheses, processes, etc. in trade.
3. To apply the acquired knowledge of trade and its classification and its understanding to familiar situation.
4. To acquire practical skills essential for the study of trade.
5. To develop interest in the subject and problems related to trade and its classification to life of the people of one's country and those of the world.
6. To develop desirable positive attitudes necessary for developing a broader outlook as a trader and as a citizen.

Specification of Instructional Objectives

1. Recalls the meaning of various types of trade.
2. Understands the meaning of various types of trade.
3. Defines the term various types of trade.
4. Lists the features of various types of trade.
5. Analyses the features of various types of trade.
6. Illustrates the features of various types of trade.
7. Compares various types of trade.
8. Draws a chart on the characteristics of various types of trade.
9. Visits of trade establishments.
10. Reads articles or books trade.

Development of the Lesson

Matter	*Method*
1. Meaning of trade. Trade means dealing in buying, selling, transferring and exchanging of goods and services. Trade and its classification Home or Internal External or Foreign Retail Whole Import Export	The teacher will develop the lesson with the help of the following questions. 1. What is commerce? 2. What is the difference between the activities of a shopkeeper and a manufacturer of toys.

Matter	*Method*
Contd.	
	3. Give examples of trading
Retail trade refers to the sale of goods in small quantities. A retail dealer deals in a variety or different lines of products.	4. Name some of the articles that are not manufactured in your state.
Wholesale trade involves buying goods from the producers or manufacturers in large quantities and selling in small quantities to traders.	5. Do you use articles produced in other countries? 6. Name some of the articles. 7. Name some of the articles that we send abroad.
Import. Purchase of goods from another country.	8. What are the advantages in buying goods in bulk?
Export. Sale of goods to another country.	9. Give some examples of wholesale markets.
Entrepot. Importing goods for the purpose of exporting goods to third country.	10. Why do we import articles from other countries?
Difference between wholesale and retail trade.	11. Why do we export articles to other countries?
	12. What differences do you find when you buy goods in bulk and in small quantity?

Wholesale	**Retail**
1. Dealing in large quantities	1. Small quantities
2. Single product line of products	2. Large variety
3. Usually credit basis	3. Usually no credit basis
4. Large storage facilities	4. Mini storage
5. Large capital	5. Small capital

Recapitulation

1. State the meaning of trade.
2. What is the difference between home trade and foreign trade?
3. What are the merits of wholesale trade?
4. Is foreign trade essential for a country? Give arguments.

Home Assignment

1. Differentiate between home trade and foreign trade.
2. Differentiate between wholesale and retail trade.

Project/Practical work

1. Prepare a list of wholesale traders of your locality.
2. Prepare a list of 5 articles that we import from other countries.

3. Find out the government sponsored organisations that deal with some goods of foreign trade.

LESSON PLAN NO. 10

Enrolment No.	Name	
School	Class XI	
Strength of the class	Period	
Duration Forty minutes	Time	Date
Subject	Commerce (Business Studies)	
Topic	Industry and its Classification	

Teaching Aids. Chart showing the classification of industry and products.

General Objectives of Teaching Commerce. As in other lessons.

Instructional Objectives

1. To acquire the knowledge of facts, terms, concepts, conventions, trends, principles, generalisations, assumptions, hypotheses, processes etc. of industry.
2. To develop understanding of facts, terms, concepts, conventions, trends, principles, generalisations, assumptions, hypotheses, processes, etc. of industry.
3. To apply the acquired knowledge of industry and its understanding to familiar situation.
4. To acquire practical skills essential for the study of industry.
5. To develop interest in the subject and problems related to the industrial life of the people of one's country and of those of others.
6. To develop desirable positive attitudes necessary for developing a broader outlook as a commerce entrepreneur and as a citizen.

Specification of Instructional Objectives

1. Recalls the meaning of an industry.
2. Understands the meaning of an industry.
3. Defines the term an industry.
4. Lists the features of an industry.
5. Analyses the features of an industry.
6. Illustrates the features of an industry.
7. Compares of various industries.
8. Draws a chart on the characteristics of an industry.

9. Visits an industrial establishment.
10. Reads articles or books on various industries.

Previous Knowledge assumed. Students have learnt about trade.

Introduction.

1. What are business activities?
2. What do you understand by agriculture?

Statement of the aim. Well students, today we shall study the various aspects of an industry?

Development of the Lesson

Matter	*Method*
Meaning of the term industry. Industry refers to economic activities connected with raising, producing and processing or manufacturing of goods and services.	The teacher will develop the lesson with the help of the following questions. 1. Name some of the articles you use in daily-life.
Classification of industry	2. Name the activities involved in the production of flour.
Primary Secondary	3. Name the activities involved in the manufacture of sugar.
Genetic Extractive Manufacturing Construction	4. Name the activities involved in extracting coal.
Primary industry. Primary industry is that industry in which nature plays a more important role than man. Example: Fishing and Fisheries.	5. Name the activities involved in dairy farming. 6. Give some examples of primary industry.
Secondary industry. Man plays an important role than nature. Example: Cycle mainufacturing, construction of buildings.	7. Give some examples of manufacturing industry. 8. Give some other examples of construction industry.

Recapitulation

1. Define an industry.
2. Explain genetic industry with the help of an example.

Black-board Summary. Chart will be drawn on the blackboard illustrating the classification of an industry.

Assignment. Classify industries and give two examples of each type of industry.

Project work/Practical work

1. Visit any genetic industry or farm house.

2. Collect information on the operations involved in any one industry.
3. Find out town famous for manufacturing cotton or sugar.

LESSON PLAN NO. 11

Enrolment No.	Name
School	Class
Strength	Period Date
Time	Subject : Commerce (Business Studies)
Topic	Transport
Teaching Aids	Model showing modes of transport

Instructional Objectives

1. To acquire the knowledge of facts, terms, concepts, conventions, trends, principles, generalisations, assumptions, hypotheses, processes etc. in transport.
2. To develop understanding of facts, terms, concepts, conventions, trends, principles, generalisations, assumptions, hypotheses, processes, etc. in transport. '
3. To apply the acquired knowledge of modes of transport and their understanding to familiar situation.
4. To acquire practical skills essential for the study of transport.
5. To develop interest in the subject and problems related to transport in the life of the people of one's country and those of the world.
6. To develop desirable positive attitudes necessary for developing a broader outlook as a transporter and as a citizen.

Specification of Instructional Objectives

1. Recalls the meaning of transport.
2. Understands the meaning of transport.
3. Defines the term transport.
4. Lists the features of transport.
5. Analyses the features of transport.
6. Illustrates the features of transport.
7. Compares different modes of transport.
8. Draws a chart on the characteristics of different modes of transport.

9. Visits a transport agency or airport etc.
10. Reads articles or books on different modes of transport.

Previous Knowledge Assumed. Students are aware of the modes of transport.

Introduction. 1. What are the aids to trade?

2. How do they help in carrying out trade?

Statement of aim. We shall learn in detail how does transport help in trade.

Teaching Aid. Model on modes of transport.

Development of Lesson

Matter	*Method*
(a) Meaning of transport. Transport means physical movements of goods and passengers from one place to another.	Lesson will be developed with the help of the following questions:
	1. How do we get oil from the refineries?
(b) Functions of transport:	
1. Widening of market.	2. How does a manufacturer send his goods within the country and outside the country?
2. Large scale production.	
3. Specialisation.	
4. Mobility of resources.	3. How does a manufacturer get the raw material?
5. Price stability.	
6. National integration.	4. How does an agriculturist send his produce to the market?
7. Employment opportunities.	
Classification of transport.	5. How does the mail and newspapers reach different towns and cities?
(i) Landways	
(a) Roadways	
(b) Railways	6. How can the goods be transported quickly in the mountainous areas.
(c) Pipeline	
(ii) Waterways	
(a) Inland	Teacher will explain the comparative, merits and demerits of each mode of transport.
(b) Coastal	
(c) Overseas	
(iii) Air Transport	
(a) Domestic	
(b) International	
(c) Ropelines	

Recapitulation

1. What is transport?
2. State any three functions of transport.

Blackboard Summary. Teacher will draw a chart on the blackboard showing the modes of transport.

Home Assignment. 1. "Transport is essential for carrying out trade" Do you agree? Give arguments in support of your answer.

Project/Practical Work

1. Collect some articles on any mode of transport.
2. Find out the name of the nearest airport.
3. Find out the route of any highway.

LESSON PLAN NO. 12

Enrolment No.	Name
School	Class XI
Strength of the class	Date
Time	Period
Subject	Commerce (Business Studies)
Topic	Insurance

Teaching Aids. Pamphlets and forms on insurance.

General Objectives of Teaching. As in other lessons plans.

Instructional Objectives

1. To acquire the knowledge of facts, terms, concepts, conventions, trends, principles, generalisations, assumptions, hypotheses, processes etc. in insurance.
2. To develop understanding of facts, terms, concepts, conventions, trends, principles, generalisations, assumptions, hypotheses, processes, etc. in insurance.
3. To apply the acquired knowledge of insurance and its understanding to familiar situations.
4. To acquire practical skills essential for the study of insurance.
5. To develop interest in the subject and problems related to insurance in the life of the people of one's country and of those of the world.
6. To develop desirable positive atitudes, necessary for developing a broader outlook as a commerce entrepreneur and as a citizen.

Specification of Instructional Objectives

1. Recalls the meaning of insurance.
2. Understands the meaning of insurance.
3. Defines the term insurance.

4. Lists the features of insurance.
5. Illustrates the term insurance.
6. Analyses various aspects of insurance of different types.
7. Compares different types of insurance.
8. Draws a chart on the characteristics of insurance.
9. Visits an insurance agent or company.
10. Reads articles or books on insurance.

Previous Knowledge Assumed. Students are acquainted with different types of aids to trade and the term business risk.

Statement of the Aim. Well students, you shall learn how business risks can be minimised through insurance.

Development of Lesson

Matter	*Method*
Meaning of the term insurance. Protection provided against different categories of risks to individuals as well as business on payment of a nominal sum called premium to recover the loss, if any, arising out of risks. It is an agreement between two parties whereby one of them called insurer agrees to protect the other called insured against an unexpected loss.	The teacher will develop the lesson with the help of the following questions: Life is full of uncertainties and unexpected sad events in life. For instance an individual who is the sole earning member in the family dies in an accident and the family faces hardships. In such an event, how can an individual minimise monetary risks?
Different Types of Insurance 1. Life insurance	
2. Fire insurance	2. What are the types of risks involved in business?
3. Marine insurance 4. Miscellaneous insurance (a) Accidence insurance	3. You are an exporter. What are the risks involved in sending goods by sea? How do you minimise
(b) Burglary insurance these? (c) Motor insurance (d) Employer's liability insurance.	

Recapitulation

1. Define the term insurance.
2. Explain the difference between life insurance and fire insurance.

Blackboard Summary. Teacher will draw a chart showing miscellaneous types of insurance.

Home Assignment. Write an essay on various kinds of insurance and different kinds of policies.

Project/Practical Work

1. Prepare a chart showing different types of insurance policies.
2. Meet an insurance agent and find out the process of taking out an insurance policy.

LESSON PLAN NO. 12

Enrolment No.	Name
School	Class XI
Strength	Period
Duration	Time
Subject	Commerce
Topic	Bank and its Functions

Teaching Aids. Various Forms, Cheques and Pass Books.

General Objectives of Teaching. As in other lesson plans.

Instructional Objectives

1. To acquire the knowledge of facts, terms, concepts, conventions, trends, principles, generalisations, assumptions, hypotheses, processes etc. in banking.
2. To develop understanding of facts, terms, concepts, conventions, trends, principles, generalisations, assumptions, hypotheses, process, etc. in banking.
3. To apply the acquired knowledge of banking and its understanding to familiar situations.
4. To acquire practical skills essential for the study of banking.
5. To develop interest in the subject and problems related to banking in the life of the people of one's country and of those of the world.
6. To develop desirable positive attitudes necessary for developing a broader outlook as a commerce entrepreneur and as a citizen.

Specification of Instructional Objectives

1. Recalls the meaning of a bank.
2. Understands the meaning of a bank.
3. Defines the term bank.

4. Lists the features of banking.
5. Illustrates the term bank and banking.
6. Analyses banking transactions.
7. Compares commercial transactions and non-commercial transactions.
8. Draws a chart on the characteristics of banking.
9. Visits a bank.
10. Reads articles or books on banks.

Development of Lesson

Matter	*Method*
Need and Definition of a Bank A bank may be defined as an institution which is engaged in accepting deposits, making loans, and providing other services to its customers and the general public. Banking refers to the business of accepting deposits and lending money. *Functions of a Bank* 1. *Accepting deposits* Types of deposits (i) Fixed deposits (ii) Recurring (iii) Saving account (iv) Current account II. *Granting loans* (i) Overdraft (ii) Cash credit (iii) Term loans III. *Discounting Bills of Exchange* IV. *Miscellaneous services* (a) Locker facilities (b) Payment of school fees (c) Electricity bill payment (d) Traveller's cheque (e) Credit cards.	1. You save some money out of your pocket money. Where do you keep that money? 2. State the services and facilities which are necessary for business activity. A person wants to take up some business who has not enough capital. From where can he arrange finance? 4. What are the sources of finance of a business? 5. What are the services rendered by a bank? (Teacher will show different kinds of cheques, passbooks and withdrawal receipts) 6. Can a bank advance loans to a business man without any surety? If not what types of sureties it accepts? 7. How do you pay your school fee? 8. You are going out of station. You do not want to take cash with you. How can you make purchases in such a situation?

Recapitulation

1. What is banking?
2. What are the functions of a bank?
3. Why does a businessman need the services of a bank?

Blackboard Summary. The teacher will illustrate the functions of a bank by drawing a chart on the blackboard.

Home Assignment. Define a bank and state its functions.

Project/Practical Work. Visit a bank and watch the activities and functions of various employees.

General Objectives of Teaching. As in other lesson plans.

Instructional Objectives. As in the previous plan.

Specification of Instructional Objectives. As in the previous lesson plan.

Project Activities

Matter	*Method*
As in the previous lesson plan. Previous permission for taking the students to a bank will be obtained from the head of the school and the bank manager.	Students will be taken to a bank and asked to observe its functioning. The manager will be requested to explain in brief the working of a bank. Thereafter teacher will fill up the gaps.

Home Assignment: Students will be asked to describe their visit to the bank and to write the functions of bank employees.

LESSON PLAN NO. 15

Enrolment No.	Name
School	Class XI
No. of Students in the Class	Subject : Business Studies
Unit: Share Capital	Time :
Period	Date

Instructional Objectives

The pupil:

1. Acquires the knowledge about the terms and concepts of finance (share capital);
2. Understands the terms and concepts of share capital;
3. Applies the knowledge in practical life;
4. Develops skill in drawing a chart and filling documents;
5. Develops desirable positive attitudes in share capital.

Specification of Instructional Objectives

The pupil:

1. Recalls the importance of finance in business;
2. Recognises the meaning of the term capital;

3. Lists the various sources of capital;
4. Defines the term share capital;
5. Classifies share capital-,
6. Defines the term share;
7. Explains the term equity shares and preference shares;
8. Differentiates between equity shares and preference shares;
9. Explains the meaning of the term share -certificate;
10. Observes a chart showing sources of capital and a share certificate; and
11. Develops skills in filling an application form.

Development of Lesson

Specification	*Content*	*Learning Experiences*
1. Recalls	Importance of finance in business. There is often considerable time interval between, incurring of expenditure and receipt arising from sales. – Complexity of production activity; tools of production – Increasing financial needs. – Industrial Revolution. – Inventions, developments. – Mass scale production of goods. – Expansion of market. – Catering to both local and outside demand. – Capital intensive	Why do we call finance the bloodstream of business activity?
2. Recognises	Meaning of the term capital: Fixed capital, Working capital Funding of the company	Teacher explanations the meaning of the term capital.
3. Lists down	Sources of capital: (i) Issue of shares; (ii) Issue of debentures; (iii) Ploughing back of own profits; (iv) Public deposits; (v) Loans from financial institutions and banks.	
4. Defines the term share capital	*Share capital*. The capital raised by a company through the issue of shares so that it has the necessary finance for its various activities.	The teacher define the term share capital.

Evaluation/Recapitulation

1. Explain the term capital.
2. Mention any two important sources of capital.

Section II

Classifies	*Share capital:*	
	Equity shares. Preference shares. *Deferred shares* (management shares)	
Defines	*Share:* A share may be defined as one of the equal parts into which the capital of a company is divided, entitling the share-holders to a proportion of profits.	Defines the term share.
Explains	*Equity Shares.* 1. Do not bear any fixed rate of dividend. 2. In case of winding, up, equity shareholder is paid back undertaken his capital after all other debts. 3. Right to vote. *Preference Shares:* (1) Fixed rate of dividend; (2) Payment after debenture holders; (3) No voting rights preference over dividend.	Discussion is undertaken.

Differentiates	*Equity Share*	*Preference Share*	
(i) Right of dividend	(i) After preference shares have been paid	(i) Preference over equity and other shareholders	Discussion explain to the difference between equity and preference shares.
(ii) Refund of a capital	(ii) After preference share has been refunded	(ii) Priority of equity share holder.	
(iii) Rate of dividend	(iii) Rate of dividend varies with the earnings of the company	(iii) Fixed rate of dividend	
(iv) Normal Value	(iv) Not so high	(iv) Generally high	
(v) Voting rights	(v) Yes	(v) No	
(vi) Element of risk	(vi) Real risk bearers	(vi) Comparatively less risk	
(vii) Redemption	(vii) Not redeemable	(vii) May be redeemed	

Specification	*Content*	*Learning Experiences*
Explains	Meaning of share certificate. It is a document, issued under the official seal of a company, showing ownership of shares in that	The pupil looks at the share certificate and goes through its contents. Discussion is undertaken.

	company (Issued after three months of allotment of shares)	
Observes chart.	A chart showing share certificate and sources of finance	The teacher displays the
Fills	A share application form	The teacher explains how to fill the application.

Recapitulation/Evaluation. 1. Why are equity share holders called the risk bearers of the company?

2. Give any three important differences between preference and equity shares.
3. What is a share certificate?

Blackboard Summary. Main points will be written on the blackboard along with the development of the lesson.

Home Assignment. 1. State the various sources of capital of a joint stock company.

2. Explain the difference between preference and equity share.

Project/Practical Work

1. Find out from your parents if they are shareholders of any company.
2. Fill up a share application form.
3. Collect two advertisements of public subscription from newspaper.

LESSON PLAN NO. 16

Enrolment No.	Name
School	Class XI
Period	Date
Subject	Commerce (Business Studies)
Topic	Objectives and Importance of Management

Teaching Aids. Chart showing Functions of Management.

Previous Knowledge Assumed. Students understand the meaning of business and business activities.

State who manages business activities.

Statement of the Aim. Today you will learn the objectives and functions of management.

Development of Lesson

Matter	*Method*
Objectives of management	Lesson will be developed with the help of the following questions:
1. To make the maximum utilisation of the physical resources available.	
2. To bring together the human resources to utilise their respective specialised knowledge and capacity to the optimum level.	1. Who is the head of your family?
3. To combine the physical and human resources into an effective enterprise to produce goods and generate services.	2. What are the objectives of the family that the head keeps in view?
4. To visualize the development and expansion of the enterprise.	3. State the functions of the head of the family.
5. To build up the competitive strength of the enterprise by providing guidelines for its effective cooperation.	4. What are the objectives of the school?
6. To make the enterprise commercially viable and a forceful organisation with endurance and stability.	5. What functions are performed for the realization of these objectives?
	6. What happens if the members of the family do not work in cooperation? (Similar is the case with the business management)
Importance of Management	
1. Unified efforts of a large number of individuals working in an enterprise.	1. What are the effects of a well managed family?
2. Fully utilisation of the skills of each member.	2. What advantages do we get from a well managed family?
3. Disciplined and motivated performance of individuals.	3. How are the skills of each member of the family utilised?
4. Economic utilisation of resources through scientific planning and execution.	
5. Making enterprise dynamic and responsive to the changing needs of the consumers.	

Recapitulation. State the objectives of management.

Home Assignment. Write an essay on the objectives and importance of management.

Project/Practical Work. Contact an entrepreneur and find out the objectives of his enterprise.

LESSON PLAN NO. 17

Enrolment No.	Name
School	Class XI
Strength	Time
Period	Date
Subject	Commerce
Topic	Levels of Management

General Objectives of Teaching. As in other lessons.

Instructional Objectives

1. Acquire the knowledge of facts, terms, concepts, conventions, trends, principles, generalisations, assumptions, hypotheses, processes etc. in levels of management.
2. Develop understanding of facts, terms, concepts, conventions, trends, principles, generalisations, assumptions, hypotheses, processes, etc. in levels of management.
3. Apply the acquired knowledge of levels of management and its understanding to familiar situations.
4. Acquire practical skills essential for the study of levels of management.
5. Develop interest in the subject and problems related to levels of management in life of the people of our country and those of the world.
6. Develop desirable positive attitudes necessary for developing a broader outlook as an entrepreneur and as a citizen.

Specification of Instructional Objectives

The pupil:

1. Recalls the meaning of levels of management.
2. Understands the meaning of levels of management.
3. Defines the term levels of management.
4. Lists the features of levels of management.
5. Analyses the features of levels of management.
6. Illustrates the features of levels of management.
7. Compares levels of management.

8. Draws a chart on the characteristics of levels of management.
9. Visits an organisation to study the levels of management.
10. Reads articles or books on levels of management.

Teaching Aids. Chart showing levels of management of a big company.

Previous Knowledge Assumed. Students are familiar with the concept of management.

Statement of the Aim. Today you will study the various aspects of levels of management.

Introduction. 1. Explain the term management.

2. What are the functions of management?

Development of Lesson

Matter	*Method*
Meaning of levels of management. The term levels of management indicates managerial hierarchy or graded arrangement of managerial positions in the organisation i.e. top level, middle and supervisory management.	Lesson will be developed with the help of the following questions asked from students and also their answers.
Levels of Management	1. Who is the head of your family? 2. What are his functions? 3. Who is the head of the school?
Top / Middle / Supervisory Board of Directors / Functional Department Heads / Senior Intermediate	4. What functions does he perform? 5. Who are the other officers who assist him?
Chief Executive Heads / Divisional Sectional Supervisor / Foreman First line	6. Is there any managing committee of the school? 7. If so, what is the designation of the head of the Managing Committee?
Top Level Management Function a. Responsibility for overall management.	8. What are the other members of the Managing Committee?
b. Responsible for organisational structure. c. Responsible for staffing.	9. What is the significance of middle level management?
d. Responsible for overall review and control.	10. Who supervises the work of the workers?
e. Responsible for public relations.	11. Who directly guides,

f. Laying down the objectives rule, regulations, policies and strategies of the organisation.

Middle Level Management Functions

i) Useful link between top management and other functionaries.
ii) Development and training of personnel.
iii) Helping employees to integrate personal goals with enterprise goals.
iv) Executing and interpreting plans, and policies formulated by top level management.
v) Coordinating middle level and controlling functionaries of superivisory level.

motivates and controls workers?

12. Who is directly responsible for proper working conditions?
13. Name the Chairman of the company.
14. State his functions.
15. Does he supervise the work of workers ?
If not, who supervises ?

Distinction between Top Level Management and Middle Level Management

Top Level	*Middle Level*
1. Formulates plans, policies and rules of the organisation.	1. Implements plans, policies and rules of the organisation.
2. Decision-making skill more important.	2. Less important
3. Owners of the organisation.	3. Employees of the organisation.
4. Less directing at this level.	4. More directing at this level.

Recapitulation. 1. At which level the work of the workers is supervised?

2. Which level coordinates the work?

3. At which level, policies are formulated?

Blackboard Work. The teacher illustrates the distinction between the functions of the top level management and middle level management.

Home Assignment. Explain clearly the difference between the functions of the top level management and middle level management.

Project/Practical Work. Visit a business organisation and find out the structure of management of any enterprise/company or bank.

LESSON PLAN NO. 18

Enrolment No.	Name
School	Class XII
Strength of the class	Period
Time	Date
Subject	Commerce (Business Studies)
Topic	Fayol's Principles of Management

General Objectives of Teaching. As in other lessons.

Instructional Objectives

The pupil

1. Acquires the knowledge of facts, terms, concepts, conventions, trends, principles, generalisations, assumptions, hypothesis, processes etc. in Fayol's principles of management.
2. Develops understanding of facts, terms, concepts, conventions, trends, principles, generalisations, assumptions, hypotheses, processes, etc. in Fayol's principles of management.
3. Applies the acquired knowledge of Fayol's principles of management and their understanding to familiar situations.
4. Acquires practical skills essential for the study of Fayol's principles of management.
5. Develops interest in the subject and problems related to Fayol's principles of management in life of the people of one's country and those of the world.
6. Develops desirable positive attitudes necessary for developing a broader outlook as an entrepreneur and as a citizen.

Specification of Instructional Objectives

1. Recalls the meaning of Fayol's principles of management.
2. Understands the meaning of Fayol's principles of management.
3. Defines the term Fayol's principles of management.
4. Lists the features of Fayol's principles of management.
5. Analyses the features of Fayol's principles of management.

6. Illustrates the term Fayol's principles of management.
7. Compares Fayol's principles of management with other principles of management.
8. Draws a chart on the characteristics of Fayol's principles of management.
9. Reads articles or books on principles of management.

Teaching Aids. A chart depicting Fayol's principles of management.

Previous Knowledge Assumed. Students are aware of the term management and its function.

Statement of the Aim. Today we take up the various aspects of Fayol's principles of management.

Development of Lesson

Matter/Learning	*Method*
Importance of the principles of management	Lesson will be developed with the aid of the following questions and also the replies of the students.
1. To assist in teaching and training of managers.	
2. To increase efficiency.	1. Why do you follow some principles in life?
3. To make more scientific decisions.	
4. To ensure the constant supply of goods and services.	2. Why does the principal of your school prescribe certain principles for the running of the school?
5. To meet more effectively the changes in technology.	
6. To meet social responsibility.	3. Name some top most industrialists of your state/ India. (Teacher will follow the lecture method.)
7. To improve research.	
Brief life sketch of Henry Fayol (1841- 1925) the real father of modern management theory.	
French industrialist. Degree in mining engineering in 1860. Beginning of career as an engineer in coal mining Company Managing Director of the same company for thirty years. Made financial position of the company sound. Undertook a lot of research. Wrote a book 'Administration industrielle generale' in French in 1916.	Lesson will be developed and principles explained with the aid of the following questions. 1. Why does the principle of the school divide the work of the school among staff members?
Translated into English in 1929. Set up a Centre of Administrative Studies in Paris.	2. If the principal has no power to control his staff, what will be the consequences?
Fayol's principles of management Flexibility of principles. Principles	3. What will be the state of affairs in the school if the

to be used in the light of changing and special conditions. 1. Principle of unity of command. 2. Principle of unity of direction. 3. Principle of division of labour. 4. Principle of authority and responsibility.	principal does not divide the work? 4. What will be the state of affairs in the country if there are two Prime Ministers (Heads of the country)?

Recapitulation

1. State the importance of the principles of management.
2. Explain the principle of division of labour in management.

Blackboard Summary. Merits of principles of management will be listed on the blackboard side by side explaining their significance to the students.

Home Assignment. Who was Henry Fayol? Why did he formulate the principles of management? Explain any two principles.

Project/Practical Work. Collect information on the life of any Indian industrialist who has made some contribution to the theory of management.

LESSON PLAN NO. 19

Enrolment No.	Name
School	Class XII
Strength of the class	Period
Time	Date
Subject	Commerce (Business Studies)
Topic	Fayol's Principles of Management (Contd.)

General Objectives of Teaching. As in other lesson plans.

Instructional Objectives of Teaching. Fayol's Principles of Management. As in the previous lesson plan.

Specifications of Instructional Objectives of Teaching Fayol's Principles of Management. As in the previous lesson plan.-

Teaching Aid. 1. As in the previous lesson plan.

2. Solar chain will be drawn on the blackboard.

Introduction. 1. What is the significance of the principles of management?

2. Why did Fayol's formulate principles of Management?

Statement of the Aim. In the previous lesson we took up some principles of management. Today we would take up the remaining principles of management as formulated by Fayol.

Development of Lesson

Matter	*Method*
Principle of Scalar Chain. Fayol looks upon the chain as "a chain of superiors ranging from the ultimate authority to the lowest ranks". It is the line of authority. Normally A will issue directions to B and B to C and so on.	Actual functioning of the school will serve as the basis of principles of management. Following questions will be asked to explain the Principles of management 1. State the chain of authority in the school. 2. Is it possible for all the employees to be of the same rank? If not why? 3. Why should the principal have more powers than the Vice-Principal?
But in emergency 'A' may by-pass all channels and take up the matter with 'E'.	4. Why should the head of a management enjoy more powers than the other functionaries? 5. Why should the principal delegate some powers to the staff and students?
Principle of remuneration. Equitable and fair wages to all workers.	6. Why do people work? 7. What should be the basis for remuneration?
Principle of decentralisation. Lower to be delegated.	
Principle of esprit de corps. Team spirit.	8. Why should all the members of team work unitedly?
Principle of discipline. Following rules and regulations.	9. What is the significance of discipline in school?
Principle of stability of tenure. Enough time to be given to each worker to acquire competence and confidence.	10. What will be the consequences if teachers change classes frequently? 11. What will be the effect if the head of a family puts heavy restrictions?
Principle of equity. Fair treatment.	12. Why should the principal have more powers than the vice-principal?
Principle of initiative. Freedom to think of new ideas and plans.	

Recapitulation

1. Explain the principle of scalar chain. State its significance.
2. "The principles of management of business are not applicable to school management?" Do you agree? Give arguments in support of your answer.

Blackboard Summary. The principle of scalar chain will be explained by drawing a diagram on the black-board.

Home Assignment. Discuss any five principles of management as advocated by Fayol.

Project/Practical Work. Prepare a diagram indicating the scalar chain.

LESSON PLAN NO. 20

Enrolment No.	Name
School	Class XII
Strength of the Students	Period
Time	Date
Subject	Commerce (Business Studies)
Topic	Planning

General Objectives of Teaching

1. To develop in the students an interest in the theory and practice in business, trade and industry.
2. To acquaint students with the theoretical foundations and practices of organising, managing and handling routine operations of a business firm.
3. To inculcate attitudes and values leading to the integration of business with the social system with a positive approach.
4. To enable students to apply the principles and functions of management to specific aspects of business.
5. To equip the students with essential fundamental knowledge of setting up, organising and handling routine operations of a small scale factory.
6. To equip the students with basic information on modern methods of office operations for effectively carrying out paper work in a business office.

7. To impart knowledge of methods considered useful in maintaining records of proprietory and partnership firms, companies and non-trading organisations.
8. To generate and promote awareness of students in modern techniques of maintaining accounting records with the help of computers.
9. To develop desirable positive attitudes necessary for developing a broader outlook as a businessman and as a citizen.

Instructional Objectives

1. To acquire the knowledge of facts, terms, concepts, conventions, trends, principles, generalisations, assumptions, hypotheses, processes etc. in planning.
2. To develop understanding of facts, terms, concepts, conventions, trends, principles, generalisations, assumptions, hypotheses, processes, etc. in planning.
3. To apply the acquired knowledge of planning and its understanding to familiar situations.
4. To acquire practical skills essential for the study of planning.
5. To develop interest in the subject and problems related to planning in the life of the people of one's country and of those of the world.

Specification of Instructional Objectives

The pupil:

1. Recalls the meaning of planning.
2. Understands the meaning of planning.
3. Defines the term planning.
4. Lists the features of planning.
5. Illustrates the term planning.
6. Analyses planning process.
7. Compares planning and non-planning.
8. Draws a chart on the characteristics of planning.
9. Visits an organisation.
10. Reads articles or books on planning.

Teaching -Aid

Chart illustrating characteristics of planning.

Introduction

1. Why do you plan your work?
2. What points do you consider while planning your schedule of studies?

Statement of the Aim. Today we take up the need and other aspects of planning a business.

Development of Lesson

Matter	*Method*
Meaning of planning and objectives. Planning means determining a course of action to achieve some desired result. It is deciding in advance what to do, how to do, when to do, and who is to do. It indicates our destination – where we are and where we want to go. ***Definitions of Planning*** A few definitions of planning – for example of the following authors will be taken up. (1) Alderson (2) Allen (3) Brown (4) Erwing (5) Fayol (6) Robert Reference to the Planning Commission will be made. ***Characteristics of planning*** 1. Planning is an intellectual process. 2. Planning is goal-oriented. 3. Planning is the primary function of management. 4. Planning involves a choice between alternative courses of action. 5. Planning pervades all management activity. 6. Planning is an interdependent and a consistent process. 7. Planning leads towards efficiency. 8. Planning is based on forecasting. 9. Planning enables us to face risks. 10. Planning is flexible.	The lesson will be developed with the help of the following questions: 1. What do you intend to take up after completing your studies? 2. What preparations would you make to achieve your aim? 3. Why is school year divided into different terms? 4. How do you plan to secure good marks in the Board's examination? 5. Who makes plans for your school? 6. How will you organise your school games? 7. What steps have been taken by the Government of India to remove unemployment? 8. Is planning a physical exercise? 9. If not, what is required in planning? 10. What is the objective of planning? 11. Who plans or plan your school programmes? 12. Who are the persons associated with the planning of your school programme? 13. Is planning of school programmes confined to the head?

Recapitulation

1. Explain the term planning.
2. State the main features of planning.

Blackboard work. A chart showing the main features of planning will be drawn on the blackboard.

Home Assignments. Explain the meaning of planning by giving some definitions of planning. What is the purpose of planning? List its important features.

Project/Practical work. List the various steps and factors that you consider important in planning your career.

21

Questioning, as an Art

Undoubtedly the art of questioning is the most important potent weapon in the armoury of the teacher. It is well said,

"I keep six honest serving men,
They taught me all I know.
Their names are 'what' and 'why' and 'when',
And 'how' and 'where' and 'who'."

"Good questions", writes F. Theodore Struck, "by their very nature, are educative, and they have a very prominent place in all kinds of learning." Questioning plays an indispensable part in 'learning', teaching', and 'testing'. If used in the right way, at the proper time, questions lead to new realms of understanding; they serve as means of organizing knowledge, or correlating the results of educative experiences; of tying together units of learning; and of integrating personality. One who questions faultlessly teaches effectively, is not without meaning. Salmon holds that a bad questioner is a bad teacher; he may be a good lecturer. In the words of Rybum, "It is no exaggeration to say that the success of a teacher in any particular lesson, and in teaching in general, depends upon his ability to question well." According to Raymont, "The acquisition of a good style of questioning may be laid down definitely as one of the essential ambitions of a young teacher."

Questions, with a Purpose

1. To test the previous knowledge of the students.
2. To enable them to recall something.

3. To enable them to recognise something.
4. To enable them to think over something.
5. To enable them to reason about something.
6. To elicit something from students.
7. To stimulate interest and effort on the part of students.
8. To keep the children mentally alert.
9. To promote initiative and originality.
10. To stimulate the curiosity of the students.
11. To ascertain whether they are folllowing the lesson or not.
12. To link new knowledge with old.
13. To revise the lesson and thus to fix the facts in the minds of the students.
14. To secure the co-operation of the students.
15. To diagnose the weak points of the students.
16. To formulate general rules.

CLASSIFICATION OF QUESTIONS

Formal Questions　　Natural Questions

Teaching Questions　　Developing Questions　　Testing Questions

Preliminary Questions　　Recapitulatory Questions

Formal questions. Formal questions are those where the questioner already knows the information which he asks for. Classroom questions may be put under this category.

Natural Questions. In natural questions, the questioner does not know the information about which he asks and makes a query.

Teacher's questions are formal and those of the students natural.

Teaching questions: These are classified under preliminary and recapitulatory questions.

Preliminary questions and introductory questions. These questions are generally asked at the beginning of the lesson. The purposes are:

(i) To test the previous knowledge of the students.
(ii) To link the new knowledge with the already learnt knowledge.
(iii) To motivate the child and arouse his curiosity.

These questions enable the teacher to test the readiness of the student's mind. Questioning at this stage enables the teacher to follow the maxim "From known to unknown".

Questions should be relevant to the topic. Their number should be very small, say three or four.

Racapitulatory questions. Such questions are generally put at the end of a lesson or at the end of each section of the lesson. These questions serve two purposes:

(1) To enable the teacher to know if the children have picked up the ideas he wanted them to learn.
(2) To serve the purpose of revision and to give students a good opportunity for practice.

Developing questions. These questions are said to be the backbone of the lesson. They are used:

(i) to develop a particular line of thought;
(ii) to lead the pupils to discover facts for themselves;
(iii) to formulate new generalizations in an inductive way;
(iv) to focus attention on important points;
(v) to develop knowledge step by step;
(vi) to enable the students to use their powers of observation, of comparison and concentration;
(vii) to break the narrative in order to ensure that the class is following; and
(viii) to make the inattentive students attentive ones.

A great skill is required on the part of the teacher to ask developing questions. The teacher has to lead the students to think and discover facts for themselves. While narrating a story, the teacher should not ask questions.

Questions for Test

These are discussed separately.

Characteristics of Good Questioning.

Following are the chief characteristics of good questioning:-

1. The language of the question should be simple.
2. Questions should be graded. They should neither be too easy nor too difficult. If the problem is too easy, the child

will not take interest in it. If it is too difficult; he will get discouraged. Of course students must be trained to answer very difficult questions.

3. Questions should not be ambiguous, lengthy and vague. They should be clear, brief and to the point.
4. Questions should be suited to the ability of the children to whom they are put.
5. Questions should be relevant to the topic.
6. Questions once asked should not be repeated unless the teacher is- sure the class has not followed them.
7. The teacher should try to vary the form of his questions.
8. Two questions should not be asked in one.
9. Questions should be interesting as far as possible.
10. Questions should be framed in such a way that these do not encourage guess work. The teacher should not generally admit answers like 'Yes' or 'no' or other single words.

Practice of Questioning

The teacher should bear in mind the following points in this regard:-

1. The question should be asked first and then the student be asked to answer it. The main advantage in asking the question first is to set the whole class thinking to find out the answer. On the other hand, if a particular student is asked to stand or sit, as the case may be, and then the question is put to him, other students may not show much interest.
2. Questions should be evenly distributed. No child should be neglected. At the same time questions should not be given in a regular order round the class. Generally there is a tendency to put either too many questions or too less to the students sitting at the back or in the front. Such a tendency should be avoided.
3. Plenty of time should be allowed for pupils to think out the answer. However, the time allowed will depend upon the nature of the question.
4. The inability of a child to answer a question should be accepted. The teacher should avoid to waste a lot of time in trying to get an answer out of a child who cannot

answer. A skilful teacher recognises when the case is hopeless and the child is unable to answer the question in spite of his best efforts.

5. A volley of questions asked in a rapid-fire manner is upsetting.
6. Avoid phrases like "Can any one answer this question?"
7. Questions should be addressed to the entire class.
8. Questions should be asked in a pleasing manner.
9. Questions should be put in such a way that every student thinks that he will be asked to answer whether he is good or weak.
10. Adequate time should be allowed to answer.

Attitude of the Teacher

Following facts should be kept in mind:

1. The students should be encouraged to ask questions.
2. Relevancy in questions should be insisted upon.
3. The teacher must insist on courtesy. Several pupils should not be allowed to ask questions at the same time. Everyone should be asked to listen to a question.
4. Pupils' questions may be made the starting point for a small project.
5. The teacher should be frank enough to admit his inability to answer a question when he does not know the answer. However, in due course, he should be able to answer that question. For the sake of prestige in the eyes of the students, he should not give a wrong answer.

Judicious Blending of Talking and Questioning. Questioning is not a one-way traffic. There is an ample scope for the teacher as well as the students to put questions. The teaching-learning process is effective only when the teacher as well as the pupils are active and co-operative. The aim of the teaching-learning process is to enable the child learn in such a way that it enables him to adjust himself to the environment. As both the teachers and the pupils are attempting to realize the same goal, it is evident that they must be active and not passive.

Answers with Significance

Answers reveal the deficiency of the students as well as the teachers. They are the touchstone to test the effectiveness of the teaching-learning process. If the answers are not satisfactory, it clearly indicates that either there is something wrong with the teaching process or with the learning process. Either the teacher has not taught in the proper manner or the students have not understood the subject-matter. Therefore, answers provide an important tool to make necessary changes in the teaching-learning process.

Classification of Answers. A close analysis of the various types of answers shows that these can be put under the following six categories:

(i) Right and correct answers.
(ii) Correct but incomplete.
(iii) Partially correct and partially wrong.
(iv) Wrong but intelligent.
(v) Ridiculously wrong.
(vi) Mischievous.

How to Deal with Answers ? No hard and fast rule can be laid down for dealing with various categories of answers. Ward and Rascoe write in this connection, "There are no rules. It is unwise to pass over all wrong answers as it is unwise to deal with all. Some are genuine misconceptions, which the teacher must clear up at that time or later on, others are imperfect and incomplete answers, genuine also, which must be rounded off, others are haphazard or stupid and should be treated with contempt or else with such brief but emphatic words of disapproval as the teacher may have a command." The following are the different ways of dealing with answers.

Appreciation. The teacher should always appreciate the answers of the students as appreciation will encourage the students to think further. Even if the answers are wrong but teacher feels that the child is making genuine attempts, due appreciation should be given.

Analysis of wrong answers. When the answers given by most of the students are wrong, the teacher should try to analyse their causes. The causes may be as under:

(i) Defective or difficult language used by the teacher.
(ii) Defective explanation of the subject-matter taught.
(iii) Inattentiveness on the part of the students.
(iv) Lapses of memory.
(v) Toughness and complexity of the subject-matter.

In such cases, the teacher should accept the responsibility and should not feel shy of teaching the subject-matter again.

Encouragement of children. When the answers are partly right and partly wrong, the students should be encouraged to analyse themselves the nature of their mistake. The teacher may ask further questions to analyse the nature of the mistake. When all the factors which are responsible for wrong answer, or answers are not clear to all the students, they may be asked to build up the real answers once again. It is unwise on the part of the teacher to be impatient and to make the necessary completion or correction himself.

Treatment of wrong answers. When a particular student gives a wrong answer, the teacher should not pass on till he gets the right answer without explaining why the first answer is wrong. The child must be made to understand why his answer is wrong. He is not likely to gain anything from the right answer if his doubts remain unexplained.

Answers carrying some other version, other than expected by the teacher. The teacher should accept and appreciate correct and complete answer although it may differ from the answers as expected by the teacher. There are a few intelligent students in every class who believe in novelty and do a lot of extra-reading. The difference in approach should be explained by the teacher.

The form of the answers according to the nature of the lesson. Whether the answer should be in bits or incomplete sentences depends upon the nature of the lesson. No general rule can be laid down. It is up to the teacher to decide the form of the answer. But it must be stressed that whatever be the form answers should be in a clear, simple and concise language.

Answers based on right understanding. The teacher must make sure that the answers as given by the students are really based on genuine mental activity. Parrot fashion words, though they may have senses, are not based on any thought or understanding on the part of the child. The teacher must go deeper and ensure that the child really knows what he says.

Answers given in unison. Answers given in unison should be discouraged. Such answers lack educational value and, therefore, should be disallowed. Assertive students should be given their due only. They should not be allowed to usurp the right of others who are slower or are perhaps making a mistake. No student should be allowed to interrupt while another is answering a question.

Observance of courtesy. The teacher should see that the ordinary courtesy is observed in answering questions. The students should stand or sit and address in the proper way.

Encouragement to shy and submissive students. There are always some students who feel shy and become nervous when questions are put to them. Though they know the answers quite all right, yet they remain mum. The teacher should, in all such cases, give more encouragement and appreciation.

Repetition of good answers. Good answers of the students should be referred to the class, got repeated, preferably by another pupil. The teacher should avoid to repeat a correct answer himself, unless he wants it to be specially stressed.

Discouragement to irrelevant answers. The students should be made to realize the cause of the irrelevant answer. The teacher should study thoroughly that the irrelevant answer is not due to some mischief on the part of the students.

Development of the summary of the lesson with the help of the answers. The answers given by the students at the recapitulatory stage may be used to develop a summary of the lesson. All the answers in brief may be written on the blackboard and the students encouraged to develop an integrated summary with the help of these answers.

Conclusion

Correct, clear and thoughtful answers rèsult from clear thought-provoking questions. The better means of evoking responses from the students are sympathy, patience and encouragement rather than impatience, harshness or snubbing them. Right and correct answers imply that the teacher is using right and correct methods of teaching and the students are learning in an appropriate manner. It may, therefore, be concluded that the pupils answers to the questions are equally important if not more than the questions of the teacher in teaching-learning process.

Questions properly planned, carefully worded, evenly distributed, scientifically and phychologically asked, honestly answered and intelligently followed up are very profitable and in fact indispensable in the effective teaching-learning process. Colvin gave recognition to questioning in these words, "The efficiency of instruction is measured in a large degree by the nature of the questions that are asked and the care with which they are framed. No teacher of elementary of secondary school subjects can succeed in his instruction if he has not a fair mastery of the art of questioning."

QUESTIONS

1. Elucidate the importance of questioning in Commerce teaching.
2. Give a few examples of introductory, developmental and recapitulatory questions in Commerce teaching.
3. Explain the technique of asking questions.
4. How should a teacher deal with the answers of the students?
5. "Too much continuous talking on the one hand and discursive questioning on the other hand should be avoided." Discuss the statement and state the main characteristics of the art of questioning.
6. "Questioning is a difficult art and one worth working at." Explain the significance of this statement.
7. Is questioning a one-way traffic-that is the teacher questioning the pupils always, or there is a place for the pupils to question the teacher? Explain.
8. "Questioning is a tool in the hands of a teacher to be used for making his teaching effective." Explain the characteristics of good questioning.

22

Current Scenario

Micro-teaching

Meaning and Definition – Micro-teaching is a procedure in teacher education/training which aims at modifying teacher's behaviour by simplifying the complexities of the traditional regular training process. In a micro-teaching procedure, the trainee is engaged in a scaled down teaching situation. It is scaled down in terms of class size, since the trainee is teaching a small group of four to six pupils. The lesson is scaled down in length of class time and is reduced to five or ten minutes. It is also scaled down in terms of teaching tasks.

It is a process of subjecting samples of human behaviour to 5 R's of Video tape-'recording', 'reviewing', 'responding', 'refining' and 'redoing'. Micro-teaching is a controlled practice that makes it possible to concentrate on teaching behaviour in the student-teacher training programme.

Following definitions throw light on the wider meaning and nature of micro-teaching–

Allen, D. W (1966): Micro-teaching is a scaled down teaching encounter in class size and class time.

Allen, D. W and ***Eve, A. W*** (1968): Micro-teaching is defined as a system of controlled practice that makes it possible to concentrate on specified teaching behaviour and to practise teaching under controlled conditions.

Bush, R.N. (1968): Micro-teaching is a teacher education technique which allows teachers to apply clearly defined teaching skills to carefully prepared lessons in a planned series of five to ten minutes encounter with a small number of real students, often with an opportunity to observe the result on video-tape.

Clift, J C. and ***Others*** (1976): Micro-teaching is a teacher training programme which reduces the teaching situation to a simpler and more controlled encounter achieved by limiting the practice teaching to a specific skill and reducing time and class size.

Encyclopaedia of Education (Ed. Deighton, L.C:-1971): Microteaching is a real, constructed, scaled down teaching encounter which is used for teacher training, curriculum development and research.

Flanders, Ned A. (1960): Micro-teaching programme is organised to expose the trainees to an organised curriculum of miniature teaching encounters, moving from the less complex to the more complex.

Jangira, N.K and ***Singh, Ajit*** (1982): Micro-teaching is a scaled down teaching encounter or miniatured classroom teaching.

ML Alease, WR. and ***Unwin D*** (1970): The term micro-teaching is most often applied to the use of closed circuit television to give immediate feed-back of a trainee teacher's performance in a simplified environment.

Passi, BX and Lalita, MS. (1976): Micro-teaching is a training technique which requires student teachers to teach a single concept using specified teaching skill to a small number of pupils in a short duration of time.

Singh, L.C. (1977): Micro-teaching is a scaled down teaching encounter in which a teacher teaches a small unit to a group of five pupils for a small period of 5 to 20 minutes. Such a situation offers a helpful setting for an experienced or inexperienced teacher to acquire new teaching, skill s and to refine old ones.

Micro-Teaching Cycle

The micro-lesson or the short lesson (scaled down lesson) is recorded on an audio or video-types recorder and the trainee gets to hear and see himself immediately after the lesson. The pupils who attend the lesson are asked to fill in rating questionnaires evaluating specific aspects of the lesson. The trainee' own analysis of the lesson based on the authentic feedback from the tape together with the pupils' reaction -and a supervisor's analysis and suggestions, assists the trainee in restructuring the lesson, which he then immediately reteaches to a new group of pupils. Further assessments by the 'learners' and the supervisor lead to further improvements when he teaches again, either immediately after or several days later. This micro-teaching sequence is practised usually in a micro-teaching laboratory in a teacher-training institution, or an in-service training programme in regular schools.

MICRO-LESSON PLAN

TEACH MICRO-LESSON	RE-TEACH ANOTHER GROUP
DISCUSS	REPLAN FEEDBACK

Three volunteers from the participants play the teachers' roles in front of VTR camera and other participants also take part of pupils' roles. After discussing how the teaching behaviours should be improved, three volunteers teach other participants again. The comparison is made between two teaching traits in each teacher on the evaluation sheet.

Phases of micro-teaching. Following are the three phases of micro-teaching.

Knowledge acquisition phase. In this phase, the student-teacher attempts to acquire knowledge about the skill-its rational, its role in classroom and its component behaviours. For this he reads relevant literature. He also observes demonstration lesson-mode of presentation of the skill (modelling). The student teacher gets theoretical as well as practical knowledge of the skills.

Skill acquisition phase. On the basis of the model presented to the student-teacher, he prepares a micro-lesson and practises the skill and carries out the micro-teaching cycle. There are two components of this phase: feedback and micro-teaching setting. Micro-teaching setting includes conditions like size of the micro-class, duration of the micro-lesson, supervisor, types of students etc.

Transfer phase. Here the student-teacher integrates the different skills. In place of artificial situation, he teaches in the real classroom and tries to integrate all the skills.

The three phases involve certain steps which are given as under:

Orientation of the student teacher. This involves providing necessary information and theoretical background about microteaching on the following aspects:

- (i) Concept of micro-teaching;
- (ii) Rationale or significance of using micro-teaching;
- (iii) Procedures of micro-teaching;
- (iv) Requirement and setting for the adoption of micro-teaching technique.

Discussion of teaching skills. Under this step the knowledge and understanding of the following steps is to be developed-.'

- (a) Analysis of teaching into component teaching skills.
- (b) Discussion of the rationale and role of these teaching skills in teaching.
- (c) Discussion regarding the component teaching behaviours comprising various teaching skills.

Selection of a particular skill. Each skill needs to be practised at a time. Student teachers should be given necessary background for the observation of a model of demonstration lesson on the selected particular skill.

Presentation of a model demonstration lesson–a particular skill. Demonstration lesson by the teacher educator before the student teachers on the use of a particular skill is given. This is also known as 'modelling'. Demonstration can be given in a number of ways:

- (i) By exhibiting a film on a video-tape.
- (ii) By providing writing material such as hand-books, guides, illustrations etc.
- (iii) By making the trainees listen on audio-tape.
- (iv) By arranging a demonstration from a live model i.e. a teacher educator or, some expert.

Observation of the model lesson. An observation schedule designed for the observation of the specific skill is distributed for the guidance of the student teacher to observe the lesson.

Criticism of the model lesson. A critical appraisal of the model lesson is made by the student teachers.

Preparation of the micro-lesson plan. For the preparation of the micro-lesson plan, on the skill demonstrated, help may be taken from sample lesson plans and from the teacher educator.

Creation of a micro-teaching setting. The Indian Model of Micro-Teaching developed by NCERT gives the following setting:

(a) Number of pupils: 5-10
(b) Type of pupils : Real pupils or preferably peers.
(c) Type of supervisor : Teacher educators and peers.
(d) Time duration of a micro-lesson: 6 minutes.
(e) Time duration of a micro-teaching cycle: 36 minutes. This duration is divided as under:
    Teaching session: 6 mts.
    Feed-back session: 6 mts.
    Replan session: 12 mts.
    Reteach: 6 mts
    Refeed back: 6 mts
    Total: 36 minutes

Practice of the skill (Teach Session). Under this step, the student teacher teaches the prepared lesson for 6 minutes to a micro class of 5-10 real pupils or peers (students teachers). This lesson is supervised by the teacher educator and other student-teachers (peers). Where possible, the student-teachers may also have the lesson taped on a video or audio tape.

Providing feedback. The peers and the teacher educators observing the micro-lesson- may provide immediate feed-back. Where possible mechanical gadgets like the video-tape, audio-tape, closed circuit television may be used for getting feedback.

Replanning (Re-plan Session). In the light of the feedback the student teacher replaces his micro-lesson. He is given 12 minutes for this purpose.

Reteaching (Re-plan Session). This session lasts 6 minutes and the student-teacher reteaches his micro-lesson on the basis of his replanned lesson.

Providing Re-feedback (Re-feedback Session). The student teacher is provided re-feedback on the re-taught micro-lesson.

Integration of teaching skills. This is the last step and is concerned with the task of integrating several skills individually mastered by the student teacher. It is helpful in bridging a gap between training in isolated teaching skills and the real teaching situation faced by a teacher.

Important Features

Important characteristics and features of micro-teaching may be summarised as:

1. It is scaled down teaching:
   (a) which reduces the class size 5 to 10 pupils
   (b) which reduces the duration of period 5 to 10 minutes.
   (c) which reduces the size of the topic.
   (d) which reduces the teaching skill
2. It provides adequate feed-back.
3. Micro-teaching provides opportunity to select one skill at a time and practise it through its scaled down encounter and then take another in a similar way.
4. Micro-teaching is a highly individualised training technique.
5. Micro-teaching permits a high degree of control in practising a particular skill.
6. Use of videotape and closed circuit television makes observation very objective.
7. Micro-teaching is an analytic approach to training.

Role of the Supervisor

A supervisor plays a leading role in micro-teaching. He assists student-teachers in relating component skills of teaching to both the theory underlying the skills and to practical classroom situations. The supervisor has to provide continuous consultation so that he can help the student teacher transfer the skill learnt in micro-teaching setting to the actual classroom. First of all he gives demonstration of a particular skill. Thereafter he prepares a special schedule of microteaching lessons in the practising schools. He supervises the lesson and discusses with the student teacher in a group of other student teachers. He completes the evaluation schedule and gives and feedback. The supervisor discusses the lesson with the student teacher in a group of other student teachers. The supervisor is expected to work hard to be a model for the student teachers.

Merits

1. Micro-teaching lessens the complexities of normal training technique.
2. Micro-teaching focuses on training for the accomplishment of specific tasks.
3. Micro-teaching allows for the increased control of practice.
4. Micro-teaching greatly expands the normal knowledge of results of feedback dimension in teaching.
5. Micro-teaching in real teaching.

Demerits

Following are the main drawbacks of micro-teaching:

1. For successful implementation, micro-teaching requires competent and suitably trained teacher-educators.
2. Micro-teaching tends to reduce creativity of teachers.
3. Micro-teaching can be carried on successfully in a controlled environment only.
4. Micro-teaching is very time consuming.
5. The application of micro-teaching to new teaching practices is limited.
6. Micro-teaching alone may not be adequate. It needs to be supplemented and integrated with other teaching techniques.

Micro-teaching and Traditional Teaching Compared

Micro-teaching	*Traditional Teaching*
1. Objectives are specified in behavioural terms.	1. Objectives are general and not specified in behavioural terms.
2. Class consists of a small group of 5 to 10 students.	2. Class consists of 40 to 60 students.
3. The teacher takes up one skills at a time.	3. The teacher practices several skills at a time.
4. Duration of time for teaching is 5 to 10 minutes	4. The duration is 40 to 50 minutes.
5. There is immediate feed-back	5. Immediate feed-back is not available.

6. Teaching is carried on under controlled situation.	6. Teaching has no control over situation.
7. Teaching is relatively simple.	7. Teaching becomes complex.
8. The role of the supervisor is specific and well defined to improve teaching.	8. The role of the supervisor is vague.
9. Patterns of classroom interaction can be studied objectively.	9. Pattérns of classroom interaction cannot be studied

Development and Growth

The term micro-teaching was first coined by A.W. Dwight Allen of the Stanford University in 1963. A number of experiments have been conducted in many institutions in the USA, UK and the Netherlands. In India also, a number of institutions have started work in the area of micro-teaching in recent year. D.D. Tiwari was the first to take up this work in 1967 at the Government Central Pedagogical Institute at Allahabad. This was followed by G.B.Shah who tried an experiment in micro-teaching with the help of a tape-recorder in the Faculty of Education and Psychology, Baroda in 1970. Other names in the field who worked, are R.R. Chandasama, L.P. Singh, N.S. Sarkar and N. Pangotra. A major break-through was made at the Technical Teacher Training Institute, Madras where a studio for educational television programme was set up in which micro-teaching was introduced for the training of technical teachers. A major contribution to the micro-teaching as a teaching device was made in 1974 at the Technical Teachers' Training Institute, Chandigarh under the guidance of Dr. N.L. Dosajh. The institute has published a number of research papers in the area of micro-teaching. The Royal Netherlands Government has provided a closed circuit television to this Institute. The Technical Teachers' Training Institute, Calcutta has started micro-teaching with the help of audiotape.

Perhaps the first book on micro-teaching in India was written by N.L. Dosajh under the caption 'Modification of Teacher Behaviour through Micro-teaching' (1977).

The Department of Teacher Education in the National Council of Educational Research and Training (NCERT) designed a project to study the effectiveness of micro-teaching in 1975 in collaboration with the Centre of Advanced Study in Education (CASE) Baroda.

Programmed Instruction/Programmed Learning. Programmed learning emerged in the beginning of the 20th century from the efforts of American psychologists. E.L. Thorndike (1874-1949) was the first psychologist whose findings bear direct relevance to programming. Other important psychologists who have made significant contribution in the field are Sidney L. Pressy Robert M. Gagne, Robert Mager and B.F. Skinner.

Programmed learning is related with the 'Law of Effect' as explained by Thorndike.

Meaning of Programmed Learning: G.O.M. Leith (1966) provides a very comprehensive definition of programmed learning. According to him programme is a sequence of small steps of instructional material (called frames), most of which require a response to be made by completing a blank space in a sentence. To ensure that expected responses are given, a system of cueing is applied, and each response is verified by the provision of immediate knowledge of results. Such a sequence is intended to be worked at the learner's own pace as individual self- instruction."

Essential elements of programmed instruction are as under:

(a) an ordered sequence of stimulus items to teach (b) of which a student responds in some specific way (c) his responses being reinforced by immediate knowledge of results, (d) so that he moves by small steps, (e) therefore, making few errors and practicing mostly correct responses, (f) from what he knows by a process of successively closer approximation, toward what he supposed to learn from the programme.

Principles of Programmed Learning

1. Principle of small steps.
2. Principle of active responding.
3. Principle of reinforcement.
4. Principle of self-pacing.
5. Principle of self-evaluation and self-testing.

Programmed Instruction	*Traditional Method*
1. It presents the instructional matter step by step in logical order.	1. It presents the instructional matter as a whole.
2. It is based on the teaching principles that have been known for years.	2. It becomes difficult to apply teaching principles in crowded classrooms.
3. The size of the unit of information presented to the pupil is a small bit of information.	3. The unit is a lengthy one. There is no provision for response from the students in the form of answer to questions.

4. Immediate feedback is given to the learner.	4. The learner does not get immediate feedback.
5. Objectives are defined very clearly in operational terms.	5. Objectives are not well-defined and are usually vague.
6. The programmer prepares his programme with care and precision.	6. Little preparation is made
7. Programme is prepared in such a way that the student automatically participates actively by making responses continually.	7. The student usually remains a passive listener and the teacher himself does the summarising and reviewing.
8. A programme is developed empirically through a series of tryouts and refined gradually. Effective sequences of frames are retained and ineffective ones discarded.	8. It is usually found to be very difficult to modify traditional instruction on the basis of student reaction.
9. It is an individualised technique of instruction.	9. It is a group technique.

Merits

Programmed learning is considered to be a more efficient method of teaching-learning. It is increasingly being used in the advanced countries of the world. It is realised that the programmed instruction has potentialities to revolutionise the theory and practice of teaching.

Following are the main merits of programmed learning.

1. A well-programmed instruction is a great thrust in the direction of individualised instruction, as it is tailored to the needs of the individual learner in class. It permits individual learner to progress at his own speed.
2. Since a programme requires continuous response from the learner, it overcomes the inertia and passivity on the part of the learner.
3. The teacher can give explanation in the classroom if the error is common or he may arrange individual conferences on specific points.
4. Learning material in a programmed instruction is presented in such a way that learning becomes an interesting game and the learner is motivated to meet the challenges set by his own capabilities.
5. Programmes are developed by experts. They are empirically tested and modified till they are standardised. A number of learners can use a single good programme and thus save test books.

6. In programmed instruction the learner is immediately reinforced to correct his response and this reinforcement sustains the motivation of the learner.
7. The self-instructional technique presents material in which its complexity is simplified through the analysis of the subject matter into small and more easily assismilated segments of information.
8. The introduction of programmed instruction is of great significance for developing countries which are set on the path of educating millions of learners and are short of teachers.
9. Good teachers are freed from the boredom of routine classroom teaching and they are in a position to devote more time to more creative activities.
10. The programmed instruction has been used more successfully in teaching the discernment of the logic of various disciplines and inspiring students to creative thinking and judgment.
11. Certain motor skills and intellectual abilities normally taught by frequent drills and rote memorisation can be very efficiently taught by self-instructional devices.
12. Self-instructional Materials have been found to be very useful 'in the West in revolutionising the social setting of the classroom. Problems of discipline have been solved and a new hope for eliminating emotional and social problems has been generated.
13. Programmed instruction enables the teacher to diagnose the problems of the individual learner.
14. The introduction of programmed instruction is very helpful in certain situations where human instructors are not easily available in the required number, for instance small schools in the isolated or hill areas.

Demerits

Programmed materials have been severely criticised as a threat to replacing the teacher.

It is also argued that there is too much emphasis in learning facts and very little—emphasis on the mastery of principles and concepts.

Some critics of programmed instruction maintain that the user of a programme does not know where he is headed to.

They also point out that the learners are not aware of the organisation and programmed instruction is unrelated to other aspects of instruction.

It is also argued that the programmed instruction material is very costly and only rich nations can afford it.

It is also stated that the development and use of programmed instructional material require expert knowledge and training. An average teacher finds it very difficult to make 'use' of this device.

Can Programmed Learning Replace a Teacher?

Programme learning cannot replace the teacher. Any innovation in the school programmes and practices must remain in the hands of the teachers. The radio and T.V. did not displace the teacher. Similar is the case with programmed instruction. It is upto the enlightened teachers to take up the challenging task of preparing programmes. We have got a wide market. The programmes can be sold all over the country. A student who is convinced that he can learn better, achieve more with the help of this programme, will definitely prefer to buy this programme to buying a textbook.

It may also be remembered that these gadgets can be used mainly in the cognitive field and possibly in the psycho-motor field to develop certain abilities and skills of the student as an individual. A teacher is something more than all these gadgets put together. He has to bring about socialization of the individual; he has to promote socially desirable attitudes and interests and mould the personality of the students. The effective domain is almost reserved for his care.

Role of the teacher in the changed context of programmed learning may be stated as under:

1. Teacher as an adviser in helping students in the selection of programme learning material.
2. Teacher as a discussion leader for focusing the attention of the learners on important points.
3. Teacher as a guide to clarify doubts and elaborate on various points asked by the learner.
4. Teacher as an evaluator of the learning outcomes.

5. Teacher as an consultant to the various agencies engaged in production of programmed material.

Illustrative Programmes in Commerce

Programme No 1. **Class XI**

Introduction

This is a programme meant for you for the study of economic and non-economic activities.

In this programme you will find paragraphs which are called frames. Study each frame, carefully and write down what is required. Answers are given at the end. After stating your answers, check them. If the answer is wrong or you do not understand the matter, you can again go back to the frame. It is a self-study programme and not a test.

Frame I. All activities which are undertaken by people to earn income and to meet their needs are economic activities. These activities are undertaken for creation of wealth i.e. acquisition of properties and assets. But there are various other activities which are carried on to derive personal satisfaction. These are called non-economic activities.

Q1. What are economic activities?

Q2. For what purpose the above activities are undertaken?

Q3. Which activities are called non-economic Activities?

Frame II. A farmer producing wheat for his own consumption or for sale, will be regarded as engaged in economic activities. But people who are engaged in private or social activities like performing household work or helping the poor, will be regarded as undertaking non-economic activities.

Q4. Give some examples of economic activities.

Q5. Give some examples of non-economic activities.

Answers

Frame I

1. All activities which are undertaken by people to earn income are known as economic activities.
2. The main purpose to undertake economic activity is to earn wealth i.e. acquisition of properties and assets.
3. Non-economic activities are those activities which are carried on to derive personal satisfaction.

Frame II

4. A farmer producing wheat for sale is an example of economic activity.
5. Household work or helping the poor is regarded as a non-economic activity.

Programme No. 2 **Class XI**

Frame I. Activities connected with the production or purchase and sale of goods and services with the object of earning profit are called business activities.

Q1. What is a business activity?

Q2. What is the purpose of carrying a business?

Frame II. Some business activities are mining, manufacturing, trading, transporting, banking, insurance etc.

Q3. Give some examples of business activities?

Frame III. Business activities require use of scarce resources like Men, Materials and Capital.

Q4. What are the resources required for carrying out a business activity?

Answer

1. Any activity concerned with the production or purchase and sale of goods or services to earn profits is known as a business activity.
2. The main purpose of carrying a business activity is to earn profits.
3. Manufacturing, trading are examples of business activity.
4. The resources required for carrying out a business activity are men, materials and capital.

Simulated Teaching

Definition and Meaning. The International Dictionary of Education defines the term as, "teaching technique used particularly in management education and training in which a 'real life situation and values are simulated by 'substitutes' displaying similar characteristics." It also means "Techniques in teacher education in which students act out or role play teaching situations in an attempt to make 'theory' more practically oriented and realistic.

Simulation is a role playing in which the process of teaching student teachers is enacted artificially and an effort is made to practise some important skill of communication through this.

Under this, the student-teacher and the students simulate a particular role and try to develop an identity with the actual classroom environment. Thus, the whole simulated teaching programme becomes a training in role perception and role playing.

In the world of science and technology, simulation is almost a must. Engineers build models, study their performance, make some adjustments and build a prototype.

In order to perform operations on human beings, doctors are made to learn the operation techniques by experimenting on frogs and rats etc.

Application of Simulation Technique

For removing some of the deficiencies of the demonstration lessons based on traditional lines mechanism of simulated teaching is adopted in teacher training. Student-teachers are trained in some artificial laboratory like conditions. Student-teachers are not directly allowed to use school children for practising their teaching skills and modify their teaching behaviours. They are first provided opportunities to acquire the necessary teaching experiences. Through simulated teaching i.e., playing the role of teacher in their own institution within their own group of fellow trainees student-teachers are sent to schools for practice teaching. In simulated teaching, every student teacher plays three different roles-teacher, pupil (student) and observer. The student teacher delivers his lesson to his peers who play the role of students. Some students play the role of observers. The superior or the teacher educator is also present. The peers and the teacher educator (supervisor) observers the lesson and notes down all the good and weak points concerning the classroom interaction-teaching behaviours, content taught, skills practised and methodology used etc. After the lesson is over, there is frank and free discussion for getting feedback and thereby modifying and improving classroom interaction.

Following steps are usually followed in the mechanism of simulated teaching.

1. Orientation of the student-teachers with the concept of simulation – its use in teacher training, steps to be followed in simulated teaching, role of student teachers as students, teachers and observers and the setting for adopting simulated teaching.

2. Selection of the specific teaching skills to be practised.
3. Demonstration lesson by the teacher educator (supervisor).
4. Formation of groups of student teachers.
5. Assignment of roles-teacher, student and observer, to student teachers.
6. Determining the procedure and technique, of on observation of the classroom interaction.
7. Delivering the lesson by the student-teacher.
8. Follow up and further modification in the teaching technique.

D.R. Cruickshank (1968) developed a teacher training system which is capable of presenting the student with upto thirty-one different simulated problems related to teaching.

N.A. Flanders (1970) recommends the following steps for simulation:

1. Letters, A, B, C, D, etc. are assigned to each person in the group and role assignments are rotated by letters so that each individual has a chance to be an actor or observer.
2. The skills to be practised are discussed and topics of conversation that fit the skills are also suggested.
3. Consideration as to who will start the conversation, who will intervene, who will stop the interaction and when it will be stopped are decided.
4. The procedure of evaluation, the kind of data to be recorded, the method of recording, etc. are decided.
5. First, practice-session is conducted and the actor is provided with feedback on his performance. If necessary, the procedure of the second session is altered in order to improve the training procedure.
6. If need arises, one should be prepared to change the procedure and the topic and move on to the next skill so as to present a meaningful challenge to each actor to keep his interest as high as possible.

Reasons for the simulation technique

N.A. Fattu (1966) has given the following reasons for the use of simulation:

1. When an environment cannot be duplicated exactly, then it may be made as realistic as possible.
2. When a process is to be examined systematically, it may yield information through developing and operating a situation.
3. When a system is too difficult to manage, simulation may suggest a way of breaking it down into sub-systems. Then it may be noted how the skills and the information required may be pooled.
4. When a difficult problem is confronted beyond a teacher's ability, simulation may help him synthesize and infer a good solution.
5. Cost may be reduced by simulating rather than by alternative forms of experimenting.
6. Simulation may also indicate which variables in a complex operation or system are important and how they are related to each other.
7. The amount of time accomplished is controllable by the simulator.

Simulation technique has been applied in the USA and the UK with reference to teacher education, teacher educators, training of principals and educational administrators. In India, it is still in its infancy.

In India Prof. K.P. Pandey of the Himachal Pradesh University tried the first experiment in simulated teaching in the year 1971 with B.Ed. in-service trainees enrolled for correspondence courses. The Teacher Education Department of NCERT and the Centre for Advanced Study in Education, M.S. University of Baroda have also done some work in 'simulated teaching' in the context of teacher training.

Value of Simulation

1. Simulation helps to build confidence in the student-teacher.
2. Simulation bridges the gulf between theory and practice.
3. Simulation enables the learner to learn directly from experience.
4. Simulation promotes a high level of critical thinking.
5. Simulation games develop in the students an understanding of the decision-making process.

6. Role playing enables the individual to emphasis with the real life situations.
7. Simulation provides feedback to the learners on the consequences of actions and decisions made.
8. Simulation technique motivates students by making real-life situations exciting and interesting.
9. Post-simulation analysis enables teachers and learners to assess the realism of the situation by uncovering misconceptions.

Limitations of Simulation

1. The most common error in serious skill training is the misconception that adults can play the role of pupils.
2. It is quite possible that during an exercise, the observer may record incorrectly.
3. Simulation attempts to portray real situations in a simple way and which is very difficult.
4. There is a tendency to use the results of a single simulation as the sole basis of generalization.

Team Teaching

Definition and Meaning : Team teaching is one of the most interesting and significant recent developments in education. It is an organisational structure to improve teaching-learning process in the classroom. It is an innovation in school organisation in which two or more teachers teach a group of students. The group is benefited by the expertise of different teachers.

Following definitions throw adequate light on the meaning of team teaching.

In the words of Carlo-obson, "Team teaching is an instructional situation where two or more teachers possessing complimentary teaching skills cooperatively plan and implement the instruction of a simple group of students using flexible scheduling and grouping techniques to meet the particular instruction."

According to David Warwick, "A team teaching is a form of organisation, in which individual teachers decide to pool resources, interest and expertise, in order to devise and implement scheme of work suitable to the needs of their pupils and the facilities of their school".

Francis Chase of the University of Chicago explains team teaching in these words, "such an arrangement (team teaching) would allow for maximum use of the available talent; provide guidance for young and inexperienced teachers."

Goodland regards team teaching as a "hierarchy of personnel as well as a differentiation of staff functions based on differences in qualifications or personal interests. The hierarchy involves a team leader, assistant teacher, teacher's aid, internal teacher and clerk or some other array of sources."

M.B. Naik holds, "In a team teaching method, two or more teachers make a plan of the subjects cooperatively, carry it out, and always evaluate its effect on the students periodically."

Michal J. Apter writes, "Team teaching involves bringing together a number of classes, whose teaching is the joint responsibility of the teachers of these classes who now constitute a team."

In the words of T.T. Shaplin, "Team teaching is a type of instructional organisation involving teaching personnel and the students assigned to them, in which two or more teachers are given responsibilities, working together, for all or a significant part of the instruction of some group of students."

Characteristics. From the above mentioned definitions of team teaching, its following characteristics emerge:

1. It is an instructional arrangement.
2. It involves teaching to be conducted by two or more teachers.
3. It calls for team spirit in teaching.
4. Team spirit of teachers is bound to benefit the students to the maximum.
5. It is sort of pooling of expertise and resources such as experience, interest, knowledge and skills etc. of teachers.
6. It is economical in the sense that it results in more work in less time.

Origin and growth. USA is said to be the birth place of team teaching. In 1955, it was initiated at the Harvard University. The second milestone was at Lexington in 1957.

Francis Chase of the University of Chicago and J. Leyond Trump, Director of the Commission on the experimental study popularised the movement in the secondary schools in the USA.

In the 1970's, almost all institutions in the USA used team teaching in one or the other way.

Now several advanced countries in the world make use of team teaching to improve the quality of instruction.

In India and in other developing countries, team teaching has not gained ground in the instructional process on account of several reasons.

Objectives. Team teaching aims at the realisation of the following objectives:

1. To bring about improvement in instruction.
2. To make the best use of the expertise and talents of teachers.
3. To develop the feeling of cooperation and group work among teachers.
4. To make the best use of the resources of the school.
5. To develop the feeling and sense of shared responsibility among teachers.
6. To expand the scope of teaching good things to students in the most effective manner.
7. To increase flexibility ' in grouping and scheduling as the team teaching groups students according to their interest and aptitudes in the subject.

Different Types. Johnson and Hunt (1968) suggest the following three types of team teaching:

1. *Team teaching within a single discipline.* Here a team of teachers carries on cooperative teaching in the same subject. For instance, two or three teachers of English may teach the subject together in the same class.
2. *Different team experts related to the course.* Here different teachers who are experts in their own fields are asked to teach together some course which is related to all of them.
3. *Combined team teaching with related innovations.* Here a few teachers who are interested in some innovations are asked to discuss their innovations of classroom teaching to one group of learners.

Guiding principles of team teaching. Following are the important principles:

1. Allocation of duties to teachers on the basis of their interests,, qualifications and personality characteristics.

2. Having varying size of the group according to the purpose of the team teaching.
3. Allotment of time according to the importance of the subject.
4. Providing appropriate learning environment by making arrangement of laboratory, good library, workshops etc.
5. Providing appropriate learning behaviour to each learner within the group.
6. Exercising constructive supervision on the activities of the group.
7. Keeping the level of team teaching appropriate to the level of the learners.

Advantages

1. Team teaching stimulates thought and discussion among teachers who are jointly responsible for a group of students.
2. A strong sense of involvement and responsibility develops among the students.
3. Team teaching gives adequate opportunities to students for free expression.
4. Team teaching affords opportunities to the students to develop human relations essential for social adjustment.
5. Teachers are motivated to work hard for the development of their professional proficiency.
6. Students get the opportunity to be benefited by the special knowledge of teachers, constituting the team.
7. Team teaching makes proper use of the staff, equipment and the school building.
8. Team teaching helps in the maintenance of discipline as it makes the best use of the time and energy of the students.
9. Team teaching helps teachers to evaluate the work of one another and provides opportunities for improving one's own teaching.
10. The plan provides a flexible class size.
11. Teachers work in the totality of a situation.
12. Ultimately team teaching helps in the improvement of instruction.

Bhaskara Rao, Digumarti, Editor (1996). *National Policy on Education*. 2 Volumes. New Delhi: Anmol Publications Pvt. Ltd. ISBN 81-7488-323-1.

Bhaskara Rao, Digumarti, Editor (1997). *Care the Child*, 2 Volumes. New Delhi: Discovery Publishing House. ISBN 81-7141-394-3.

Bhaskara Rao, Digumarti, Editor (1997). *Education for the 21st Century*. New Delhi: Discovery Publishing House. ISBN 81-7141-389-7.

Bhaskara Rao, Digumarti, Editor (1997). *Reflections on Scientific Attitude*. New Delhi: Discovery Publishing House, ISBN 81-7141-319-6.

Bhaskara Rao, Digumarti, Editor (1997). *Success Story of a Primary Education Project*. New Delhi: APH Publishing Corporation. ISBN 81-7024-850-7.

Bhaskara Rao, Digumarti, Editor (1997). *World Food Summit*. New Delhi: Discovery Publishing House. ISBN 81-7141-386-2.

Bhaskara Rao, Digumarti, Editor (1998). *Adolescence Education*. New Delhi: Discovery Publishing House. ISBN 81-7141-432-X.

Bhaskara Rao, Digumarti, Editor (1998). *Community and School Nutrition Education*. New Delhi: Discovery Publishing House. ISBN 81-7141-435-4.

Bhaskara Rao, Digumarti, Editor (1998). *District Primary Education Programme*. New Delhi: Discovery Publishing House. ISBN 81-7141-396-X.

Bhaskara Rao, Digumarti, Editor (1998). *Earth Summit*, 2 Volumes. New Delhi: Discovery Publishing House. ISBN 81-7141-435-4.

Bhaskara Rao, Digumarti, Editor (1998). *National Policy on Education: Towards an Enlightened and Humane Society*, New Delhi: Discovery Publishing House. ISBN 81-7141-426-5.

Bhaskara Rao, Digumarti, Editor (1998). *Reforming School Education*. New Delhi: Discovery Publishing House. ISBN 81-7141-403-6.

Bhaskara Rao, Digumarti, Editor (1998). *Teacher Education in India*. New Delhi: Discovery Publishing House. ISBN 81-7141-406-0.

Bhaskara Rao, Digumarti, Editor (1998). *World Summit for Social Development*. New Delhi: Discovery Publishing House. ISBN 81-7141-420-6.

Bhaskara Rao, Digumarti, Editor (2000). *Education for All: Achieving the Goal*, 3 Volumes, New Delhi: APH Publishing Corporation. ISBN 81-7648-152-1.

Vol. I *The Global Consensus*. ISBN 81-7648-155-6.

Vol. II *Mid-Decade Review Reports of Regional Seminars*. ISBN 81-7648-154-8.

Vol. III *Issues and Trends*. ISBN 81-7648-155-6.

Bhaskara Rao, Digumarti, Editor (2000), *International Encyclopaedia of AIDS*, 11 Volumes in 13 Parts. New Delhi: Discovery Publishing House. ISBN 81-7141-6 (Set).

Vol. 1 *Introduction to HIV/AIDS*. ISBN 81-7141-523-7.

Vol. 2 *HIV/AIDS—Issues and Challenges*, 2 Parts. ISBN 81-7141-524-5.

Vol. 3 *HIV/AIDS—Socio Economic Realities*. ISBN 81-7141-524-3.

Vol. 4 *HIV/AIDS—Law Ethics and Human Rights*, 2 Parts. ISBN 81-7141-526-1.

Vol. 5 *AIDS and NGOs*. ISBN 81-7141-527-X.

Vol. 6 *AIDS and Home Care*. ISBN 81-7141-528-8.

Vol. 7 *STD Case Management*. ISBN 81-7141-529-6.

Vol. 8 *HIV/AIDS Prevention and Care—Teaching Modules for Nurses and Midwives*. ISBN 81-7141-530-X.

Vol. 9 *HIV Prevention Education for Education for Educational Institutions*. ISBN 81-7141-531-8.

Vol. 10 *Instructional Modules for AIDS Education*. ISBN 81-7141-532-6.

Vol. 11 *School Health Education to Prevent AIDS and STD—A Package for Curriculum Planners*. ISBN 81-7141-5338-4.

Bhaskara Rao, Digumarti, Editor (2000). *International Encyclopaedia of Science and Technology Education*, 11 Volumes. New Delhi: Discovery Publishing House. ISBN 81-7141-548-2 (Set).

Vol. 1 *Science and Technology Education*. ISBN 81-7141-568-7.

Vol. 2 *Science Education in Developing Countries*. ISBN 81-7141-570-9.

Vol. 3 *Organisational Structure of Science*. ISBN 81-7141-570-9.

Vol. 4 *Science Education in Asia and the Pacific*. ISBN 81-7141-571-7.

Vol. 5 *Science and Technology Education for All*. ISBN 81-7141-572-5.

Vol. 6 *Values, Ethics, Talent and Girls in Science and Technology Education*. ISBN 81-7141-573-3.

Vol. 7 *Popularization of Science and Technology Education*. ISBN 81-7141-574-1.

Vol. 8 *Science, Power and Society*. ISBN 81-7141-575-X.

Vol. 9 *Information Technology*. ISBN 81-7141-576-8.

Vol. 10 *Teacher Training in Science and Technology Education*. ISBN 81-7141-577-6.

Vol. 11 *Teacher Training in Science and Technology: A Curriculum Framework*. ISBN 81-7141-578-4.

Bhaskara Rao, Digumarti, Editor (2001). *Distance Education in Different Countries*. New Delhi: APH Publishing Corporation. ISBN 81-7648-229-3.

Bhaskara Rao, Digumarti, Editor (2001). *Decentralised Management of Education (Management of Education in Panchayati Raj and Municipal Bodies)*. New Delhi: Discovery Publishing House. ISBN 81-7141-617-9.

Bhaskara Rao, Digumarti, Editor (2001). *Electrochemistry for Environmental Protection*. New Delhi: Discovery Publishing House. ISBN 81-7141-619-5.

Bhaskara Rao, Digumarti, Editor (2001). *Global Educational Studies*. New Delhi: Discovery Publishing House. ISBN 81-7141-616-0.

Bhaskara Rao, Digumarti, Editor (2001). *Global Synthesis of Educational Assessment*. New Delhi: Discovery Publishing House. ISBN 81-7141-613-6.

Bhaskara Rao, Digumarti, Editor (2000). *International Encyclopaedia of Human Rights.* 7 Volumes in 13 Parts. New Delhi: Discovery Publishing House. (Royal Size). ISBN 81-7141-567-9 (Set).

Vol. 1 *International Instruments of Human Rights,* 2 Parts. ISBN 81-7141-595-4.

Vol. 2 *Regional Instruments of Human Rights.* ISBN 81-7141-604-7.

Vol. 3 *Human Rights and the United Nations,* 2 Parts. ISBN 81-7141-605-5.

Vol. 4 *Fact Files of Human Rights,* 3 Parts. ISBN 81-7141-605-3.

Vol. 5 *Study Stories of Human Rights,* 3 Parts. ISBN 81-7141-607-3.

Vol. 6 *International Meetings on Human Rights,* 2 Parts. ISBN 81-7141-608-X.

Vol. 7 *Professional Training in Human Rights.* ISBN 81-7141-609-8.

Bhaskara Rao, Digumarti, Editor (2001). *Jomtein Decade of Education.* New Delhi: Discovery Publishing House. ISBN 81-7141-618-7.

Bhaskara Rao, Digumarti, Editor (2001). *Nuclear Materials: Issues and Concerns,* 2 Volumes. New Delhi: Discovery Publishing House. ISBN 81-7141-611-X.

Bhaskara Rao, Digumarti, Editor (2001). *World Conference on Education for All.* New Delhi: APH Publishing Corporation. ISBN 81-7141-274-9.

Bhaskara Rao, Digumarti, Editor (2001). *World Conference on Higher Education,* New Delhi: Discovery Publishing House. ISBN 81-7141-610-1.

Bhaskara Rao, Digumarti, Editor (2001). *World Conference on Science.* New Delhi: Discovery Publishing House. ISBN 81-7141-612-8.

Bhaskara Rao, Digumarti, Editor (2003). *Inspiring Experience in Teacher Education.* New Delhi: Discovery Publishing House. ISBN 81-7141-656-X.

Bhaskara Rao, Digumarti, Editor (2003). *International Studies in Education,* 3 Volumes, New Delhi: Discovery Publishing House. ISBN 81-7141-647-0.

Bhaskara Rao, Digumarti, Editor (2003). *Military Conversion: Impact on Science and Technology*, New Delhi: Discovery Publishing House. ISBN 81-7141-578-4.

Bhaskara Rao, Digumarti, Editor (2003). *United Nations Millennium Summit*. New Delhi: Discovery Publishing House. ISBN 81-7141-632-2.

Bhaskara Rao, Digumarti, Editor (2003). *World Assembly on Aging*. New Delhi: Discovery Publishing House. ISBN 81-7141-637-3.

Bhaskara Rao, Digumarti, Editor (2004). *World Conference on Human Rights*. New Delhi: Discovery Publishing House. ISBN 81-7141-661-6.

Bhaskara Rao, Digumarti, Editor (2003). *World Education Forum*. New Delhi: Discovery Publishing House. ISBN 81-7141-639-X.

Bhaskara Rao, Digumarti, Editor (2004). *Education Employment and Human Resource Development*. New Delhi: Discovery Publishing House. ISBN 81-7141-681-0.

Bhaskara Rao, Digumarti, Editor (2004). *Successfully Schooling*. New Delhi: Discovery Publishing House. ISBN 81-7141-677-2.

Bhaskara Rao, Digumarti, Editor (2004). *European Education and Teachers*. New Delhi: Discovery Publishing House. ISBN 81-7141-702-7.

Bhaskara Rao, Digumarti, Editor (2004). *Teachers in a Changing World*. New Delhi: Discovery Publishing House. ISBN 81-7141-694-2.

Bhaskara Rao, Digumarti, Editor (2004). *Learning to Live Together*, 4 Volumes. New Delhi: Discovery Publishing House.

Vol. 1 *International Conference on Learning to Live Together.*

Vol. 2 *Globalisation and Living Together.*

Vol. 3 *Curriculum for Learning to Live Together.*

Vol. 4 *Science Education for the Contemporary Society.*

Bhaskara Rao, Digumarti (2004). *International Guidelines on Open and Distance Education*, New Delhi: Discovery Publishing House.

Bhaskara Rao, Digumarti, Editor (2004). *Adult Learning in the 21st Century*. New Delhi: Discovery Publishing House.

Bhaskara Rao, Digumarti, Editor (2004). *Educational Practices: Research and Recommendations*. New Delhi: Discovery Publishing House.

Bhaskara Rao, Digumarti, Editor (2004). *Chernobyl: Never Again*. New Delhi: APH Publishing Corporation.

Bhaskara Rao, Digumarti, Editor (2004). *Virology and Immunology*. New Delhi: APH Publishing Corporation.

Bhaskara Rao, Digumarti, C.A.P. Swami and B.S.V. Dutt (1997). *Self-Evaluation in Student Teaching*. New Delhi: Discovery Publishing House. ISBN 81-7141-374-9.

Bhaskara Rao, Digumarti and B.S.V. Dutt, Editors (2003). *Education: Programmes and Policies*. New Delhi: APH Publishing Corporation. ISBN 81-7648-470-9.

Bhaskara Rao, Digumarti and D. Naresh Kumar (2004). *School Teacher Effectiveness*. New Delhi: Discovery Publishing House.

Bhaskara Rao, Digumarti and D. Sridhar (2002). *Job Satisfaction of School Teachers*. New Delhi: Discovery Publishing House. ISBN 81-7141-652-7.

Bhaskara Rao, Digumarti and Digumarti Pushpa Latha (1994). *Achievement in Biology*. New Delhi: Discovery Publishing House. ISBN 81-7141-264-5.

Bhaskara Rao, Digumarti, C. Sridevi and K. Vijaya (1995). *Achievement in Social Studies*. New Delhi: Discovery Publishing House. ISBN 81-7141-281-5.

Bhaskara Rao, Digumarti and Digumarti Pushpa Latha (1995). *Achievement in English*. New Delhi: Discovery Publishing House. ISBN 81-7141-283-1.

Bhaskara Rao, Digumarti and Digumarti Pushpa Latha (1994). *Achievement in Science*. New Delhi: Discovery Publishing House. ISBN 81-7141-280-70.

Bhaskara Rao, Digumarti and Digumarti Pushpa Latha (1995). *Achievement in Mathematics*. New Delhi: Discovery Publishing House. ISBN 81-7141-278-5.

Bhaskara Rao, Digumarti and Digumarti Pushpa Latha, Editors (1998). *International Encyclopaedia of Women*. 5 Volumes. New Delhi: Discovery Publishing House. ISBN 81-7141-410-9.

Vol. 1 *Status of World's Women*. ISBN 81-7141-494-X.

Vol. 2 *Women, Education and Empowerment*. ISBN 81-7141-498-1.

Vol. 3 *Women Challenges and Advancement*. ISBN 81-7141-497-4.

Vol. 4 *Women and Family Health*. ISBN 81-7141-497-4.

Vol. 5 *Women and International Action*. ISBN 81-7141-498-2.

Bhaskara Rao, Digumarti, Digumarti Pushpa Latha and Digumarti Harshitha, Editors (2001). *Biological Warfare*. New Delhi: Discovery Publishing House. ISBN 81-7141-597-0.

Bhaskara Rao, Digumarti, Digumarti Pushpa Latha and Digumarti Harshitha, Editors (2001). *Women as Educators*. New Delhi: Discovery Publishing House. ISBN 81-7141-602-0.

Bhaskara Rao, Digumarti and Digumarti Harshitha, Editors (2001). *Education in India*. New Delhi: APH Publishing Corporation. ISBN 81-7141-207-2.

Bhaskara Rao, Digumarti, Digumarti Pushpa Latha and Digumarti Harshitha, Editors (2001). *Assessing Learning Achievement*. New Delhi: Discovery Publishing House. ISBN 81-7141-601-2.

Bhaskara Rao, Digumarti, Digumarti Pushpa Latha and Digumarti Harshitha, Editors (2001). *Energy Security*. New Delhi: Discovery Publishing House. ISBN 81-7141-598-9.

Bhaskara Rao, Digumarti, Digumarti Harshitha and K.R.S.S. Rao, Editors (1999). *Advanced Biotechnology*. New Delhi: Discovery Publishing House. ISBN 81-7141-516-4.

Bhaskara Rao, Digumarti and K.R.S. Sambhasiva Rao, Editors (1996). *Current Trends in Indian Education*. New Delhi: Discovery Publishing House. ISBN 81-7141-311-0.

Bhaskara Rao, Digumarti and K. Vijaya (1995). *A Text Book of Evaluation*. Ambala Cantt: The Associated Publishers.

Bhaskara Rao, Digumarti and N.V.M. Mohana Rao (2002). *Problems of Mentally Handicapped Children*. New Delhi: Discovery Publishing House. ISBN 81-7141-645-4.

Bhaskara Rao, Digumarti and S. Chandra Mohan (2002). *Sports Management*. New Delhi: APH Publishing Corporation. ISBN 81-7648-467-9.

Bhaskara Rao, Digumarti and Sk. Johni Basha (2004). *Teachers' Population Education Awareness*. New Delhi: APH Publishing Corporation.

Bhaskara Rao, Digumarti, V.V. Rao, V.V. Lakshmi and V.V. Krishna, Editors (1999). *Status and Advancement of Women*. New Delhi: APH Publishing Corporation. ISBN 81-7648-169-6.

Babu, P.C., Author and Digumarti Bhaskara Rao, Editor (2004). *Flowers of Wisdom*. New Delhi: Discovery Publishing House. ISBN 81-7141-695-0.

Bhagya Lakshmi, Lingineni, Author and Digumarti Bhaskara Rao, Editor (2000). *Reading and Comprehension*. New Delhi: Discovery Publishing House. ISBN 81-7141-543-1.

Bhuvaneswara Lakshmi, Gadde, Author and Digumarti Bhaskara Rao, Editor (2000). *Attitude Towards Science*. New Delhi: Discovery Publishing House. ISBN 81-7141-541-6.

Devraj, T.A.S., Author and Digumarti Bhaskara Rao, Editor (1997). *Trace Analysis of Uranium and Thorium*. New Delhi: Discovery Publishing House. ISBN 81-7141-375-7.

Durga Rani, K., Author and Digumarti Bhaskara Rao, Editor (2000). *Educational Aspirations and Scientific Attitudes*. New Delhi: Discovery Publishing House. ISBN 81-7141-555-55.

Dutt, B.S.V. and Digumarti Bhaskara Rao (2001). *Empowering Primary Teachers*. New Delhi: Discovery Publishing House. ISBN 81-7141-615.2.

Ediger, Marlow and Digumarti Bhaskara Rao (1996). *Science Curriculum*. New Delhi: Discovery Publishing House. ISBN 81-7141-321-8.

Ediger, Marlow and Digumarti Bhaskara Rao (2000). *Teaching Mathematics Successfully*. New Delhi: Discovery Publishing House. ISBN 81-7141-552-0.

Ediger, Marlow and Digumarti Bhaskara Rao (2001). *Teaching Science Successfully*. New Delhi: Discovery Publishing House. ISBN 81-7141-600-4..

Ediger, Marlow and Digumarti Bhaskara Rao (2001). *Teaching Social Studies Successfully*. New Delhi: Discovery Publishing House. ISBN 81-7141-596-2.

Ediger, Marlow and Digumarti Bhaskara Rao (2002). *Philosophy and Curriculum*. New Delhi: Discovery Publishing House. ISBN 81-7141-631-4.

Ediger, Marlow and Digumarti Bhaskara Rao (2002). *Improving School Administration*. New Delhi: Discovery Publishing House. ISBN 81-7141-633-0.

Ediger, Marlow and Digumarti Bhaskara Rao (2002). *Elementary Curriculum*. New Delhi: Discovery Publishing House. ISBN 81-7141-658-6.

Ediger, Marlow and Digumarti Bhaskara Rao (2003). *Language Arts Curriculum*. New Delhi: Discovery Publishing House. ISBN 81-7141-657-8.

Ediger, Marlow and Digumarti Bhaskara Rao (2004). *Teaching Language Arts Successfully*. New Delhi: Discovery Publishing House. ISBN 81-7141-678-0.

Ediger, Marlow and Digumarti Bhaskara Rao (2004). *Teaching Mathematics in Elementary Schools*. New Delhi: Discovery Publishing House. ISBN 81-7141-687-X.

Ediger, Marlow and Digumarti Bhaskara Rao (2004). *Teaching Science in Elementary Schools*. New Delhi: Discovery Publishing House. ISBN 81-7141-709-4.

Ediger, Marlow and Digumarti Bhaskara Rao (2004). *School Curriculum and Administration*. New Delhi: Discovery Publishing House. ISBN 81-7141-709-4.

Ediger, Marlow and Digumarti Bhaskara Rao (2004). *Modern Elementary School*. New Delhi: Discovery Publishing House.

Ediger, Marlow and Digumarti Bhaskara Rao (2004): *Relevancy in Elementary Curriculum*. New Delhi: Discovery Publishing House. ISBN 81-7141-751-5.

Ediger, Marlow and Digumarti Bhaskara Rao, (2004). *Teaching Social Studies in Elementary Schools*. New Delhi: Discovery Publishing House.

Ediger Marlow, B.S.V. Dutt and Digumarti Bhaskara Rao (2004). *Teaching English Successfully*. New Delhi: Discovery Publishing House. ISBN 81-7141-707-8.

Harshitha, Digumarti and Digumarti Bhaskara Rao, Editors (2004). *Educational Innovations*. New Delhi: Discovery Publishing House.

Indira Devi, Author and J. Prasanth Kumar and Digumarti Bhaskara Rao, Editors (2004). *Values in Language Text Books*. New Delhi: Discovery Publishing House.

Jayasree, Kandi, Author and Digumarti Bhaskara Rao, Editor (1999). *Correlates of Socialisation*. New Delhi: Discovery Publishing House. ISBN 81-7141-517-2.

John Babu, Chikati, Author and T.J.R. Prasad, G.M. Madhukar and Digumarti Bhaskara Rao, Editors (1996). *Problem Solving in Mathematics*. New Delhi: APH Publishing Corporation. ISBN 81-7648-273-0.

Lalitha, T., Author and K.S. Prabhakaram, D.S.N. Sastry and Digumarti Bhaskara Rao, Editors (2004). *Educational Philosophic Beliefs*. New Delhi: Discovery Publishing House. ISBN 81-7141-765-5.

Madhu Bala, Jampala, Author and Digumarti Bhaskara Rao, Editor (2004). *Adjustment Problems of Hearing Impaired*. New Delhi: Discovery Publishing House.

Marja, Talvi and Digumarti Bhaskara Rao, Editors (1996). *Educational Leadership and Social Changes*. New Delhi: Discovery Publishing House. ISBN 81-7141-320-X.

Nirmala Jyothi, M., Author and Digumarti Bhaskara Rao, Editor (2003). *Non-detention Systems in School Education*. New Delhi: Discovery Publishing House. ISBN 81-7141-654-3.

Prabhakaram, K.S., Author and Digumarti Bhaskara Rao, Editor (1998). *Concept Attainment Model in Mathematics Teaching*. New Delhi: Discovery Publishing House. ISBN 81-7141-424-9.

Prasanth Kumar, J., Author and Digumarti Bhaskara Rao, Editor (1998). *Effectiveness of Distance Education System*. New Delhi: Discovery Publishing House. ISBN 81-7141-437-0.

Prasanth Kumar, J., Author and G. Sundara Rao and Digumarti Bhaskara Rao, Editors (2000). *Open University Student Support Services*. New Delhi: Discovery Publishing House. ISBN 81-7141-550-4.

Ramatulasamma, K., Author and Digumarti Bhaskara Rao, Editor (2002). *Job Satisfaction of Teacher Educators*, New Delhi: Discovery Publishing House. ISBN 81-7141-655-1.

Rama Krishnaiah, D., Author and Digumarti Bhaskara Rao, Editor (1998). *Job Satisfaction of College Teachers*, New Delhi: Discovery Publishing House. ISBN 81-7141-438-9.

Rama Kumar Ratnam, M., Author and Digumarti Bhaskara Rao, Editor (1998). *Dukka: Suffering in Early Buddhism*. New Delhi: Discovery Publishing House. ISBN 81-7141-653-5.

Rathaiah, Lavu and Digumarti Bhaskara Rao, Editors (1996). *International Innovations in Education*. New Delhi: Discovery Publishing House. ISBN 81-7141-359-5.

Ramesh, Ganta and Digumarti Bhaskara Rao, Editors (1998). *Environmental Education: Problems and Prospects*. New Delhi: Discovery Publishing House. ISBN 81-7141-423-0.

Rathaiah, Lavu and Digumarti Bhaskara Rao (1997). *Achievement Correlates*. New Delhi: Discovery Publishing House. ISBN 81-7141-385-4.

Reddy, Sudhakar Y., Author, and Digumarti Bhaskara Rao, Editor (2003). *Creativity in Adolescents*. New Delhi: Discovery Publishing House. ISBN 81-7141-659-4.

Reddy, M.S., Author and Digumarti Bhaskara Rao, Editor (2004). *Creativity in College Students*. New Delhi: Discovery Publishing House. ISBN 81-7141-697-7.

Radramamba, B., Author and Digumarti Bhaskara Rao, Editor (2003). *Problems of Teaching*. New Delhi: APH Publishing Corporation. ISBN 81-7648-462-8.

Sanjeeva Rao, P.C., Author and Digumarti Bhaskara Rao, Editor (1996). *A Text Book of Geology*. New Delhi: Discovery Publishing House. ISBN 81-7141-313-7.

Satya Narayana V., Author and Digumarti Bhaskara Rao, Editor (2001). *Physical Education, Social Attitudes and Leadership Qualities*. New Delhi: Discovery Publishing House. ISBN 81-7141-593-8.

Srinivasulu Reddy, M., and K.R.S. Sambasiva Rao, Authors and Digumarti Bhaskara Rao, Editor (1999). *A Text Book of Aquaculture*. New Delhi: Discovery Publishing House. ISBN 81-7141-482-6.

Srinivasa Rao, Mandalapu, Author and Digumarti Bhaskara Rao, Editor (2004). *Achievement Motivation and Achievement in Mathematics*. New Delhi: Discovery Publishing House. ISBN 81-7141-674-8.

Vanaja, M. Author and Digumarti Bhaskara Rao, Editor (1999). *Inquiry Training Model*. New Delhi: Discovery Publishing House. ISBN 81-7141-515-6.

Vanaja. M. and N. Sneha Latha, Authors and Digumarti Bhaskara Rao, Editor (2004). *Student Shyness*. New Delhi: APH Publishing Corporation.

Valeri V. Koustiouk, Author and Digumarti Bhaskara Rao, Editor (2002). *A Text Book of Cryogenics*. New Delhi: Discovery Publishing House. ISBN 81-7141-642-X.

Valeri V. Koustiouk, Author and Digumarti Bhaskara Rao, Editor (2004). *Refrigeration and Environment*. New Delhi: APH Publishing Corporation.

Veena Kumari, Balusu and Digumarti Bhaskara Rao (1996). *Operation Black Board*. New Delhi: Ashish Publishing Corporation. ISBN 81-7024-711-X.

Veena Kumari, Balusu, Author and Digumarti Bhaskara Rao, Editor (2000). *Psycho-Social Correlates of Achievement*, New Delhi: Discovery Publishing House. ISBN 81-7141-547-4.

Vanaja, M., Author and Digumarti Bhaskara Rao, Editor (1999). *Inquiry Training Model*. New Delhi: Discovery Publishing House. ISBN 81-7141-515-6.

Venkata Rao, P. and Digumarti Bhaskara Rao (1989). *A Text Book of Zoology—Junior Intermediate*. Guntur: Vignan Publishers.

Venkata Rao, P. and Digumarti Bhaskara Rao (1989). *A Text Book of Zoology—Senior Intermediate*. Guntur: Vignan Publishers.

Venugopala Rao, K., Author and Digumarti Bhaskara Rao, Editor (2000). *Teacher Morale in Secondary Schools*. New Delhi: Discovery Publishing House. ISBN 81-7141-551-2.

Vidya, C., Author and Digumarti Bhaskara Rao. Editor (1996). *A Text Book of Nutrition*. New Delhi: Discovery Publishing House. ISBN 81-7141-309-9.

Vidya Bharathi, D., Author and Digumarti Bhaskara Rao, Editor (2000). *Educational Philosophies of Swami Vivekananda and John Dewey*. New Delhi: APH Publishing Corporation. ISBN 81-7648-309-9.

Books in Telugu Language

Bhaskara Rao, Digumarti (1986). *Dhrushya Sravana Bodhanapakaranalu* (Audio Visual Teaching Aids). Guntur: Nagarjuna Publishers.

Bhaskara Rao, Digumarti (1993). *Jeevasashtra Bodhana* (Teaching of Biology). Guntur: Nagarjuna Publishers.

Bhaskara Rao, Digumarti (1995). *Vignanasasthra Bodhana* (Teaching of Science) Guntur: Nagarjuna Publishers.

Bhaskara Rao, Digumarti (1997). *Vidya Manovignana Seshtram* (Educational Psychology). Guntur: Creative Press.

Bhaskara Rao, Digumarti (1998). *DSC Study Material*. Guntur: Nagarjuna Publishers.

Bhaskara Rao, Digumarti (1998). *Upadhyayudu Vidya*. (Teacher and Education). Guntur: Nagarjuna Publishers.

Bhaskara Rao, Digumarti (1998). *Vidya Drukpadalu* (Prespectives of Education). Guntur: Nagarjuna Publishers.

Bhaskara Rao, Digumarti (1999). *EdCET Teaching Aptitude*. Guntur: Nagarjuna Publishers.

Bhaskara Rao, Digumarti (2001). *Bharata Samajamulo Upadyayudu Vidya* (Teacher and Education in Emerging Indian Society). Guntur: Nagarjuna Publishers.

Bhaskara Rao, Digumarti (2001). *Bhoutika Sastra Bodhana Paddathulu* (Methods of Teaching Physical Science). Guntur: Nagarjuna Publishers.

Bhaskara Rao, Digumarti (2001). *Jeeva Sastra Bodhana Padhathulu* (Methods of Teaching Biology). Guntur: Nagarjuna Publishers.

Bhaskara Rao, Digumarti (2001). *Vidya Manovignana Sastram* (Educational Psychology). Guntur: Nagarjuna Publishers.

Bhaskara Rao, Digumarti (2003). *Patsala Yajamanyam/Paripalana* (School Management and Administration). Guntur: Nagarjuna Publishers.

Bhaskara Rao, Digumarti (2004). *Vidya Sanketika Sastram mariyu Computer Vidya* (Educational Technology and Computer Education). Guntur: Nagarjuna Publishers.